Contents

Early Market Street scene, circa 1975

The barn is in the background to the right.
The buildings in the right foreground occupy the present site of McIntyre's bookstore.

Flavors of Fearrington

Acknowledgements

Our sincere gratitude goes to all the committee chairs and committee members who have spent many hours preparing the contents of this book. The committee chairs, David Alter, Jean Green, Tuck Green, Sam Mason, Phil Morse, Peggy Quinn, Rod and Anne Louise Snelling, Alvin Schultzberg, and Jim Terry have given their sustained support to the guidance of this project. We also thank Anita Martin and Julie Snyder for their special fundraising help.

To all those Fearringtonians who graciously submitted their recipes for consideration, we say, "Thank you so much." It was not possible to use all of them but it was a pleasure to have such a large number of households involved.

Special thanks to Jesse Fearrington for the many family photographs and memorabilia he offered for this project. We particularly appreciate the recipes of his late wife, Willa.

The historical information, stories and photographs provided by Fred Vatter have greatly enhanced the section called Fearrington Past and Present.

We are grateful to Mary Ann Young who has delighted us with her creative use of words in the text portions of this book.

We thank the Fearrington Cares Board of Directors for their guidance and support.

The unique perspective provided by Ginny Gregory in her *Reflections on Community* has added immeasurably to the book. Her valuable insights into the creation of community in Fearrington Village are much appreciated.

For the wonderful line drawings, which provide a thread of continuity throughout the book, we thank Carol Owen.

The color photographs printed in the book have been donated by Fearrington residents Wally Mann, John Shillito, Jim Terry and Fred Vatter. Our sincere gratitude goes to each of them for their beautiful work.

For his unfailingly positive support in providing the project with event venues, staff assistance, historical information, chef's recipes and much more we express our deep appreciation to Richard Delany.

We are grateful that the current and former chefs of the Fearrington House Restaurant have been willing to share their unique recipes with us. Special thanks to Cory Mattson, Executive Director, Food Service, Graham Fox, Chef de Cuisine and those who preceded them; Edna Lewis, Ben Barker, Shane Ingram, Warren Stephens.

Finally, we offer our deep appreciation to R.B. Fitch for his very generous offers of historical photographs and information, marketing assistance, encouragement and support.

Flavors of Fearrington

Fearrington Cares

Fearrington Cares is an organization created by and for the residents of Fearrington Village. We are all proud to live in this diverse and vibrant community. The organization provides information and support services that help optimize healthcare choices and assist residents and their families in navigating our complex health care system. We materialized out of the natural concerns that compassionate people have for their friends and neighbors. Fearrington Cares is a lively group of volunteers and professionals providing programs and services to all residents, maintained and funded through the generosity of the community.

In the summer of 2003 three innovative volunteers approached the Board of Directors with the idea for a cookbook. The book would contain favorite recipes of our residents and would reflect the community of Fearrington, its past history and the present village. Proceeds from its sale would be channeled towards the ongoing support of Fearrington Cares. As a non-profit, tax-exempt service organization, we depend on the contributions of this community for our existence. The cookbook sounded like a great idea.

So many people have donated countless hours of their time to making the ideas of this project become a reality. The unwavering support of the community has been heartwarming. *Flavors of Fearrington* will simultaneously be a wonderful way to share recipes and ideas, while generating a stream of financial support for our organization.

The Fearrington Cares Board of Directors would like to extend grateful thanks to all of those involved in this enormous undertaking. Their foresight, creativity and perseverance have made this book a reality. Enjoy the food with friends and family in the spirit in which these ideas were shared.

Mervin Shumate
President, Fearrington Cares

Introduction

The ornament of a house is the friends who frequent it.
Ralph Waldo Emerson

There is a common occurrence in Fearrington Village, a community just eight miles south of Chapel Hill, North Carolina. A moving van rolls down the tree-lined streets, past the English gardens, the ponds, and Village center. The "Belties" give a nod to the driver who may never have seen the rare breed of Scottish black and white striped cows that graze in the fields among the beautiful homes, shops, and 5-star restaurant and inn. After a few days of settling in, new residents are greeted by friendly neighbors and the conversation leads to the inquiry, "So what brought you to Fearrington?"

Neither a gated community, nor country club, or houses surrounding a golf course, Fearrington is a lifestyle choice that is based on a desire to be part of a unique community. The name, Fearrington Village, is meaningful. Close to many cultural, recreational, and medical facilities, the Village is also isolated enough to take on its own identity as a small town where residents know and greet each other. It is a community where a wide range of interests is reflected in the many clubs organized by the residents... everything from books to investment banking, from tennis to concerts, and from arts and crafts to wines. Here is found the pursuit of further knowledge and the extension of creative skills. The conversation in Fearrington at any gathering is lively and broad, reflecting the backgrounds and growing interests of the residents. And where people gather there is a tradition of serving good food.

Delicious meals enhance one of life's great pleasures, sharing food with friends. As Fearrington is more than a development, *Flavors of Fearrington* is more than a cookbook. This book goes beyond the usual collection of favorite recipes to mirror the lifestyle of the Village. Included are wonderful resources from this farmland that still exists today. There is a section on the fresh herbs and edible flowers that abound in our patios and gardens. The menu section reflects the frequent activities that occur in the Village...pool picnics, appetizers at the outdoor concerts, holiday cocktail parties, gourmet dinners for eight, meals for grandchildren, holiday celebrations, and buffets for the visiting family.

First and foremost in our minds in creating the book was the desire to capture on paper the cordial atmosphere that exists in the natural beauty of our community. In addition, the book serves as a fund raising project for the village organization called Fearrington Cares, a non-profit group created to provide residents with information and services to optimize their health care. Funds from book sales are a means of sustaining the organization while providing a resource for the tradition of Fearrington social gatherings that includes good food lovingly prepared for family and friends.

Many Fearrington residents contributed to the creation of *Flavors of Fearrington,* not just by submitting their recipes, but by giving their time and expertise to kitchen test each one. More than 200 people submitted recipes, including all current and former Fearrington House Restaurant chefs. Others served on the various committees, provided photographs, design layout, editing, computer entry and marketing services. Numerous residents pledged funds for publication, and supported fund raising events. Such an effort on the part of so many demonstrates the talents and caring nature of village residents. *Flavors of Fearrington* is truly a community product, one inspired and initiated by those who love living here, and who want to share what is so unique about Fearrington Village.

To those many people, our friends and neighbors who created *Flavors of Fearrington,* we express our sincere thanks and salute their community spirit.

Janet Lorant   *Joyce Mason*   *Barbara Terry*

Reflections

on

Community

The Old Granary, Circa 1975

This building was renovated to create the Market Café.

Reflections on Community

In the late spring of 1986, a brown Mercedes station wagon arrived at Catalpa Farms. The driver had come to investigate what was happening up on this hill. She said she had been passing my sign and today she had decided to check me out. With that single visit, my life was forever changed.

The woman was Jenny Fitch, who, with her husband, R.B., was creating Fearrington Village. She was scouting out the possibility of cut flowers. We talked about my business and about me...."do you have flower design experience?" she asked. "I learned from my mother and grandmother," I answered. "Great," she said, "I want you to meet me behind the Fearrington House Restaurant this Tuesday afternoon with as many buckets of fresh flowers as you can bring and we'll put flower arrangements together." And so started my third career at the age of 35.

I met Jenny every Tuesday afternoon through the spring and summer of '86. We put flowers into vases and drank Diet Coke with fresh lemon slices. Over the months Jenny asked me every question imaginable and I, feeling so comfortable, would answer without hesitation.

Jenny Fitch, Director of The Village Center.

This ease was mutual. I asked her about growing up in Siler City and what her life prior to Fearrington was like, about her college years, meeting R. B. Fitch, about growing older, cancer and about her wonderful optimism and pure joy of life. I adored working for her. It was as if I was always with her, even later when she was not there.

We arranged flowers and talked and before we knew it several hours had passed, vases were ready to be put out on tables in the restaurant and the sun was going down. Jenny was off in a tear for the next thing on her list to do.

It's strange. I look back now and cannot remember any instructions, but I learned more than I could ever write about flowers and arranging them, food and seasoning and most important of all, I came to learn that we are all connected by a common need to belong.

Jenny was passionate about food, flowers and décor. She had studied at the Cordon Bleu in Paris and believed that if good food were served in a beautiful atmosphere people would come. She brought her exuberant personality, her skill and her devotion to all things beautiful to the development of the village center. Those who knew her well relate that Jenny was "always right in there doing things herself." She could be found weeding or potting up in the gardens, puttering in the kitchen and redecorating the rooms in the Inn.

She was always behind and yet always going forward with great enthusiasm and excitement. She once forgot a needlepoint group luncheon scheduled at her home. It became the opportunity, in just an hour's time, to present a meal that had the touch of a well-planned gourmet event. She frequently prepared floral arrangements for the restaurant, the Inn and for weddings. A friend remembers her running to the Border Garden and thrusting a bouquet into a bride's hand just as "Here Comes the Bride" began.

The time I spent with Jenny showed me that she truly understood community. She believed that you must know your employees, know and care about their lives. She understood that loyalty was something earned, that employees were people to be appreciated, that her livelihood was due to the creative and often arduous work of those who made up the Fitch Creations workforce. She asked about sick babies as if they were hers and about the progress of a house being built after hours by many of the staff. She asked about graduations, deaths, and marriages. She knew everyone's name and they in turn made sure that she was taken care of. It might be hanging pictures in a model home or moving a tree three inches to the right, at 6:30 in the morning or 6:30 at night.

I am not sure if we knew we were learning about community... the act of forming a community, but indeed we were all involved in VILLAGE EVOLUTION 101 and she was our teacher without even knowing it.

When people came to look at Fearrington, imagining that this southern village could become their new home, the first people they met would often be Jenny and R.B. Fitch. He would be hurrying across the parking lot, but R.B. was never too busy to welcome potential buyers. He told them that he lived here, wasn't going anywhere, and would be here from start to finish. The next words would be, "Come here Jenny! I have someone I want you to meet". She would be racing across the parking lot with a bolt of fabric under her arm for a chair in a new inn room and she would stop. Then you would hear her laugh. It rang out across the village, not ladylike, just plain joyful. R.B. has it too, a loud, throw back your head laugh. Together they would make the prospective buyers feel right at home, make them feel as if they would be part of something, part of a community. While they talked, workers would come by and R. B. would nod to them as they spoke to him. Jenny would call out, "What did you name the new baby?" and before you knew it the connection that those new homeowners observed became the connection that began to hold the community of homeowners together.

These new Fearrington residents began to see themselves as a village, a community of people caring about each other. Dinner parties began to happen and celebrations of new beginnings. Clubs began to evolve. R.B. Fitch donated a building so the homeowners would have a place of their own in which to congregate. It was rightly called The Gathering Place.

Soon the Market Café became the central meeting place for the men's coffee club that gathered each morning to solve the world's problems or the lunch date after the women's doubles in tennis. It was the late afternoon glass of wine together with neighbors or the early evening dinner honoring old friends. From weddings to grand openings to bagels and hot coffee, food has been translated into the vehicle for connection here at Fearrington.

This book, *Flavors of Fearrington*, reflects the connection of people from all over the country who have come together to be a community of neighbors in a unique village called Fearrington.

As you read this book and try these recipes, share with others and the connections of community continue.

Ginny Gregory
Former Fearrington Horticulturist

Market Cafe

Clearing Storm

The village where neighbors care and community is alive

Fearrington

Past and Present

The Fearrington Family Home

Old Granary

Early Market Café Construction

Fearrington Past and Present

Drive eight miles south of Chapel Hill, North Carolina on route 15-501 and you will come upon Fearrington Village. As you enter, notice the silo remaining from the days when the property was a working dairy. On your left there may be people at the bocce court and a family by the swings and slide. In the large meadows, surrounded by white fences, you will see part of the championship herd of Belted Galloways, their blue ribbons displayed in the Market Café. The youngsters refer to this rare breed of Scottish black and white striped cows as Oreos.

Continue on Village Way and see the turtles sunning themselves on their raft and geese preening by the pond in one of the many parks scattered throughout the village. Further along on the road, you will discover residential areas, each with individual flavor, from classic to modern. Everything appears to fit into its own natural setting.

Along the meandering roads of the Village and in the parks there will be people, some in groups, some alone, some running, some strolling, and they will greet you warmly. The workmen in their trucks will wave as they pass.

In the Village Center, you will find the Barn, used for social events, art shows and gatherings featuring renowned authors and speakers. Come upon the five star Fearrington House Inn and Restaurant, the Market Cafe in the old granary, and unique shops. Delight in discovering Jenny's Garden, the Rose Garden and Camden Park with its walking paths, little bridges, graceful trees, benches and the clutch of "crete sheep." The woods by the lower pond are home to the herd of black and white striped Tennessee Fainting Goats who clean up the underbrush and care for their new kids.

Ask residents "Where are you from? What brought you here?" In response you will hear enthusiastic accolades about the flavors of Fearrington. Your education about what gives Fearrington Village its unique identity has begun.

The area now known as Fearrington Village was first settled by English speaking people in 1745. In the 1770's John Andrew Fearrington came to Chatham County from Flushing, New York. He received land grants from Governor Richie Caswell giving him thousands of acres between the Haw River and what is now the Orange County line. In 1786 William Cole, Sr., Jesse Fearrington's maternal great, great, great grandfather, purchased the 640 acres of land that eventually became Fearrington Village. It is said that he was able to purchase the land for a pittance because the owner, John Oldham, did not believe there was enough water on his property to run a gristmill and a whiskey still.

The Coles named the land Eureka Farm. The farm produced corn, cotton, tobacco and cornmeal from their gristmill. In the early 1800's the farm passed to William Cole, Jr., then to Elijah Cole in 1840. Elijah's daughter inherited the farm and married Edwin M. Fearrington in 1859, placing the land in the hands of the Fearrington family. The Cole family cemetery is located in Fearrington Village.

The original farmhouse, built in 1820, was destroyed by fire in 1925. John Bunyan Fearrington, Edwin's son, replaced the home with a columned mansion nestled in an oak grove close to the Chapel Hill-Pittsboro Road. Along with the field crops, he ran a cotton gin on the property until the 1930's when he began to transform the farm into a dairy.

Jesse Fearrington, John's son, grew up on the farm. Today he lives across the Chapel Hill-Pittsboro Road, now route 15-501. He graduated from Pittsboro High School and N.C. State University with a major in dairying and animal husbandry. In talking about life on Eureka Farm, Jesse says he was the one who got up and milked the cows. The milk was sent to Durham, first in large metal milk cans that people now use for umbrella stands, and later it was pumped into a truck for the journey to Durham.

Jesse and his bride, Willa, moved into a two-story wing that was added onto the mansion in 1947. They raised their son and daughter in the home that is now the Fearrington House Restaurant. They operated a dairy, raised beef cattle, hogs and chickens, and tended a big vegetable garden and a fruit orchard. These days, Jesse prefers to shop at Farmers' Markets. "I can tell fresh vegetables, I know a good sweet potato." he says.

Jesse and Willa Fearrington

John Bunyan Fearrington, Jesse's father
and the soil conservation agent

Jesse reminisces that the first job of the day was for the cook to light the fire. Willa enjoyed cooking for family and friends. Fried chicken was a favorite. Cornbread and biscuits, vegetables from the garden, fruits from the apple and peach trees, and wild blackberries graced their table. Jesse smiles when he mentions Willa's spoon bread. Food from the land is part of the Fearrington tradition.

By the end of the 1960's, Jesse and Willa were ready to retire from running Eureka Farm. They began to look for a buyer who would love the natural woodlands and preserve the historic value of family lands, the stately pines, ponds, meandering streams, sloping hills and valleys which attracted numerous birds and many species of wildlife. It was important to Jesse that the land not be neglected or allowed to fall into disrepair as was the fate of many old farms. And so the beautiful wooded tract, located eight miles south of Chapel Hill on the road to Pittsboro, was made available for sale.

In 1974 Jesse and Willa Fearrington found their buyers in R.B. and Jenny Fitch. Jesse and R.B.'s fathers had been long-time friends and business associates. Jesse was confident that his land was going into good hands; that the environment would be protected and maintained. "You've got to make people happy," Jesse says, "otherwise you won't be happy yourself."

Jenny Fitch grew up in Siler City, R.B. in Chapel Hill. He graduated from the University of North Carolina at Chapel Hill and worked for his father in the family lumber business. He saw numerous housing developments sprout up on the outskirts of Chapel Hill, a desirable, prospering town dominated by UNC and home to a respected, growing medical facility. R.B started Fitch Creations in 1960 as a kitchen and bathroom remodeling and landscaping business. Fitch Creations then expanded into home building and developed Polk's Landing, a few miles north of the Fearrington tract.

Fueled by success with the innovative Polk's Landing development, R.B. and Jenny decided to buy the Fearrington farm where he planned to continue building houses. The Fitches had long admired the Fearrington Farm with its neat, manicured lawns and imposing columned portico. It was regarded by many as one of the most attractive sites between Chapel Hill and the coast. R.B. marketed the new homes at Fearrington, advertising in the *Wall Street Journal* and the *New Yorker* magazine. Young professionals, singles, and retirees were attracted to the area and to R.B.'s award winning, energy efficient homes.

The Fitches acquired 450 acres from the Moore and Gust families, adding to the land purchased from Jesse Fearrington. This additional land was part of the original holdings of the 16th century Fearrington family, though not part of the land owned by Jessie Fearrington. The present size of the Village is about 1100 acres of rolling countryside, pastures and farmland.

In 1979 architect Jon Condoret designed and Fitch Creations built the Family Circle Solar Dream House and The Southern Living House of the Year. Fitch Creations received other awards and recognition for solar ideas by *Better Homes and Gardens* and *Southern Living*.

Solar Home

After their three children were no longer a full time job, Jenny turned more of her attention to the beautification of the village and was able to give free rein to her creativity. She began by decorating the model homes. A *Better Homes and Gardens* editor referred to Jenny Fitch as "one of the most talented decorators... she has a sensitive feel for color and knows how to relate it to the elements of a room setting, she demonstrates exquisite design taste." Together R.B. and Jenny were creating a memorable community. Inspired growth and change were flavoring the air.

Eureka Farm with the Fearrington home at the center, the granary, now the Market Café and farmer's cottage to the right, the other farm buildings to the left, now the Dovecote and Fearrington Grocery

The plan for Fearrington Village, bigger than a hamlet and smaller than a town, was to make it a special place to live, work and play. This plan, announced in 1982, included a dedication to pattern the village center on the charming farm scape of the original buildings. The existing farm buildings were updated for their current use. The old granary became the Market Café and Deli, where the second story restaurant provides expansive views of the meadows and the Galloways. A casual pick-up deli service is available on the first floor and local artists display their works on the lower level. The milking barn became Pringle's Pottery and later Dovecote, Jenny's home and garden shop. The building also houses A Stone's Throw and the Fearrington Grocery Company. The corncrib grew into the Potting Shed. The center of the village also includes a bookstore, bank, antique store, children's shop, beauty salon, travel agency and a fine linen shop.

The Old Granary

The Fearrington family home was remodeled in the mid 1970's to make it suitable for a restaurant. Great care was given to maintaining the integrity of the original structure. During the remodel, much of the building was saved and in turn this act of preservation created a warm and wonderful collection of small and intimate dining rooms.

Bill Neal, a well-known chef and his wife Moreton, a cooking class friend of Jenny's, brought their extraordinary culinary talent and avid following from Chapel Hill to open their own "destination restaurant," La Residence. In 1976 the Neals moved with their young son into the second floor of the mansion and in the evenings they served elegant French dinners to thirty or forty guests in the living areas of the Fearrington home. The tariff for a four-course meal was ten dollars, plus a small corkage fee for those who chose to bring wine into dry Chatham County. People gladly drove "all the way out there" for dinner at La Residence, which operated until the Neals returned to Chapel Hill in 1978. A tradition for fine dining had been established.

Following additional renovation the Fearrington House Restaurant opened on May 7, 1980. The renowned Edna Lewis, "the first lady of fine Southern Cooking" agreed to come from New York City for one year as a visiting chef. She was a champion of fresh seasonal ingredients and under her leadership the Fearrington House Restaurant gained national acclaim. Succeeding chefs, Ben and Karen Barker, Cory Mattson, current Director of Food Services, Walter Royal, Shane Ingram, Warren Stevens and Graham Fox, current Chef de Cuisine, contributed innovative and creative "New Southern" dishes to the menu. The restaurant's reputation for fine dining and catering for weddings and special celebrations catapulted upward.

In 1986, a fourteen-room country inn was added to the village center. Each room is distinctive and unique, decorated with quality English pine and eclectic furnishings and has views of the courtyard gardens or the Park. Today the Inn boasts 33 rooms. The Fearrington House Inn and Restaurant attained a highly desirable affiliation with Relais et Chateaux, a collection of the most beautiful and distinguished country houses and

Dovecote

restaurants worldwide. AAA has awarded the Fearrington House Inn and Restaurant 5 Diamonds and the Mobil Travel Guide has proclaimed the property the only five-star destination in North Carolina.

R.B. says "I don't think I would be in the restaurant business if it weren't for Jenny. Dovecote, the garden and gift shop was also because of her. And the bookstore was because of my daughter Keebe's interest in books." Keebe credits her mother with giving McIntyre's bookstore the remarkable at-home ambiance that invites visitors to browse at leisure and settle into one of the comfortable chairs for a while.

McIntyre's

Jenny's White Garden

Flowers and plantings beautifully accent the shops and restaurants of Fearrington Village. Visitors are always welcome to stroll and relax in the gardens. The splendid displays include the Fragrant White Garden, the Perennial Border Garden, site of many weddings, the Herb Garden and the Inn's English courtyard and Knot Garden. The informal Southern garden around the Market Café reflects the casual hustle and bustle inside with roadside daylilies, hollyhocks (seeds gathered from Monet's Garden in Giverny, France), Shasta daisies and redbud. Tours of the gardens are conducted by horticulturists who point out the more than 200 varieties of flowers, hardy herbs, trees, vines and flowering perennials to be seen in the village.

Clusters of forest remain throughout the village. Homes range from classic to contemporary, reflecting the individuality of their owners, and may be modest or grand. About fifteen hundred residents live on the 1100 acres in town homes, row houses, homes on wooded lots and more.

Deciding to move to Fearrington is more than choosing a house or a floor plan. It is opting for a new lifestyle. Residents come from everywhere. They wave and talk with their neighbors. Dozens of clubs and groups sponsor Fearrington-wide activities, reflecting the huge diversity of residents' interests and hobbies. And the activities keep expanding. If you can't find what you want, you can create it.

Fearrington Village hosts an annual folk art show in February, regular free concerts in the Cafe, open-air concerts in the summer, classical concerts at the Gathering Place, fashion shows, fund raisers and more. Sculptures and artwork by local artists are regularly displayed.

R.B. and Jenny Fitch's vision of a country community with lush English gardens, southern charm and scrumptious food is realized today. It is a place where residents know and greet each other, where flowers and plant life abound and where good food is shared. This is Fearrington Village.

Reflection

Culinary and Landscape

Herbs

and Edible Flowers

The chosen site for Jenny's White Garden

Culinary and Landscape Herbs and Edible Flowers

*Life is not measured by the number of breaths we take
but by the places and moments that take our breath away!*
Anonymous

Living in an area surrounded by flowers, herbs and beautiful trees is one of life's greatest gifts. The gift is compounded if one enjoys cooking, for the fortunate cook can "smell the flowers" and eat them too.

Fearrington Village is located in growing zone seven, where the gardener and cooking enthusiast have access to herbs, vegetables, and flowers picked fresh from the garden throughout most of the year. The mild climate affords gardeners and growers long and productive seasons. Homegrown vegetables and seasonal cut flowers are available to Fearrington residents from local farmers who provide a weekly Farmer's Market at Fearrington from April to November.

Farmer's Market

While fresh herbs such as parsley, rosemary and thyme add a new dimension to familiar dishes, edible flowers such as pansies and nasturtiums take the simplest dishes to new heights.

Culinary herbs grow profusely in all areas of Fearrington Village. Most are easily grown and tolerate a wide variety of weather conditions. Available year round are parsley, rosemary, lavender and thyme. Summertime brings chives, mint, oregano, sage, tarragon, marjoram and the many varieties of basil. Delicious combinations include roast lamb with rosemary, pork and fresh sage, chicken in a tarragon cream sauce, Italian dishes scented with oregano, and summer tomatoes with basil. Herb flavored vinegars, oils and butters enhance countless dishes.

Lavender is intense, sweet and fragrant and a little goes a long way. Use it to flavor custards, ice cream or honey. Add chopped florets to sugar cookies or fresh orange slices. Try the lavender ice cream in the dessert section.

Herbs may also be used as landscape shrubs. Rosemary and lavender grow into large plants in two to three years, some as large as three to four feet in diameter. The creeping varieties of thyme and mint are very attractive when grown between steppingstones and along walkways.

The flowers of many plants are edible and add interesting flavor and beauty to a meal. Squash blossoms may be added to salads, soups and stews and stuffed for delicious fritters. Rose petals may be candied or used to flavor teas, jellies and sorbets. They are delightful as a garnish.

Violets are sweet and perfumed. Their leaves are tart and good in soups and salads. The flowers are popular in desserts, candied or in syrups. Johnny-jump-ups and pansies are slightly wintergreen in flavor. As garnish they add interest to mild soups such as cucumber, sorrel, consommé and cold summer fruit soups.

Nasturtiums are a favorite for the peppery flavor of both the leaves and the flowers. They are beautiful in salads and perk up omelets. The options for new flavors and creative adornment of food become almost limitless.

Taking a walk in the village any time of year can take your breath away. In early spring daffodils peek up through a light frosting of snow amidst the hearty green parsley and spiky rosemary that have survived the winter months. In early summer the colorful flowers of thyme and chives delight the eye and the purple haze of lavender brings bees by the dozens. Roses bloom profusely all summer and in the late fall and winter the many colors of pansies may be enjoyed in the garden and on the table.

Fall, winter, summer or spring, a visit to Fearrington Village is a treat for the eye and the bounty overflows to the table. The rich flavors of Fearrington are a gift to all who live in the village and those who come to visit.

Menus

Menus

A Spring Dinner After a Concert on the Lawn

Cocktails
Wild Mushroom Toasts

Arugula and Escarole Salad with Port and Figs

Chicken Breasts with Grapes and Raisins
Brandied Pureed Carrots
Riesling or Pinot gris

Tipsy Blueberry Gin Pie
Coffee

Breakfast for Weekend Guests

Bacon and Egg Strata
Wild Mushroom Grit Cakes
Sliced Fresh Fruit
Yummy Sweet Rolls
Coffee

Picnic with the Grandkids

Black Bean Dip and Veggies with Pita Wedges
Assorted Fruit Drinks
Chicken Kabobs
Dilled Potato Salad
Boston Baked Beans
Chocolate Chip Pumpkin Cake
Frozen Fruit Cups

A Ladies' Summer Luncheon

Electric Lemonade
Spinach Salad with Cranberries
Basil Tomato Tart
Raspberry Ice Cream
in
Lacy Dessert Baskets
Coffee

Neighborhood Grill Supper

Tai Chee Cocktails
Caponata with Rustic Baguette Slices

Grilled Swordfish
Nutted Wild Rice
Clare's Salad
Pinot noir

Red Raspberry Pie
Coffee

A Southern Buffet Brunch

Milk Punch
Ham Loaf
Crawfish Étouffé
Turnip Casserole
Parmesan Spoonbread
Lemon Tartlets
Coffee

A Progressive Dinner Party

Cosmopolitans
Parmesan Pesto Puffs and Chutney Ball with Toast Points

Shrimp, Red Pepper and Asparagus in Spicy Asian Sauce
Green Rice
Sour Cream Dinner Rolls
Gewürztraminer

Almond Cappuccino Dacquoise
Coffee

A Wickedly Delicious Dessert Party

Cheeses and Fresh Fruit with Fig Chutney
Pistachio Orange Cookies
Amaretti Torte
Bread Pudding New Orleans Style
Triple Chocolate Biscotti
Luscious Lemon Cream
Ruthie and Moe's Carrot Cake
Coffee

A Celebration Dinner for Eight

Whiskey Sours
Snow Peas with Smoked Salmon

Shrimp Pernod
Sancerre

Butternut Squash Soup with Apple Confit

Filet of Beef with Sherry and Mushrooms
Green Beans with Shallots and Bacon
Merlot or St. Emilion

Cheese Selections
Processor Italian Bread Slices

Chamomile Dried Fruit Compote with Mascarpone

Grandmother Donnelly's Irish Cream
Chocolates from the Fearrington Grocery
Coffee

A Halloween Dinner Party

Carrot Soup with Bacon
Chardonnay

Caesar Salad

Herbed Stuffed Flank Steak
Corn Pudding
Semi-Dried Tomatoes
Zinfandel or Syrah

Pumpkin Pot de Crème
Coffee

Holiday Open House

Holiday Punch
Chicken Satay and Sauce
Warm Mixed Nuts with Rosemary and Shallots

Leek Tartlets
Crab au Gratin, Warm Toasts
Chicken Liver Pâté
Gewürztraminer

Cranberry Biscotti
Holiday Pie

A Rustic Supper in Front of the Fire

Manhattans
Eggplant-Walnut Pâté
Crisp Toasts
Spicy Glazed Pecans

Cream of Zucchini Soup
Chardonnay

Lamb Shanks Braised with White Beans
Garlic Scented Rapini
Tuscan red or Côte du Rhone

Buttermilk Pie with Raspberry Sauce
Coffee

Cocktails after the Luminaries

Cocktails
Kalamata Olive Aioli
Raw Fennel Sticks
Crab Bites
Asparagus Wrapped with Prosciutto
Blue Cheese Spread, Crackers
Shrimp de Jonghe
Marinated Mushrooms
Cocktail Pecans

Roasted Figs with Candied Lemon and Sherry
White Christmas Fruitcake
Coffee

A Southern New Year's Dinner

Champagne

Baked Ham
Hoppin John
Ingrid's Collard Greens
Sweet Potato Apple Scallop
Ida's Cornmeal Rolls
Chardonnay or Pinot noir

Old Fashioned Pecan Pie
English Walnut Pudding Cake
Coffee

Traditional English Afternoon Tea

Assortment of Tea Sandwiches

Smoked Salmon on Dark Bread
Egg and Watercress

Scones
Served with Devonshire Cream and Strawberry Preserves

Scones with Golden Raisins
Current and Brandy Scones

Tea Breads and Cookies

Blueberry Lemon Tea Bread
English Fruit Loaf

Cakes and Trifle

Amaretti Torte
English Trifle
Chocolate Christmas Trifle
Lemon Tart

Selection of Freshly Brewed Teas
Earl Grey
Darjeeling
Keemum

You Are Cordially Invited

To The Pleasures of Afternoon Tea

The ritual of afternoon tea is a civilized break in a busy day. Henry James captured teatime beautifully in his novel *The Portrait of a Lady* when he wrote; "There are few hours in life more agreeable than the hour dedicated to the ceremony known as afternoon tea."

A tea can be what ever you want it to be. Small sandwiches, scones, tea breads, cookies, small cakes, tartlets, large cakes or English Trifle can be served *but, please, not all at once.* Teatime can be any time but, generally, traditional Afternoon Tea is served mid-afternoon between the hours of 3:00 and 5:00 p.m. High Tea known as the workingman's early supper is served later in the day and is the most substantial of the tea meals unlike the tea foods described above.

Tea played a dramatic role in the establishment of the United States of America. In 1767 the British Government put a tax on the tea used by the American Colonists. The rest is history, the "Boston Tea Party." But, did you know that North Carolina had a famous tea party too? On October 25, 1774, 51 ladies of the town of Edenton, North Carolina met and openly resolved that "We, the Ladys of Edenton, do hereby solemnly engage not to conform to the Pernicious Custom of Drinking Tea," or that "We, the aforesaid Ladys will not promote ye wear of any manufacturer from England until such time that all acts which tend to enslave our Native country shall be repealed." The site of the Edenton Tea Party is marked by a Colonial teapot mounted on a Revolutionary cannon in the town of Edenton.

According to Lipton Tea Company, tea is the world's second most popular drink (after water). Two Americans made major contributions to tea drinking. In 1904 during a heat wave at the World's Fair, Richard Blechynden, poured tea over ice in order to compete with the lemonade stands. Today about three-fourths of all tea drunk in the U.S. is iced. The second contribution also dating back to 1904 started out as a marketing gimmick by Thomas Sullivan, a New York Tea Merchant, who sent customers samples of his teas in little silk pouches. Orders poured in for what we know today as tea bags.

A tea can be as elegant as a formal reception to entertain a great number of people or as cozy as cookies with family or friends. The secret is to set a tempting table and brew a good pot of tea. Occasions such as weddings, birthday parties, showers, afternoon cards games and other home parties are good reasons to have a tea. Remember, tea is a meal for all seasons. It is suitable for all occasions.

Appetizers

and

Beverages

Appetizers and Beverages

Appetizers

Asparagus Wrapped in Prosciutto, 40
Barbecued Ribs, 32
Black Bean Dip Plus, 36 ♥
Blue Cheese Spread, 43
Caponata, 37 ♥
Chicken Liver Pate, 31
Chicken Satay with Satay Sauce, 44 ♥
Chutney Ball, 35
Cocktail Pecans, 46
Crab Bites, 36
Eggplant-Walnut Pate, 34 ♥
Fabulous Spinach Artichokes, 45
Festive Salmon Mousse, 41
Kalamata Olive Aioli, 34
Leek Tartlets, 38
Marinated Mushrooms, 40
Parmesan Pesto Puffs, 42
Reuben Spread, 39
Shrimp de Jonghe, 33
Snow Peas with Smoked Salmon, 46
Spicy Glazed Pecans, 31 ♥
Stuffed Clams, 47 ♥
Stuffed Tortillas, 35
Warm Mixed Nuts with Rosemary and Shallots, 32
Wild Mushroom Toasts, 42

Beverages

A Perfect Pot of Tea, 52
Cosmopolitan, Modern Martini, 50
Electric Lemonade, 48
Grandmother Donnelly's Irish Cream, 48
Holiday Punch, 51
Joyce's Whiskey Sour, 51
Milk Punch, 50
Minted Iced Tea, 49
Tai Chee Cocktail, 49
Tea Sandwiches, 53
Will's Manhattan, 51

♥ Heart Healthy

Spicy Glazed Pecans ♥

1/2 cup sugar
3 tablespoons water
1 teaspoon kosher salt
1/4-1/2 teaspoon cayenne pepper
3 cups pecan halves

- Preheat oven to 350° F.
- Butter a large baking sheet.
- Combine the sugar, water, salt and cayenne pepper in a saucepan and mix well.
- Bring to a boil over medium heat, stirring frequently and boil for 2 minutes.
- Add the pecans, stirring until coated.
- Spread the pecans evenly on the prepared baking sheet. Bake for 10-15 minutes or until the nuts just begin to brown.
- Transfer the pecans to a baking sheet lined with parchment paper and separate with a fork.
- Let stand until cool. These may be stored in an airtight container for up to one week.

Rhoda Berkowitz

Chicken Liver Pâté

Makes 2 cups

4 tablespoons butter
1 pound chicken livers
2 green onions, chopped
1/4 teaspoon nutmeg
1/4 cup cognac or dry vermouth
1/2 teaspoon salt
1/8 teaspoon pepper

- In a medium skillet brown the livers in butter for 10 minutes.
- Place the contents of the skillet in a blender or food processor with all other ingredients and blend until finely chopped and well mixed. Be careful not to over process.
- Put the mixture into a crock or bowl and refrigerate for at least one day.

*The pâté can be made ahead. It keeps in the refrigerator for up to one week and can be frozen.
Serve with flavored crackers such as Wheat Thins.*

Jacqueline Stempfle

Warm Mixed Nuts with Rosemary & Shallots

5 cups mixed nuts, such as cashews, walnuts, almonds, pistachios, pecans
1 tablespoon extra virgin olive oil
2 small shallots, thinly sliced into rings
3 garlic cloves, thinly sliced
2 tablespoons butter
1/4 cup coarsely chopped fresh rosemary
1/4 teaspoon cayenne pepper
1 tablespoon brown sugar, packed
1 tablespoon kosher salt

I gave jars of these for Christmas last year. They received rave notices. They are also great for a cocktail party

Vaughn Owen

- Preheat oven to 350°F.
- Place nuts in a single layer on 2 cookie sheets and bake in preheated oven for 8-12 minutes. Rotate pans and stir nuts halfway through baking. Transfer nuts to a large bowl.
- Heat olive oil in a small skillet over medium heat. Add shallots and garlic. Fry until golden, 3-5 minutes, and transfer to paper towels.
- Melt the butter and pour over the nuts.
- Add the rosemary, cayenne, brown sugar and salt and stir well to combine.
- Toss in the crispy garlic and shallots.
- Serve warm. The nuts may be made ahead and reheated in a 300° F. oven for 10 minutes.

Barbecued Ribs

Serves 10

4 pounds of spareribs in pieces
2 medium onions
1 cup tomato catsup
1 tablespoon lemon juice
1/2 cup vinegar
2 teaspoons salt
2 teaspoons dry mustard
1/2 teaspoon Tabasco sauce
1 bay leaf
1/4 cup chili sauce
1/2 teaspoon pickling spice

Continued on next page

Barbecued Ribs *continued*

- Preheat the oven to 300° F.
- Separate each rib at the bone and cut into three inch pieces.
- Arrange spareribs on baking pan and cook in the preheated oven until they begin to brown. Pour off fat.
- Combine onions, catsup, lemon juice, vinegar, salt, mustard, Tabasco sauce, bay leaf, chili sauce and pickling spice and simmer for 30 minutes. Add a little water if necessary.
- Strain the sauce and put half on the ribs. Return the ribs to the oven and continue to cook until done, about one hour.
- While cooking, baste the ribs at intervals with the rest of the sauce to prevent drying out. Serve in a chafing dish.

Shrimp de Jonghe

Serves 12

3 pounds fresh, uncooked shrimp
1 clove garlic, minced
3 tablespoons chopped parsley
1/2 teaspoon paprika
Dash of cayenne
1/3 cup sherry
3/4 cup butter, melted
1 1/2 cups soft breadcrumbs
Fresh parsley for garnish

- Preheat oven to 325° F.
- Cook shrimp in boiling, salted water until pink. Drain and cool in cold water; peel.
- Mix garlic, chopped parsley, paprika, cayenne and sherry. Toss with shrimp.
- Mix butter and breadcrumbs with a fork until mixture resembles small pebbles.
- Place shrimp in a greased baking dish and top with crumbs.
- Bake in preheated oven until crumbs brown, about 20-25 minutes.
- Sprinkle with chopped parsley and serve with cocktail picks.
- Serve piping hot

Jane Silverstein

The ribs should not be dripping with sauce or falling off the bone. The sauce can be made ahead of time and frozen.

Anne Louise Snelling

Eggplant-Walnut Pate ♥

Serves 10-12

1 large eggplant
2 teaspoons fresh gingerroot, peeled, grated, and finely chopped
2 cloves garlic, mashed
1 tablespoon extra-virgin olive oil
1 cup walnut pieces, finely ground
1/8 teaspoon ground allspice
Salt and hot pepper sauce to taste

- Preheat oven to 450° F.
- Pierce eggplant with a fork in several places and bake until very soft, about 45 minutes. Remove eggplant from oven, slash to let steam escape, drain off any liquid, and scrape the pulp into a food processor with the gingerroot, garlic, and olive oil. Process until smooth. Add walnuts and allspice and process again.
- Season with salt and hot pepper sauce to taste and pour into a medium bowl. Chill several hours. Spread on crackers or toast.

This is adapted from a recipe from Dr. Andrew Weil. His comment: "This elegant vegetarian version of the traditional high fat pate is filled with flavor and is nutritious".

Maggie Gaudet

Kalamata Olive Aioli

Makes 3 cups

4 ounces Kalamata olives, pitted
4-6 cloves minced garlic or to taste
1 ounce fresh basil leaves
1 ounce fresh Parmesan cheese, coarsely grated
1 (16-ounce) jar mayonnaise
Salt and pepper to taste

- Drain olives of all liquid.
- Place olives, basil, garlic and Parmesan cheese in a food processor and puree until mixture begins to thicken.
- Add mayonnaise and process for 2 minutes.
- Add salt and pepper to taste and pulse to combine.
- Chill well, at least 4 hours, before serving

This is my favorite dip. I first tasted it at the Arizona Biltmore years ago. The chef gave me the recipe. My guests always love it. Serve with raw vegetables or bread sticks. It is even better if refrigerated overnight before serving. This is a garlic lovers' dish.

Burt Weiss

Stuffed Tortillas

Makes 40 appetizers

1 (7-ounce) jar roasted red bell peppers
2 cups cooked chicken, chopped
1 (8-ounce) package cream cheese, softened
1 (0.4-ounce) envelope Ranch-style buttermilk dressing mix
1/4 cup chopped, ripe olives
1/2 small onion, diced
1 (4.5-ounce) can chopped green chilies, drained
2 tablespoons fresh cilantro, chopped
1/2 teaspoon pepper
1/4 cup pine nuts, optional
8 6-inch flour tortillas

- Drain roasted red peppers well, pressing between layers of paper towels, and chop.
- Stir together roasted red peppers and all remaining ingredients except pine nuts and tortillas.
- Cover and chill at least 2 hours, preferably overnight
- Stir pine nuts, if desired, into chicken mixture and spoon evenly over tortillas.
- Roll up and cut each roll into 5 slices.
- Serve warm or cold.

Pat Buyze

Chutney Ball

Serves 8-10

8 ounces softened cream cheese
1/2 cup quality fruit chutney
1/2 cup chopped pecans
3-4 large pieces crystallized ginger, chopped fine
1 teaspoon curry powder
1-2 teaspoons milk, if needed
1 (8-10 ounce) jar red pepper jelly

- Mix all ingredients, except jelly.
- Form the mixture into a softball size ball. Use milk if mix is too stiff to work.
- Refrigerate ball at least several hours.
- Before serving, frost ball with jelly allowing extra to surround the ball on the plate as desired.

A half-cup of flaked coconut can be added to the initial ingredients or used to coat the ball instead of the pepper jelly. Serve with mild crackers. Or, instead of forming a ball, use mixture to fill Belgian endive boats. Sprinkle tops very lightly with cayenne pepper.

Marietta Williams

Crab Bites

Makes 60 bite-size appetizers

1/2 cup margarine, room temperature
1 (4 ounce) jar Kraft Old English cheese spread
6 ounces canned crab, drained
4 green onions, chopped, not minced
1/8 teaspoon cayenne pepper
5 English muffins, split in half
Paprika for garnish

- Preheat broiler to 400° F. and put rack in lower half of oven.
- Cream margarine and cheese until light.
- Stir in crab, green onion, and cayenne.
- Spread on muffin halves.
- Cut each muffin half into 6 pie-shaped wedges and place on a baking sheet.
- Broil 10-15 minutes until bubbly and beginning to brown.
- Serve immediately.

These appetizers may be made ahead and frozen. Place them on a cookie sheet until frozen and then put into freezer bags. When ready to use, pull out as many as you need and broil them.

Sandy Gerow

Black Bean Dip Plus ♥

Makes 6 cups

3–4 ripe avocados
1 red onion
1 red or orange pepper
1 pint cherry tomatoes
Chopped cilantro to taste
2 jalapeños, diced
1 can black beans, drained
1 can corn niblets in water, drained
1 tablespoon olive oil
1 teaspoon cumin

Tortilla chips

- Chop the fresh vegetables and add the cilantro and jalapeños.
- Add the drained beans and corn.
- Stir in olive oil and cumin.
- Serve with tortilla chips.

Courtesy of Tracy Siebold, Haddonfield, NJ, daughter-in-law of Ann Siebold

Ann Siebold

Caponata ♥

Serves 20 as an appetizer or 6 as a vegetable

1 medium eggplant, unpeeled and cubed
1/4 cup salt, will be rinsed off later
3/4 cup plus 2 tablespoons olive oil
2 cups chopped onions
1 cup chopped celery
1 (14-ounce) can diced tomatoes with Italian seasoning,
  drained
1/2 cup chopped green olives
1/4 cup capers, drained
1 tablespoon pine nuts
1/2 cup raisins
1/3 cup balsamic vinegar
1 tablespoon brown sugar
Freshly ground black pepper

- Salt eggplant in a colander and drain one hour. Rinse well and pat dry with paper towels.
- Heat 3/4 cup oil in a large skillet over high heat. Sauté eggplant 5-8 minutes until golden brown. Remove to a strainer and drain.
- Wipe the pan clean. Add 2 tablespoons oil and sauté onions and celery until just tender.
- Add tomatoes, cover pan and cook 4-5 minutes on low to moderate heat. Uncover and cook 5 minutes more.
- Add eggplant, olives, capers, pine nuts and raisins.
- Combine vinegar and sugar and stir until sugar dissolves. Pour into the eggplant mixture and simmer, covered 5-10 minutes.
- Add pepper to taste. Cool to room temperature. Serve with crackers.

This is my daughter Jill Gammon's recipe. It is a favorite in our family. People who usually do not like eggplant love this dish. It keeps in the refrigerator for two weeks and improves each day with just a stir. It is also good served as a vegetable or over pasta. We usually serve this dish with mild crackers or toast rounds.

Jane Silverstein

Leek Tartlets

Makes 24 tartlets

Tart Pastry
2 cups all-purpose flour
1/2 teaspoon salt
12 tablespoons chilled butter
2 tablespoons chilled vegetable shortening
1/4-1/3 cup ice water

Mixer method:
- Place flour and salt in bowl of electric mixer.
- Cut butter into small pieces and add to bowl along with shortening. Turn beater on and off until butter and shortening have broken down to the size of peas.
- Quickly add the ice water, bit by bit; stop immediately when dough begins to mass on the blade.
- Place dough on a lightly floured surface and knead with the heel of your hand a few times to work the dough.
- Shape into a 5 inch circle and cover with wax paper. Chill in the refrigerator for 2 hours before using.

Processor method
- Place flour and salt in food processor.
- Cut butter into small pieces and add to processor along with shortening.
- Process for 2-3 seconds to break butter into pea-size pieces.
- Add ice water little by little until dough forms a mass on blades, about 15 seconds.
- Place on lightly floured board and knead with heel of hand a few times to work dough and smooth it.
- Shape into a 5-inch circle, cover with wax paper and chill for 2 hours.
- Butter twenty-four 2 1/2-inch tartlet molds or muffin tins about 1/2 inch deep.
- Roll out chilled pastry dough 1/8 inch thick. Cut with cookie cutter 1/2 inch larger in diameter than your molds. Line molds with pastry and prick with a fork.

Continued on next page

Leek Tartlets *continued*

Filling
6 tablespoons butter
4 cups chopped leeks, about 4 leeks
2 large stalks celery, chopped, optional
Salt and freshly ground black pepper
2 large eggs
1 1/2 cups heavy cream
Few drops hot pepper sauce
Salt and freshly ground pepper

- Preheat oven to 425° F.
- Melt butter in saucepan, add leeks and celery and stir to coat with butter. Cover and cook over low heat 8-10 minutes, stirring to prevent sticking. Season with salt and pepper.
- Beat eggs with cream; season with hot sauce, salt and pepper.
- Add leek mixture to eggs and blend with a fork.
- Fill molds and bake for 15 minutes or until nicely browned. Let rest 1 minute before unmolding. Serve hot.

Norma Berry

Reuben Spread

Makes 2 cups

8 ounces cream cheese cut into small pieces
1 cup sauerkraut, drained and chopped
1/2 cup finely chopped cooked corned beef
2 teaspoons onion, minced
1 tablespoon ketchup
2 teaspoons mustard
1 cup grated or finely chopped Swiss cheese

- Preheat oven to 375° F.
- Mix all ingredients together until well combined.
- Put in an ovenproof dish and bake covered for 30 minutes in the preheated oven.
- Uncover and bake another 5-8 minutes.
- Serve warm with Triscuits, rye crackers or Frito scoopers.

Joan Zollinger

Asparagus Wrapped in Prosciutto

Serves 24

24 thick asparagus spears, trimmed and peeled
12 thin slices prosciutto, about 5 ounces
1/2 cup freshly grated Parmesan cheese
1/4 teaspoon coarsely ground black pepper

- Preheat oven to 450° F.
- In 5 quart Dutch oven, heat 3 quarts water to boiling over high heat. Add asparagus and cook 3 minutes to blanch. Drain, rinse with cold water and pat dry with paper towels.
- Working in batches, spread out prosciutto on a cutting board, cut each slice in half lengthwise and separate slightly. Evenly sprinkle 1 teaspoon Parmesan cheese on each prosciutto strip. Place one asparagus spear at the end of one strip, and wrap the prosciutto in spiral along the length of the asparagus. Do not cover the asparagus tip.
- Transfer to a jellyroll pan. Repeat with remaining prosciutto, Parmesan and asparagus. Sprinkle with pepper and bake 10 minutes.
- Transfer to paper towels to drain.
- Arrange on a platter and serve warm.

You may use thin asparagus if desired. Just reduce the blanching time to 2 minutes and baking time to 8 minutes. If not serving right away, cover and refrigerate up to 6 hours.

Carol Sherrod

Marinated Mushrooms

Serves 20

1 pound butter
4 pounds button mushrooms, about 100
1 bottle burgundy or port
1 1/2 tablespoons Worcestershire sauce
1 teaspoon dill
1 teaspoon pepper
1 teaspoon garlic powder
2 cups water
3 beef bouillon cubes
3 chicken bouillon cubes
3 cubes vegetable bouillon

- Put all ingredients in large pot. Bring to boil. Reduce heat and simmer 3-5 hours until liquid is almost gone.
- Taste and add salt if needed.

This really is a WOW recipe. I have made these for years for party food and everyone loves them. It's not a recipe for the faint-hearted with all that butter and wine but is it ever good! It is easily frozen and heated for later use. Serve warm in a chafing dish.

Peggy Quinn

Festive Salmon Mousse

Serves a crowd

1 envelope gelatin
1/4 cup cold water
1/2 cup boiling water
1/2 cup Hellman's mayonnaise
1 tablespoon fresh lemon juice, do not use bottled juice
2 tablespoons finely grated onion
Dash of Tabasco sauce
1/4 teaspoon sweet paprika
1 teaspoon salt
1 tablespoon finely chopped fresh dill
1 cup finely flaked, canned salmon, skin and bones
  removed
1 cup heavy cream
Capers and very thinly sliced cucumber for garnish

- Spray a 4-cup mold with cooking spray.
- Soften gelatin in cold water in a large mixing bowl.
- Stir in the boiling water and whisk mixture slowly until gelatin dissolves. Cool to room temperature.
- Whisk in mayonnaise, lemon juice, onion, Tabasco, paprika, salt and dill. Stir to blend completely and refrigerate for about 15 minutes, or until mixture begins to thicken slightly.
- Fold in the finely flaked salmon. In a separate bowl, whip the cream until it is thickened to peaks and fluffy. Fold the cream gently into the salmon mixture.
- Transfer the mixture to a mold and cover and chill for at least four hours.
- Unmold, garnish with capers and cucumber and serve with crackers and champagne.

Lynn Zempel

Parmesan Pesto Puffs

8 ounces cream cheese, softened
3 tablespoons pesto, homemade or in a jar
3 tablespoons chopped green onions
3 drops Tabasco
2/3 cup freshly grated Parmesan cheese, divided
Thin-sliced, good quality white bread

- In a food processor, mix cream cheese, pesto, onions and Tabasco.
- Transfer to a bowl, stir in 1/2 cup of Parmesan cheese and chill until ready to serve.
- Cut out 60 1 1/2-inch bread rounds and butter on one side.
- Place on a cookie sheet and broil until browned. Turn over and lightly brown the unbuttered side.
- Spread the buttered side with the cheese mixture, forming a point in the middle.
- Dip in the remaining Parmesan cheese. At this point you can place the rounds on a baking sheet in the freezer. When frozen, store in Ziploc bags until ready to serve.
- Place on a baking sheet and broil until puffy and light brown, watching them constantly.

These puffs freeze like a dream! They are great to have in the freezer for the unexpected guests. They take only a few minutes to cook but may burn quickly if not watched.

Barbara Merten

Wild Mushroom Toasts

Serves 8-10

2 large shallots, finely chopped
2 tablespoons butter
1 pound mixed wild mushrooms, finely chopped
2 tablespoons freshly grated Parmesan cheese
2 tablespoons finely chopped parsley
1 tablespoon fresh lemon juice
Salt and pepper to taste
12 slices Pepperidge Farm white bread
1/2 pound goat cheese

- Sauté shallots in 2 tablespoons butter until wilted.
- Add chopped mushrooms and quickly sauté. Add butter if needed.
- Add Parmesan cheese, parsley, lemon juice and salt and pepper. Mix well and set the pan aside.
- Toast bread. Remove crusts. Cut each piece into two triangles.
- When ready to serve, warm mushroom mixture.
- Spread each toast point with goat cheese and top with a spoonful of the mushrooms. Serve immediately.

This takes no time to fix and is the hit of every party. My daughter sent it to me from California. Any mushrooms can be used but the blend of different tastes enhances the flavor. I usually use shitakes and portabellas; sometimes I add dried morels or porcini. Toasted baguette slices may be substituted for the toast points.

Peggy Quinn

Bleu Cheese Spread

Serves 12-15

4 ounces Camembert or ripe Brie cut up with rind
1 cup shredded Swiss cheese
4 ounces Danish bleu cheese, crumbled or more if desired
3 (8-ounce) packages cream cheese, softened
2 tablespoons sour cream
2 tablespoons milk or more if necessary
Walnut pieces, coarsely chopped
Apple and/or pear slices
Crackers of choice

- In a medium bowl, mix cream cheese with remaining ingredients except nuts and fruit. Mixture will be stiff.
- Line the bottom and sides of a 9-inch spring form pan with plastic wrap.
- Crumble walnuts on the bottom of the pan, covering it completely.
- Spoon in the cheese mixture and smooth it out with the back of a spoon.
- Cover with plastic wrap, pressing lightly to smooth the top.
- Refrigerate for several days for flavors to mellow.
- To serve, remove the plastic from the top and place a large plate over it. Invert so the walnuts are on top. Remove spring form pan and the plastic.
- Serve with apple, pear slices and crackers.

This spread needs 2 to 3 days in the refrigerator to mellow and can be made a week ahead. Do not put in too much milk to make it runny. The mixture should be thick.

Annie Adams

Chicken Satay with Satay Sauce ♥

Makes 50 pieces

1 1/4 pounds boneless, skinless, chicken breasts, cut in strips
2 tablespoons sesame oil
2 tablespoons cooking oil
1/4 cup dry sherry
1/4 cup soy sauce
2 tablespoons lemon juice
1 1/2 teaspoons minced garlic
1 1/2 teaspoons minced fresh ginger
1/4 teaspoon salt
1/4 teaspoon pepper
Dash of Tabasco sauce

- Combine all ingredients. Marinate 1–12 hours.
- Preheat oven to 375° F.
- Thread chicken strips on wet wood skewers. Lay on baking sheet. Bake 5–10 minutes in preheated oven.
- Serve with Satay Sauce at room temperature for dipping.

Sauce:
4 teaspoons cooking oil
2 teaspoons sesame oil
1/2 cup minced red onion
2 tablespoons minced garlic
1 teaspoon minced fresh ginger
1 tablespoon red wine vinegar
1 tablespoon brown sugar
1/3 cup peanut butter
1/2 teaspoon ground coriander
3 tablespoons ketchup
3 tablespoons soy sauce
1 tablespoon lemon or lime juice
1/2 teaspoon pepper
Dash of Tabasco sauce

- Over low heat, sauté onion, garlic and ginger in the oils until softened.
- Add vinegar and brown sugar and cook, stirring, until sugar dissolves. Remove from the heat and transfer to a food processor.
- Add all remaining ingredients and process until smooth.

This flavorful appetizer is tender and moist. It takes a bit of last minute work but is very enjoyable.
The recipe was given to me by a friend – a lovely way to remember friends far away. The dip has the illusion of being a bit exotic. It has very complex flavoring.
If made in advance, it may thicken slightly or separate. You may remedy this by whisking in a little hot water.

Nancy Foster

Fabulous Spinach Artichokes

Serves 8-10

2 (16-ounce) packages frozen chopped spinach
2 pounds fresh mushrooms
2 tablespoons butter for mushrooms
5 tablespoons butter for sauce
2 tablespoons flour
1 cup whole milk
Salt and pepper to taste
1 (12-ounce) can artichokes, drained, not marinated
Topping:
1 cup sour cream
1 cup mayonnaise
1/4 cup fresh lemon juice
1/2 cup pine nuts for garnish

- Let unwrapped spinach defrost overnight in strainer and squeeze as dry as possible.
- Preheat oven to 370° F. (that is correct! –not 375).
- Clean the mushrooms with a damp cloth or paper towel and slice thinly. Save 5-6 mushroom caps.
- Sauté mushrooms in 2 tablespoons butter until browned and most of the liquid has evaporated.
- In a large saucepan melt the remaining butter and stir in the flour. Stir over low heat for 1-2 minutes. Add the milk in a slow stream, stirring until the sauce thickens and bubbles. Season to taste with salt and pepper.
- Add spinach and mushrooms to sauce and stir to combine well.
- Slice the artichokes, dry on paper towels and place in the bottom of an ovenproof baking dish. Save a few for garnish.
- Pour the spinach mixture over the artichokes.
- Mix topping together and pour over spinach mixture.
- Garnish with mushroom caps, artichoke hearts and pine nuts
- Bake in preheated oven for 30 minutes, until bubbly.

This dish can be made ahead to the point where you put on the topping. It doubles or triples well for a crowd and is very popular as a hot appetizer. It can also be served as a side dish. If there are leftovers, just stir the topping into the spinach mixture and put in smaller bowl. Microwave for 4 minutes, covered. Add grated cheese if you wish.

Ginny Mellencamp

Snow Peas with Smoked Salmon

Serves 8-10

This appetizer is colorful, different and delicious. I once used it as an appetizer for an English dinner menu. It does not freeze well.

Nancy Foster

1/2-3/4 pound snow peas
8 ounces cream cheese, room temperature
4 ounces smoked salmon, no bones or skin
Juice of 1/2 lemon
2–3 tablespoons heavy cream
White pepper

- Blanch snow peas 60 seconds in boiling water. Drain and immediately plunge into ice water to cover. Drain and dry. Split snow peas lengthwise and remove the "strings". Keep the 2 halves paired up and attached.
- Puree remaining ingredients to spreading consistency.
- Chill filling for 3-4 hours.
- When well chilled, pipe or spread into the split peas.
- Refrigerate until ready to serve.

Cocktail Pecans

Serves 12

This recipe will keep for up to one week in a plastic bag or airtight container. Other nuts may be substituted or a combination of nuts may be used.

Janet Lorant

4 cups pecans
1/4 cup olive oil
1 1/2 tablespoons dried rosemary
1 1/2 tablespoons sea salt, or to taste

- Preheat oven to 350° F.
- Place pecans on a baking sheet in a single layer. Toast in oven for 10 minutes until the pecans are fragrant and starting to brown. Remove from the oven and set aside to cool slightly.
- Heat olive oil in a large skillet. Add dried rosemary and stir until oil begins to shimmer. Stir until rosemary releases its fragrance, but remove from heat before it begins to brown.
- In a large bowl, combine the warm rosemary oil and nuts and stir gently to coat. Add 1/2 tablespoon of sea salt at a time, stirring after each addition. Continue to stir until all the nuts are coated with oil and salt.
- Allow the nuts to cool completely. The nuts will absorb more oil as they cool. Store in an airtight container until ready to serve.

Stuffed Clams ♥

Serves 6 for cocktails or 4 as a first course

24 fresh clams
3 tablespoons freshly grated Parmesan Regianno cheese
3 tablespoons chopped Italian flat leaf parsley
1/3 cup fine, fresh breadcrumbs
2 teaspoons minced fresh garlic
6 tablespoons olive oil, divided
Salt and pepper to taste
1/4 cup water
1/4 cup dry white wine

- Scrub clams and soak in iced salt water for 1 hour. Rinse well.
- Combine cheese, parsley, breadcrumbs, garlic, and 3 tablespoons of the olive oil, salt and pepper. Mix well.
- Combine water, wine and clams in a large skillet. Cover and steam the clams for 2-4 minutes until they open. Discard any that do not open. Remove lid and allow clams to cool.
- Drain the liquid from each clam into the skillet. Set clams aside.
- Strain the clam broth and use for soup or another purpose.
- Remove top shell of each clam and discard. Be sure to remove all bits of shell. Using a spoon, loosen each clam and place into remaining shell.
- Spoon crumb mixture onto clams; do not pack.
- May be made ahead and refrigerated, covered, for up to 8 hours.
- Preheat oven to 400° F.
- When ready to bake, drizzle clams with remaining oil and bake until crumbs are lightly browned, about 15 -20 minutes. Do not overcook.

Garlic-loving guests rave about these clams.

Barbara Terry

Electric Lemonade

Serves 8

2 cups sugar
2 cups water
1 cup fresh lemon juice
1 large mint sprig, finely chopped, plus sprigs for garnish
8 ounces lemon-flavored vodka, also called citrus vodka
1 quart sparkling water, or to taste
1 tablespoon freshly grated lemon zest for garnish

- Place serving glasses in the refrigerator or freezer to chill.
- Mix sugar and water in a small pot and boil for 3 minutes to make a simple syrup. Cool.
- In a medium bowl, stir together 1 cup of the prepared syrup, lemon juice and mint. Pour mixture into ice cube tray and freeze for 1 hour. Leftover syrup can be refrigerated indefinitely.
- In a blender, blend frozen cubes, sparkling water, chopped mint and vodka.
- Strain the mixture to remove mint leaves if desired.
- Pour into chilled glasses. Garnish with mint sprigs and lemon zest.

This recipe is a variation of one from Oprah's cooking shows. Lemonade with an extra spark!

Kathy Bowe

Grandmother Donnelly's Irish Cream

Serves 19-12

3 pasteurized eggs
1 (14-ounce) can sweetened condensed milk
2 cups light cream
1 teaspoon vanilla
1/2 teaspoon almond extract
1 1/2 cups Irish whiskey

- Put all ingredients in a blender and process for 2 minutes.
- Refrigerate and allow to age about 24 hours.

This is wonderful on St. Patrick's Day but any other time is fine too.

Ethel D. Cunningham

Tai Chee Cocktail

Serves 2

**6 fresh lychees, pitted, or 4 canned lychees, washed and
  drained**
2 tablespoons freshly squeezed lemon juice
3 tablespoons citrus-flavored vodka
1 cup crushed ice
Sugar or artificial sweetener to taste
Mint leaves for garnish

- In a blender, combine the lychees, lemon juice, vodka, ice, and
  sweetener. Puree until thick and smooth.
- Pour into a martini glass and garnish with a mint leaf.

Anonymous

Minted Iced Tea

Makes approximately 1 gallon

1 3/4 cups sugar
2 cups water
8 regular tea bags or 3 jumbo, family sized, tea bags
8 generous sprigs of fresh mint
1 quart boiling water
2 quarts cold water
2 cups orange juice
3/4 cup lemon juice
Fresh mint sprigs, optional

- Combine sugar and 2 cups water in a saucepan and stir well.
  Bring to a boil and boil 5 minutes. Remove from heat.
- Add the tea bags and mint to the quart of boiling water. Cover
  and let stand for 10 minutes. Remove the tea bags and mint
  and discard.
- Combine sugar water, tea mixture, 2 quarts cold water, orange
  juice and lemon juice, and stir well.
- Chill and serve over ice. Garnish with mint springs, if desired.

John Webster

Cosmopolitan, Modern Martini

2 parts Citron Vodka
1 part triple sec
1 part Rose's Lime Juice
2 parts cranberry juice
Crushed ice
Fresh lime wedges

The 30's and 40's kids love them. So do the old folks. Enjoy!

Joyce Mason

- Combine all ingredients and stir.
- Place in a martini shaker with crushed ice and shake.
- Rub lime wedge around rim of glass and serve.

Milk Punch

Serves 8-10

16 ounces brandy
1 1/2 cups simple syrup made with 1 1/2 cups of water
   and 1 1/2 cups sugar. Heat until sugar dissolves.
1/2 cup white crème de menthe
1 quart whole milk
1 quart half and half

- Mix all ingredients.
- Place in a covered container and freeze overnight. The taste will mellow after it sits for a while in the freezer.
- The next day scoop out the mixture and blend it in a blender. Put it back in the freezer for 5-6 hours.
- An hour or so before serving take it out of the freezer and place it in the refrigerator until it gets to a "pourable, but slushy" stage. Stir occasionally.
- Serve in punch cups or large wine glasses.
- Garnish with fresh mint.

Anonymous

Will's Manhattan

Serves 2

3 ounces Whiskey
1 ounce Sweet Vermouth
Dash Bitters or to taste

- Stir with cracked ice and serve

This is especially good on a cold winter's night in front of a fire. For a sweeter drink, add splash of Grenadine syrup.

Sam Mason

Holiday Punch

Serves approximately 36

1 (32-ounce) bottle cranberry juice cocktail
1 (46-ounce) can unsweetened pineapple juice
2 cups orange juice
2/3 cup lemon juice
1/2 cup sugar
2 teaspoons almond extract
1 (33-ounce) bottle ginger ale, chilled

- Combine all ingredients except ginger ale and chill.
- To serve, add ginger ale, stirring well.

Anonymous

Joyce's Whiskey Sour

Serves 4

8 ounces frozen lemonade
4 ounces whiskey or Bourbon
4 ounces water
1/4 cup eggbeaters
1 cup crushed ice

- Pour all ingredients in blender and blend until smooth
- Garnish with cherries and or orange slices

Joyce Mason

Camellia sinensis, an evergreen shrub, is the origin of all tea leaves. Flavor characteristics of tea depend on where the tea is grown, varying altitudes and weather, soil conditions and how the tea is processed and blended.

Tea is harvested after each flush, the sprouting of the top two leaves and bud. Then it is processed into any of the four types of tea which are Black, Green, Oolong and White.

Herbal Teas are not technically true "teas", but are made from any part of an edible plant: leaves, flowers, seeds, bark, roots and fruit peels. Since they do not contain tea leaves from the Camellia sinensis plant, they are caffeine-free.

Carol Genovese

A Perfect Pot of Tea

Makes one pot

Freshly drawn cold water
Loose tea of your choice

- Bring water to a full rolling boil, but do not allow to over boil.
- Pour some of the boiling water into the empty teapot to pre-warm the pot.
- Discard the water from the pot and add the tea, one teaspoon per cup and one for the pot.
- Bring the pot to the kettle, not the kettle to the pot, and fill the pot with boiling water.
- Allow the tea to steep for 5 minutes. Brewing longer than 5 minutes produces bitterness.
- Serve the tea by pouring through a tea strainer.

The most popular tea consumed in the United States is Black Tea. The selections of teas you can choose from are unlimited. Of course, by all means experiment with the many types and blends. Here are a few suggestions to serve at your tea party.

Earl Grey - A highly aromatic blend of Chinese and Indian black teas distinctly scented with oil of bergamot, a citrus fruit.

Darjeeling - Grown in the foothills of the Himalayas, this fine Indian variety of black teas is consistently noted for its wonderful, soothing flavor and exquisite bouquet.

Keemum - Known as "the burgundy of teas," is the best of China black teas with a superior flavor and an attractive deep amber color.

Tea Sandwiches

Thin sliced bread such as Pepperidge Farm Original,
do not use the very thin type
Fillings of your choice

- Place fillings on bread and then trim crusts. Allow one sandwich per guest with 3-4 different fillings per occasion. Fillings should be finely minced or thinly sliced.
- Choose fillings that are suitable for the occasion and season.
- Vary breads and shapes; cut into circles, squares or triangles.
- Place all same shaped sandwiches with same filling on one platter. This will assist guests in finding their favorites.
- If making sandwiches in advance, cover with damp paper towels to prevent from drying out. Then wrap in plastic wrap. Dried or soggy tea sandwiches are not appetizing.
- Decorate platters with fresh herbs, edible flowers or use doilies. Always make an attractive presentation.

Egg and Watercress

Makes 24 sandwiches

4 hard-cooked eggs, peeled and diced
4 tablespoons mayonnaise
2 tablespoons Dijon mustard
Salt and freshly ground black pepper to taste
12 thin slices whole wheat bread
1 small bunch watercress, about 20 sprigs, stems removed,
washed, dried and coarsely chopped

- In medium bowl, combine eggs, mayonnaise, mustard, salt and pepper. Blend with a fork to desired consistency.
- Divide and spread egg mixture evenly among 6 bread slices. Sprinkle with watercress and top with remaining bread slices. Trim off crusts and cut into desired shape.

Continued on the next page

Tea sandwiches should be dainty, elegant, fresh and moist.

Carol Genovese

Tea Sandwiches *continued*

Smoked Salmon on Dark Bread

Makes 12 sandwiches

2 tablespoons unsalted butter, softened
1 teaspoon capers
3 slices of pumpernickel bread
6 ounces thinly sliced smoked salmon
Chopped fresh dill

- Using a fork, mash together the butter and the capers until they are blended.
- Divide this mixture between the 3 slices of bread and spread evenly. Place 2 ounces smoked salmon on each slice of bread.
- Sprinkle fresh dill over the top of each sandwich. Trim off crusts and cut each into 4 pieces. These are open-faced sandwiches.

Other Suggested Sandwich Fillings

- Very thinly sliced cucumber and unsalted butter.
- Caviar and cream cheese.
- Smoked salmon with a squeeze of lemon juice, cayenne pepper and unsalted butter.
- Cream cheese and finely chopped dates.
- Finely minced hard-boiled eggs with mayonnaise and olives.
- Cream cheese and mango chutney.
- Chicken and tarragon mayonnaise.

The possibilities are endless and exciting. Experiment with open-faced sandwiches and edible flowers for texture and color.

Brunch
and
Breads

Brunch and Breads

Brunch
Bacon and Egg Strata, 56
Basil Tomato Tart, 62
Eggs Mornay, 60
Gingerbread Pancakes, 58
Ham, Fontina and Spinach Bread Pudding, 59
Holiday Morning French Toast, 62
Julia's Country Granola, 60 ♥
Maple-Bacon Oven Pancake, 58
Noodle Kugel, 61
Spanakopita, 63
Spinach Pie, 64
Tomato and Onion Tart, 55
Wild Mushroom Grit Cakes, 56

Breads, Quick
Banana Blueberry Muffins, 66
Blueberry Lemon Tea Bread, 67
Currant and Brandy Scones, 65
English Fruit Loaf, 68
Fruit Muffins, 71
Morning Glory Muffins, 68
Nutmeg Muffins, 66
Parmesan Spoon Bread, 72
Pinehurst Muffins, 70
Scones with Golden Raisins, 69
Strawberry Nut Bread, 71

Breads, Yeast
California Overnight Rolls, 78
Fig and Fennel Bread, 79 ♥
Ida's Cornmeal Rolls, 74
Processor Italian Bread, 74
Rosemary, Kalamata Olive and Coarse Salt Focaccia, 73 ♥
Rustic Baguette, 76 ♥
Sour Cream Dinner Rolls, 75
Yummy Sweet Rolls, 80

♥ Heart Healthy

Tomato and Onion Tart

Serves 10

Butter pastry dough:
2 cups all-purpose flour
1 1/2 teaspoons salt
3/4 cup cold unsalted butter
6-7 tablespoons ice water
Tart:
2 large onions, about 1 1/2 pounds, sliced thin
2 tablespoons olive oil
1/2 pound Gruyere cheese, shredded, about 2 cups
1/2 pound plum tomatoes cut into 1/2-inch wedges
2 medium size yellow tomatoes cut into 1/2-inch wedges
1/4 cup Nicoise olives, pitted

- To make dough: place flour and salt in a food processor and blend in butter until mixture resembles coarse meal.
- Add ice water and process until mixture begins to form a ball.
- On a work surface smear dough in 3 or 4 forward motions with heel of hand to slightly develop gluten. Form dough into a ball and flatten to form a disk. Wrap dough in plastic wrap and chill for 1 hour.
- Cook onions in oil in large heavy skillet with salt to taste, covered, over medium heat until softened, about 20 minutes, stirring occasionally. Remove lid and cook until onions are golden and liquid evaporates. Remove from heat to cool slightly.
- Preheat oven to 375° F.
- Roll out dough and fit into a 10-12 inch tart pan.
- Spread onion mixture over dough and top with cheese.
- Arrange tomato wedges and olives in concentric circles over cheese. Season with salt and pepper.
- Bake on middle rack of oven for 1 hour, or until pastry is golden. Cool on rack.

*Dough may be made up to 1 week ahead, wrapped in plastic wrap and refrigerated.
Serve as part of a buffet or brunch; great for a picnic!*

*Ethel D.
Cunningham*

Bacon and Egg Strata

Serves 6-8

1/2 pound bacon, fried and crumbled
1 1/2 cups white bread crumbled
1 3/4 cups milk
10 eggs
Salt and pepper to taste
4 tablespoons butter
1 tablespoon mixed fresh herbs, chopped, for eggs
1/2 pound Swiss cheese slices
1/2 cup dried fine breadcrumbs combined with a small
  amount of melted butter

You can prepare the dish up to the point of baking and then refrigerate until morning. When ready to bake put it into a cold oven and set temperature for 450°F. It will take approximately 30 minutes to heat through and melt the cheese.

Jewel Hoogstoel

- Preheat oven to 450° F. Butter a 9 x 13 inch baking dish.
- Fry bacon, crumble and set aside.
- Soak crumbled bread in milk for a few minutes.
- Break eggs into a bowl. Add salt and pepper. Beat well. Strain milk from soaked bread into eggs and mix. Reserve bread.
- Melt butter in large pan and scramble eggs until cooked but NOT dry. Mix in the soaked bread. Set aside.
- Pour egg mixture into prepared baking dish. Sprinkle with herb mix and top with cheese and bacon. Sprinkle bread crumbs on top. Bake in preheated oven for 15 minutes.

Wild Mushroom Grit Cakes

Serves 6

Grits
6 cups water
2 cups heavy cream
2 cups coarse ground yellow grits
1 teaspoon salt
1 teaspoon pepper
Rosemary Cashew Cream Sauce
2 tablespoons butter
1 pound wild mushrooms, sliced, may use a mix of
  Portobello, shiitake and oyster or button mushrooms
1/2 teaspoon finely chopped fresh rosemary
Pinch of dried thyme
1 pint heavy cream
1 vine-ripened tomato, diced
1 cup cashew halves

Continued on next page

Wild Mushroom Grit Cakes *continued*

Coating:
1 cup flour
2 eggs beaten
2 cups dried breadcrumbs
1 cup olive oil or vegetable oil for frying

1/2 cup chopped scallions for garnish

Grits:
- Line the bottom of a 13 x 9 x 2-inch rectangular baking dish with wax paper.
- In a large saucepan, bring water and cream to boil.
- Slowly add grits, stirring constantly to prevent clumping. Add salt and pepper and reduce heat to a simmer.
- Cook, stirring frequently, about 30 minutes, until grits have thickened.
- Remove from heat and pour into lined baking dish. Allow to cool to room temperature. Cover and refrigerate at least one hour until completely cooled and set.
- Cut grits into 12 triangles: first make a lengthwise cut down the center of the grits, then make two crosswise cuts to make six 4 1/2 inch squares. Cut each square diagonally to make two triangles.

Rosemary Cashew Cream Sauce:
- Heat butter in a heavy saucepan over medium-high heat.
- When foaming subsides, add mushrooms, rosemary and thyme and sauté 3-4 minutes until mushrooms are soft.
- Add cream and bring to a boil. Cook about 5 minutes until thickened enough to coat the back of a spoon.
- Add tomatoes and cashews. Reduce heat and simmer about 2 minutes until tomatoes are cooked through.
- Keep warm, stirring occasionally, until serving time.

Coating:
- Place flour in a shallow dish.
- Place eggs in second shallow dish and breadcrumbs in a third.
- Pour oil to a depth of 1/2 inch in a large skillet or sauté pan over medium-high heat.
- Dip grit cakes in flour, then egg, and finally in breadcrumbs, making sure to cover cakes completely with each.
- Working in batches and/or using multiple skillets, fry grit cakes about 2 minutes per side until golden brown.
- Place 2 grit cakes on each serving plate or bowl. Ladle 1/2 cup sauce over cakes and garnish with chopped scallions. Serve immediately.

You will not believe how good this is. Of course, it contains the calories for the day or week. Save it for a splurge or when you want to impress company, especially vegetarians. This recipe is an adaptation of one from the "Top of the Hill Restaurant" in Chapel Hill. The chef claims he got it from the News & Observer newspaper.

Beverly Long

Gingerbread Pancakes

Makes about 20 four-inch pancakes.

2 1/2 cups sifted all-purpose flour
1 tablespoon instant coffee
1 1/2 teaspoons baking soda
1 teaspoon ginger
1 teaspoon cinnamon
1/2 teaspoon nutmeg
1/2 teaspoon salt
1 cup molasses
1/2 cup milk
1/2 cup butter or margarine, melted
1 egg, slightly beaten

- Sift together dry ingredients.
- Combine molasses, milk, melted butter, and egg.
- Gradually add milk mixture to dry ingredients, blending well.
- For same-size pancakes, use a ¼ cup measure and pour onto a lightly greased hot griddle or skillet.
- Cook for about 5 minutes, turning once

These pancakes are a favorite with the grandchildren. They can also be made as gingerbread men, freestyle. Leftover batter freezes beautifully and can be thawed overnight in refrigerator. If batter seems too thick, it can be thinned with a little orange juice. Serve with warm maple syrup, or warm applesauce which is our preference.

Liz Whaling

Maple-Bacon Oven Pancake

Serves 10-12

1 1/2 cups Bisquick baking mix
1 tablespoon sugar
2 eggs
3/4 cup milk
1/4 cup maple-flavored syrup
1 1/2 cups shredded Cheddar cheese, divided
12 slices apple wood-smoked bacon, cooked and crumbled

- Preheat oven to 425° F.
- Spray a 9 x 13 x 2-inch baking dish with cooking spray.
- Beat baking mix, sugar, eggs, milk, syrup and 1/2 cup cheese with hand beater until smooth; pour into baking dish.
- Bake uncovered in the preheated oven until wooden pick inserted in center comes out clean, about 10-15 minutes.
- Sprinkle pancake with remaining cheese and the bacon.
- Bake uncovered until cheese is melted, 3-5 minutes longer.
- You may serve with syrup of your choice.

Anonymous

Ham, Fontina and Spinach Bread Pudding

Serves 8-10

1 large baguette
1/2 stick unsalted butter, melted
2 onions, chopped
2 tablespoons olive oil
1 pound cooked ham, in 1/2-inch cubes
4 large eggs
1 quart whole milk
1 teaspoon salt
1/2 teaspoon nutmeg
Freshly ground black pepper to taste
6 cups fresh spinach leaves, coarsely chopped
3/4 pound Fontina cheese, grated

- Preheat broiler.
- Diagonally cut baguette into 3/4 inch slices; brush both sides with butter.
- Toast on baking sheets under broiler 3 inches from the heat until golden, about 30 seconds on each side.
- Preheat oven to 350° F.
- Sauté onions in oil until golden. Add ham and sauté until ham is slightly browned.
- Whisk eggs in a large bowl and whisk in milk, salt, nutmeg and pepper to taste. Add toasted bread and toss gently.
- Transfer bread to shallow 3-quart casserole, slightly overlapping slices. Add any remaining egg mixture.
- Tuck spinach, ham and onions between slices, reserving a little ham to sprinkle over the top.
- Sprinkle cheese over the pudding, lifting bread slices with a spatula to allow some of the cheese to fall between them. Sprinkle reserved ham over the top.
- Bake in the middle of the oven about one hour until puffed, edges of the bread are golden and custard is set in the middle.

This can be assembled one day ahead and chilled, covered. Increase the baking time to 1 hour and 10 minutes.

Amelia Carew

Julia's Country Granola   ♥

Yields about 10 cups

Dried fruits are a nice addition. This is the best granola I have ever eaten. I've been making it for about 15 years. I once estimated it had about 150 calories per 1/3 cup and about 11 grams of sugar.

Julia Salsbury

1/2 cup maple syrup
1/2 cup canola oil
1/3 cup water
2 tablespoons vanilla
5 cups regular oatmeal
1 cup Cheerios
1/2 cup unsweetened coconut
1/2 cup wheat germ
1 cup All Bran cereal
1 cup Grapenut O's
1 cup chopped nuts
1/4 cup sunflower kernels

- Preheat oven to 300° F.
- Mix maple syrup, oil, water, and vanilla in large bowl. Add oatmeal and Cheerios to liquids.
- Spread in jellyroll pan or cookie sheet with sides and bake in preheated oven for 15 minutes.
- Add coconut, wheat germ, All Bran, Grapenut O's, stirring well and continue baking for 15 minutes.
- Stir in nuts and kernels and continue baking.
- At 15 minute intervals mix and turn ingredients in pan until nice and dry. When my glasses don't fog up on opening the oven door, I figure it's done.

Eggs Mornay

Serves 6-8

6 tablespoons butter or margarine
6 tablespoons flour
1 3/4 cups milk, warm
1 cup chicken bouillon, warm
1 cup grated sharp cheddar cheese
1/2 cup freshly grated Parmesan cheese
1/4 cup sherry
1/2 teaspoon Worcestershire sauce
Salt and pepper to taste
12 eggs, hard-boiled and sliced
Plain croutons and chopped parsley for garnish

Continued on next page

Eggs Mornay *continued*

- Preheat oven to 300° F. Butter a 2-quart baking dish.
- In a medium saucepan over medium heat melt the butter and whisk in the flour. Simmer for one minute until the butter and flour begin to bubble.
- Add the milk and bouillon slowly, whisking constantly. Cook until the mixture thickens, stirring often. Add the cheeses, sherry and Worcestershire. Stir until the cheeses are melted. Add salt and pepper to taste.
- Pour a thin layer of cheese sauce into baking dish and top with layers of egg slices. Pour the remaining sauce over the eggs.
- Bake in the preheated oven for 30 minutes.
- Serve garnished with croutons and parsley.

Subtle and intriguing flavors make this dish a classic centerpiece for the brunch buffet table. It may be made a few hours in advance and refrigerated. To reheat before serving, bring casserole to room temperature, then place in a 300° oven until heated through.

Mary Bratton

Noodle Kugel

Serves 10-12

Kugel:
4 tablespoons melted butter
1/2 cup sugar
1 cup sour cream
1 pound cottage cheese
1/2 teaspoon salt
1 teaspoon vanilla
1/2 pound cream cheese
6 eggs, beaten
1/2 pound medium sized egg noodles
Topping:
1/2 cup of brown sugar
1/2 cup of slivered almonds
2 tablespoons of melted butter

- Allow butter, sour cream, cottage cheese, cream cheese and eggs to come to room temperature and mix well.
- Add sugar, salt and vanilla and stir to combine.
- Preheat oven to 350° F.
- Butter a 9 x 13-inch casserole dish.
- Cook noodles in salted boiling water until done and drain.
- Combine the cheese-egg mixture with the noodles. Pour the mixture into the prepared dish. Mix topping ingredients together and spread on noodles.
- Bake in preheated oven for 1 hour.

This is a traditional Jewish side dish at brunch. It is served with bagels and nova scotia (lox), tomato and onion slices and sliced cheeses. It can be made ahead. Cook for 3/4 hour and finish baking when ready to serve. It is best when served warm. You can add fruit such as a small can of drained crushed pineapple or sliced peaches, fresh applesauce or dried apricots.

Gloria Preminger

Basil Tomato Tart

Makes 4 large or 6 small portions

One 9-inch piecrust
1 1/2 cups shredded mozzarella cheese, divided
4 medium tomatoes
1 cup loosely packed fresh basil leaves
3 teaspoons finely minced garlic, or to taste
1/2 cup mayonnaise
1/4 cup freshly grated Parmesan cheese
1/8 teaspoon ground white pepper

- Bake piecrust in 9-inch quiche or pie plate.
- Sprinkle with 1/2 cup mozzarella. Let cool on wire rack.
- Preheat oven to 375° F.
- Cut tomatoes into wedges and drain on paper towels.
- Arrange tomatoes atop melted cheese in the pie shell.
- In food processor bowl, combine basil and garlic. Process until coarsely chopped. Sprinkle over tomatoes.
- In a medium bowl, combine remaining mozzarella cheese, mayonnaise, Parmesan cheese and pepper. Spread mixture evenly over basil mixture.
- Bake in preheated oven for 35-40 minutes or until top is golden and bubbly.
- May add basil leaves to garnish.

Anonymous

Holiday Morning French Toast

Serves 6-8

1 cup brown sugar
1/2 cup butter, melted
3 teaspoons ground cinnamon, divided
3 tart apples, such as Granny Smith, peeled, cored and
  thinly sliced
1/2 cup dried cranberries or raisins
1 loaf Italian or French bread, cut into 1 inch slices
6 large eggs
1 1/2 cups milk
1 tablespoon vanilla

Continued on next page

Holiday Morning French Toast *continued*

- Preheat oven to 375° F.
- Combine brown sugar, butter and 1 teaspoon cinnamon in a 13x9-inch baking dish.
- Add apples and cranberries. Toss to coat well. Spread apple mixture evenly over bottom of baking dish.
- Arrange slices of bread on top.
- Mix eggs, milk, vanilla and remaining 2 teaspoons cinnamon until well blended. Pour mixture over bread, soaking bread completely. Cover and refrigerate 4 to 24 hours.
- Bake covered with aluminum foil in the preheated oven for 40 minutes. Uncover and bake 5 minutes.
- Remove from oven, let stand 5 minutes. Serve warm.

Barbara Dixon

Spanakopita
Spinach Cheese Pie

Serves 16-20 as an appetizer or 8-10 for brunch

12 eggs
2 (8-ounce) packages cream cheese
1/4 pound blue cheese
2 (10-ounce) packages frozen chopped spinach, thawed and squeezed dry
1 bunch scallions, chopped
1 pound phyllo pastry
1/2 pound unsalted butter, melted

- Preheat oven to 350° F.
- Butter two 9 x 13 x 2 1/2 inch pans.
- Combine eggs, cream cheese and blue cheese in a blender or food processor.
- Pour mixture into a bowl and add drained spinach and scallions. Mix well and set aside.
- Open phyllo, unfold sheets and cover with a damp towel.
- Using a pastry brush, butter each sheet as it is used.
- Arrange one layer of sheets so as to overlap each side of the pans. Repeat once.
- Pour half the batter into each of the pans.
- Cover each with 1 sheet of buttered phyllo. Fold over the hanging phyllo leaves into the pans.
- Cover with 2 buttered phyllo sheets.
- Prick with toothpicks 6 – 8 times.
- Bake 45-60 minutes in the preheated oven.

This freezes well. You may substitute margarine, eggbeaters, lite cream cheese, and olive oil. This is a family recipe. Serve as a luncheon dish with salad or cut into squares for appetizer.

Ruth Nicholson

Spinach Pie

Serves 4-6

Processor pastry for a two crust 10 inch pie:
1 3/4 cups flour
1 teaspoon salt
5 ounces chilled butter plus 2 tablespoons shortening
1/2 cup ice water

- Put flour and salt in processor. Add butter and shortening. Pulse off and on 3-4 times until butter mixture is mealy.
- With processor running, add the water. Process just until dough forms a ball.
- Place dough in plastic wrap, refrigerate at least one hour or chill in freezer 10-20 minutes.

Filling:
2 (10-ounce) packages frozen spinach
4 tablespoons butter
2 small onions, thinly sliced
Salt and pepper to taste
1/3 cup freshly grated Parmesan cheese
1/3 cup heavy cream
1/2 pound boiled ham or prosciutto, thinly sliced
5-6 ounces Fontina cheese, diced
1 egg lightly beaten

- Preheat oven to 375° F.
- Cook spinach according to package directions. Drain and squeeze it to remove as much liquid as possible.
- In a medium skillet, heat the butter until foaming.
- Add the onions and sauté over medium heat until they turn pale yellow, 10-15 minutes.
- Add the drained spinach, salt and pepper, Parmesan cheese and cream. Mix to blend. Cook an additional 1-2 minutes to combine ingredients. Let cool.
- Cover the bottom and sides of a quiche pan or two-inch deep pie plate with pastry.
- Add one layer of ham, then one layer of diced cheese.
- Spread all the spinach mixture on top followed by another layer of ham and an additional layer of diced cheese.
- Top with a layer of pastry and pinch the top and bottom layers of the pastry together. Brush the surface of the pie with the beaten egg. This helps to make the top golden brown. Prick the pastry with a fork in 5-6 places.
- Bake 40 minutes. Let stand 10-15 minutes before cutting.

This is a great recipe from a former neighbor in Bucks County, Pennsylvania. She was a wonderful cook. This is a good Friday night supper for the family. They all love it!

Rosemary Ewing

Currant and Brandy Scones

Makes 12-15 scones

2 cups plus 6 tablespoons all purpose flour
1/4 cup sugar
1/2 teaspoon salt
2 teaspoons baking powder
3/4 teaspoon ground cinnamon
1/2 cup chilled, unsalted butter, diced
1/2 cup milk, whole or part skim
1/2 cup whipping cream
2 tablespoons brandy or cognac
1 cup dried currants

- Preheat the oven to 375° F.
- Lightly grease a large baking sheet.
- Combine the dry ingredients in a sifter and sift into a mixing bowl if mixing by hand, or into a food processor.
- Add the butter to the dry ingredients and combine by hand or in a food processor until the mixture resembles coarse cornmeal.
- Place the mixture into a large mixing bowl and add the milk, cream, brandy and currants. Stir just until the mixture is combined.
- Turn the dough out onto a well-floured surface and dust with additional all-purpose flour.
- With a rolling pin or your hands, roll or press out the dough to a thickness of 1 1/2 inches.
- Cut into 1 1/2-3 inch rounds, triangles or your favorite shapes. Use cookie cutters or other tools to form the shapes. Alternatively, divide the dough into two pieces, roll or press into 1 inch thick circles about 8 inches in diameter and cut into pie shaped wedges.
- Place 2 inches apart on the prepared baking sheet.
- Bake for 18-20 minutes or until golden brown on top.
- Serve warm or transfer the scones to a rack to cool completely.

These scones always get applause, especially when served warm with butter and jam or honey. They are especially good as part of a tea time selection served with clotted cream, preserves and other wonderful goodies. The brandy highlights the flavor of the currants. Chopped raisins, golden raisins, dried cranberries or cherries taste very good too. The scones may be frozen for 3 months and taste like 'just baked' if refreshed in a warm oven for 10 minutes after thawing.

Barbara Terry

Nutmeg Muffins

Serves 6-8

3 cups flour, divided
1 1/2 cups brown sugar
3/4 cup butter
2 teaspoons nutmeg
1/2 teaspoon baking soda
2 teaspoons baking powder
1/2 teaspoon salt
1 cup buttermilk
2 eggs, lightly beaten

- Preheat oven to 350° F. Grease muffin tins.
- Mix two cups of the flour and brown sugar in a medium bowl.
- Cut in butter until mixture resembles coarse cornmeal. Reserve 3/4 cup of the mixture for topping in a separate bowl.
- Add remaining 1 cup of flour, nutmeg, baking soda, baking powder and salt to remaining mixture and add the buttermilk and eggs. Stir just until moistened. Do not over mix.
- Spoon batter into prepared muffin tins, filling each cup half full. Sprinkle each muffin with 1 1/2 teaspoons of the reserved topping mixture and bake in preheated oven for 20 minutes.

Banana Blueberry Muffins

Makes 12 muffins

2/3 cup milk
1/4 cup vegetable oil
1/2 cup mashed ripe banana
1 egg
2 cups flour
2/3 cup sugar
2 1/2 teaspoons baking powder
1/2 teaspoon salt
1/4 teaspoon ground nutmeg
1 cup fresh or frozen blueberries
Sugar for sprinkling, optional

- Preheat oven to 400° F. Grease bottoms only of 12 medium muffin cups, or line with paper baking cups.

Continued on next page

These can be made in advance and frozen. Remove from the freezer 1 hour before serving and reheat, covered with aluminum foil at 375° F. for 15 minutes.
These are a family favorite, originally part of Easter dinner, now included at all holiday meals. All of our children make and serve them.

Judie Burke

These muffins are much loved among my family and friends. The muffins stay moist and delicious. I usually make a double batch and freeze the extras.

Karen McGrain

Banana Blueberry Muffins *continued*

- Beat milk, oil, banana and egg in a large bowl.
- Stir in remaining ingredients, except blueberries, just until flour is moistened.
- Fold in blueberries.
- Divide batter evenly among muffin cups; cups will be almost full. Sprinkle with sugar if desired.
- Bake 20-25 minutes or until golden brown. Remove immediately from pan.

Blueberry Lemon Tea Bread

Serves 8-10

Bread:
1/2 cup margarine
1 cup sugar
2 large eggs
2 cups all purpose flour
2 teaspoons baking powder
1/2 teaspoon salt
1/2 cup milk
1 1/2 cups blueberries, fresh preferred
Glaze:
1/4 cup fresh lemon juice
1/3 cup sugar

- Preheat oven to 350° F.
- Prepare a 9 x 5 inch loaf pan with cooking spray.
- In a large bowl of an electric mixer mix margarine and sugar until light and fluffy, about 5 minutes.
- Reduce speed to low, add eggs, one at a time, beating after each until well blended.
- In a medium bowl combine flour, baking powder and salt.
- Alternately add flour mixture and milk to egg mixture until well blended.
- With a large spoon gently stir in the blueberries and spoon into the prepared pan.
- Bake 1 hour and 5 minutes or until toothpick comes out clean. If using frozen berries add 5 to 10 minutes to baking time.
- Cool on a rack 10 minutes and remove from the pan.
- For the glaze, mix sugar and lemon juice together until sugar is dissolved.
- Prick top and sides of cake. Using pastry brush, wash top and sides of cake with lemon glaze. Cool on wire rack.

This is a delightful addition to the menu at any season but especially during blueberry season when berries are so plentiful. The cake is moist and stays fresh for several days when refrigerated well wrapped.

Bunny Shillito

Morning Glory Muffins

Makes about 18 muffins

2 cups all purpose flour
1 cup sugar, may use 1/2 cup Splenda
2 teaspoons baking soda
2 teaspoons cinnamon
1/4 teaspoon nutmeg
1/2 teaspoon salt
2/3 cup raisins
2/3 cup chopped dates
2 cups peeled and grated carrots
1 large tart apple, peeled, cored, and grated
2/3 cup sliced almonds or chopped pecans
2/3 cup shredded, unsweetened coconut
3 eggs
3/4 cup vegetable oil
2 teaspoons vanilla
Grated rind of one orange or one lemon

- Preheat oven to 350° F.
- Grease muffin tins or line with paper.
- Sift the flour, sugar, baking soda, cinnamon, nutmeg and salt into a large bowl.
- Stir in the raisins, dates, carrots, apples, nuts, and coconut.
- In a separate bowl beat eggs with oil, vanilla and citrus rind.
- Stir egg mixture into dry ingredients until it is just combined.
- Fill muffin tins and bake about 22 minutes. Cool slightly before removing from the pans.
- Serve warm or at room temperature. They freeze well.

Julia Salsbury

English Fruit Loaf

Makes 1 large loaf or 3 small

4 ounces soft margarine or butter
4 ounces sugar
8 ounces self-rising flour
1 tablespoon mixed spice such as pumpkin pie spice
12 ounces glazed fruit
2 eggs
1/2 cup milk
Pinch of salt

You may use nuts if you choose or use all currants or golden raisins. This recipe came to us from a dear English friend. It is great with tea, festive at the holiday time.

Bob & Sandy Holton

Continued on next page

English Fruit Loaf *continued*

- Preheat oven to 325° F.
- Put all ingredients in bowl. Mix thoroughly and pour into loaf pan(s).
- Bake in preheated oven for 1 1/2 hours.

Scones with Golden Raisins

Makes 12 Scones

1/2 cup golden raisins
2 tablespoons sherry or brandy
1 3/4 cups all purpose flour
1/2 cup sweetened flaked coconut, optional
1/4 cup sugar
1 tablespoon baking powder
1 tablespoon grated orange zest
1/2 teaspoon salt
1 cup heavy whipping cream
2 large eggs
Egg wash:
1 egg yolk
2 tablespoons water

1 tablespoon granulated sugar and 1/2 teaspoon cinnamon mixed together

- Combine raisins and sherry or brandy and let macerate for one hour.
- Preheat oven to 375° F.
- Coat a cookie sheet with non-stick spray or line with parchment paper.
- In a large bowl mix together flour, coconut, sugar, baking powder, orange zest and salt.
- In a small bowl using a fork, blend cream and two eggs. Pour over dry ingredients.
- Add raisins and sherry or brandy and stir just until mixed and dough comes together.
- Drop the dough using a scant 1/3 measuring cup. A small spoon or spatula will aid in this task.
- Brush tops with egg wash and bake for 20 to 25 minutes until puffed and browned.
- Sprinkle with cinnamon-sugar mixture.

Serve warm or at room temperature. Best served on the day they are baked. They can be frozen and warmed in a 300° F. oven for 5 minutes. You may substitute 1 pint of freshly chopped strawberries or 1/2 cup of any combination of dried mixed berries for the golden raisins.

Carol Genovese

Pinehurst Muffins

Makes 36 regular or 72 miniature muffins

4 cups unbleached flour
4 teaspoons baking soda
1 teaspoon salt
2 1/2 cups sugar
4 teaspoons cinnamon
6 eggs
2 cups corn oil
4 cups grated carrots, about 7 large
1 cup raisins
1 cup chopped pecans
1 cup coconut
2 apples, peeled, cored, and coarsely grated
4 teaspoons vanilla

- Sift together flour, soda, salt, sugar and cinnamon into a very large bowl.
- Beat eggs and oil together in a small bowl and set aside.
- Toss together the carrots, raisins, pecans, coconut and apples and combine with the dry ingredients.
- Add vanilla to egg and oil mixture and combine with the flour-fruit mixture, stirring until just combined. Allow the mixture to stand at room temperature for 2-3 hours for the dough to ripen.
- Preheat oven to 375° F.
- Spoon batter into well oiled muffin tins.
- Bake in preheated oven for 15 minutes or until top of muffin springs back when touched.
- Let cool 5 minutes and turn out onto wire rack.

Many years ago I went to lunch with friends at an inn in Pinehurst where these muffins were served. They were so delicious that we asked for the recipe. The waitress went into the kitchen and brought us a copy of the recipe. These muffins are very moist and freeze well.

Floydine Roberts

Strawberry Nut Bread

Makes five small loaves

1 cup butter or margarine
1 1/2 cups sugar
1/4 teaspoon lemon extract
1 teaspoon vanilla
4 eggs, may substitute Eggbeaters
3 cups sifted all-purpose flour
1 teaspoon salt
1 teaspoon plus a pinch, cream of tartar
3/4 teaspoon baking powder
1 cup strawberry jam, not jelly or preserves
1/2 cup dairy sour cream
1 cup broken walnuts

- Preheat oven to 350° F.
- Grease and flour pans. You may use five 4 1/2 x 2 3/4 x 2 ¼-inch or 5 3/4 x 3 1/4 x 2-inch pans.
- In the bowl of an electric mixer, cream butter or margarine, sugar, lemon and vanilla extract, until fluffy.
- Add eggs, one at a time, beating well after each addition.
- Sift flour, salt, cream of tartar and baking powder.
- Combine jam and sour cream. Add jam mixture alternately with dry ingredients to creamed mixture, beating until well combined. Stir in nuts.
- Divide among prepared pans.
- Bake in preheated oven for 50 to 55 minutes.
- Cool 10 minutes in pans. Remove and cool on wire racks.

This bread is very nice for breakfast, tea or dessert. It has a wonderful taste and is great for gifts. My mother always made these loaves around Christmastime for family and friends. The bread can be frozen successfully.

Mary Heisserman

Fruit Muffins

Makes 24 small muffins

2 eggs
1 cup Angelflake sweetened coconut
1 cup raisins
1 package chopped dates; they usually come sugared so they don't stick together
1 cup pecans or walnuts, chopped

- Preheat oven to 350 ° F.
- Place baking liners in small muffin tins.
- Beat eggs in bowl large enough to hold all ingredients. Add coconut, raisins, dates and nuts. Mix well. Fill muffin tins almost to the top. Bake 15 minutes in preheated oven.

My mother's dear friend passed this recipe on to me some forty years ago as a fast and easy dessert or snack. They freeze well. Yes, there is no flour!

Carol Feuer

Parmesan Spoon Bread

Serves 7-8

Everything can be prepared ahead, just adding the eggs prior to baking. It is good served with chives and melted butter sauce, or with stewed basil-flavored tomatoes as sauce or garnished with chopped parsley and minced red onion and butter. It can be served in 8 greased 6-ounce ramekins or cooked in a 9 x 9 x 3 inch pan. If it is cooked in a pan do not separate the eggs. Just beat them until frothy and add to the mixture. This produces a more bread-like product. My mother, Virginia born, served it on Sunday nights with whatever cold meat was left over from Sunday dinner. She often added spiced peaches or a green salad for a complete meal.

Marietta Williams

1 1/2 cups whole milk
1/2 cup low salt chicken broth
1/2 teaspoon plus a pinch of salt
1 scant cup yellow cornmeal, preferably water ground
2/3 cup finely grated Parmigiano Reggiano cheese
1/8 teaspoon cayenne pepper
4 tablespoons unsalted butter, melted
4 large eggs, separated, at room temperature

- Preheat oven to 400° F.
- Grease a 1 1/2 quart soufflé or casserole dish with butter.
- Pour 1/2 cup milk into a heavy saucepan. Stir in corn meal until lumps dissolve. Add remaining milk and stir over medium heat until mixture becomes thicker, then add salt and chicken broth. Stir until mixture is blended and thick.
- Add grated cheese, cayenne pepper and melted butter. Blend thoroughly.
- Remove from the heat. Allow to cool for 10-20 minutes.
- Whisk egg yolks for 2-3 minutes and set aside.
- Add a pinch of salt to the egg whites and heat until just barely stiff.
- Blend egg yolks into the cornmeal mixture.
- Put the soufflé dish into the preheated oven for 2 minutes or until too hot to touch.
- While the soufflé dish is heating, fold egg whites gently into the cornmeal mixture.
- When well blended, pour into the hot soufflé dish.
- Place into the oven on the center rack. Immediately reduce the heat to 375° F.
- Bake without peeking for 40 minutes.
- Serve immediately. Like any soufflé, it very quickly deflates but it is beautiful and brown right out of the oven.

Rosemary, Kalamata Olive & Coarse Salt Focaccia   ♥

Makes one 12 by 18-inch loaf

1 package active dry yeast
2 cups warm water
3 tablespoons olive oil
5 cups unbleached flour
1 tablespoon salt
1 1/2 tablespoons finely chopped fresh rosemary leaves
1 1/2 tablespoons pitted and chopped Kalamata olives
Topping:
5 tablespoons olive oil
1 tablespoon coarse salt
1 1/2 tablespoons finely chopped fresh rosemary
1 1/2 tablespoons pitted and chopped Kalamata olives

- Combine yeast and warm water in a bowl.
- Add 3 tablespoons olive oil and let stand for 5 minutes.
- Mix the flour, salt, rosemary and olives together in a bowl.
- Using a wooden spoon, pour the water/yeast mixture into the flour and stir together to form a well-mixed dough.
- Scrape the dough out onto a floured work surface and begin to work the dough with the heel of your hands, pulling and folding the dough as you push and pull. Or, use a heavy mixer with dough hook. Work the dough for 10 minutes.
- Put dough into a lightly oiled bowl. Turn the dough over to oil both sides, cover with plastic wrap and let it double in size at room temperature for 60-90 minutes.
- Preheat oven to 450° F.
- Lightly oil a cookie sheet pan, spread the dough out in the pan and pull dough evenly into the corners. Let the dough rise again for 1 hour.
- Poke the surface of the dough with the tip of your finger and drizzle the olive oil over the surface of the dough. Sprinkle with coarse salt, rosemary and olives.
- Bake in the preheated oven for 20 minutes. Check bottom of bread to ensure it is not burning and bake an additional 5 minutes. Cool in pan on rack. Serve warm.

Whitney Irwin

Ida's Cornmeal Rolls

Makes 36-40 rolls

My niece, Mary Lynn, gave this recipe to my mother, Ida, many years ago. Even at 91 years my mother still makes these rolls for family gatherings. They freeze well.

Jim Terry

1/2 cup cornmeal
1/2 cup sugar
2 teaspoons salt
1/2 cup unsalted butter
2 cups milk
1 package yeast
1/4 cup lukewarm water
2 eggs, beaten
4 cups bread flour
3 tablespoons unsalted butter, melted

- In a medium saucepan cook cornmeal, sugar, salt, butter and milk until thick. Transfer to a bowl and cool to lukewarm.
- Dissolve yeast in lukewarm water.
- Add to cornmeal mixture with eggs and beat thoroughly.
- Add flour to form a soft dough. Knead well on a lightly floured surface. Place dough in oiled bowl, cover, let rise until doubled.
- Punch down. Roll out and cut as for biscuits. Place on a greased baking sheet.
- Brush tops with melted butter.
- Preheat the oven to 400° F.
- Allow rolls to rise until nearly doubled.
- Bake in preheated oven until lightly browned, 12–15 minutes.

Processor Italian Bread

Makes one loaf

3 cups flour
1 teaspoon salt
1 tablespoon sugar
1 tablespoon butter
1 package dry yeast
1 cup plus 2 tablespoons warm water
Cornmeal, optional
1 egg white
1 tablespoon cold water

- In a food processor combine 2 cups of the flour, the salt, sugar, butter and yeast and pulse 3 or 4 times.
- Add half the warm water and pulse 3 or 4 times.

Continued on next page

Processor Italian Bread *continued*

- Add remaining water and 1 cup flour. Pulse again and then process 40-60 seconds until a ball forms.
- Knead by hand for a few seconds adding a little flour, if sticky. Form into a ball, cover loosely and allow to rest 20 minutes
- Roll into an oblong 15 x 10 inches and pat into a loaf.
- Grease a baking sheet and shake on cornmeal, if using.
- Place loaf on baking sheet and brush top with olive oil. Cover with plastic wrap and refrigerate for 2-24 hours.
- Preheat oven to 425° F.
- Remove the plastic wrap and cut 3-4 slits or 1 long one, in the top of the loaf and bake in the preheated oven for 20 minutes.
- Remove and brush the top with the egg white mixed with the water and return to oven for additional 5 minutes.

I'm not sure, but I think this recipe came from an old magazine that was published by Cuisinart. This is a great bread that adds a little special touch to a family meal.

Rosemary Ewing

Sour Cream Dinner Rolls

Makes 4 dozen

1 cup sour cream
1/2 cup sugar
1/2 cup butter, melted
1 teaspoon salt
1/2 cup warm water
2 packages yeast
2 eggs
4 cups flour

- Scald sour cream, stir in sugar, butter and salt. Cool to lukewarm.
- Measure warm water into a large, warmed bowl. Sprinkle in yeast and stir.
- Add lukewarm sour cream mixture, eggs and flour. Mix until well blended.
- Cover tightly with plastic wrap. Refrigerate overnight.
- Preheat oven to 375° F.
- Divide the dough into 4 parts. Roll each portion into a circle like piecrust, about 9 inches. Cut into 12 wedges as in pizza. Then roll up starting from the wide end. Place on greased baking sheet and cover with plastic wrap.
- Let rise until double in bulk about 45 minutes.
- Bake in preheated oven for 12-15 minutes.

These rolls can be frozen and reheated

Ruth Moose

Rustic Baguette ♥

Makes 3 to 6 baguettes depending on size

7 cups bread flour, King Arthur preferred
2 1/4 teaspoons salt
1 3/4 teaspoons yeast, instant preferred, but not quick-rise
3 cups cold water, refrigerator temperature, 40° F.

- In the bowl of a heavy-duty electric mixer combine all of the ingredients and mix on the slowest speed for a minute or two to form a rough dough.
- Allow the dough to rest 2 to 3 minutes for the flour to absorb the water. Then mix on medium speed for about 6 to 8 minutes. The dough should clean the sides of the bowl but remain sticky only at the very bottom. You may need to add a few teaspoons of extra flour, one at a time, if it is too sticky, or a few drops of water if it is not sticking at the bottom of the bowl.
- Transfer the dough into a large bowl that has been lightly oiled or sprayed with cooking spray. Cover the bowl with plastic wrap and immediately place in the refrigerator overnight.
- The next day remove the dough from the refrigerator. The dough will have risen slightly. Leave the dough at room temperature for 3 to 4 hours to warm up and continue to rise until it has doubled *from its original pre-refrigerated size.*
- Place a baking stone in the oven and preheat to 500° F. or 525° if your oven will go that high. Allow the stone to heat at least 40 minutes before baking.
- Place an empty sheet pan in the bottom of the oven to be hot and ready for water when the loaves are ready to bake. Have a spray bottle of water available.
- Cut parchment paper sheets to fit the baking stone and place on the counter.
- Lightly flour the work surface and your hands. Carefully turn out dough onto the counter so as to deflate it as little as possible. Use a dough scraper to fold the dough over on itself once. Gently stretch the dough into an oblong shape about 8 inches long and 6 inches wide.
- Use the dough scraper to cut the dough in half across the width of the dough. Cut each half into two or three pieces, depending on what size loaves you want.

Continued on next page

This sounds like a very complicated recipe but is actually very easy and the timing is very forgiving. A heavy-duty mixer is necessary for kneading the dough and the baking stone is very important. I use a convection oven with two baking stones and bake all of the loaves at one time, but one stone will work quite well in a regular oven and bake in two sessions. The baker's peel makes handling the loaves very easy. This recipe is an adaptation of a recipe in 'The Bread Baker's Apprentice' by Peter Reinhart.

Jim Terry

Rustic Baguette *continued*

- Stretch each piece to the length of your baking stone. Form the loaf by gently pulling the dough over on itself, lengthwise, pressing the seam to form a rustic baguette. The loaves may look very unpromising at this point but don't despair.
- Place the loaf seam side down onto a prepared parchment sheet. Form all the loaves and cover them with a light towel. Leave at room temperature for about 30 minutes. You may slash the tops of the loaves diagonally with a sharp knife, or scissors, if desired, just before baking.
- Pour 1 cup of _hot_ water into the pan in the bottom of the oven and quickly close the oven door. Carefully slide the parchment paper with the dough onto the back of an upturned baking pan, cookie sheet or use a baker's peel. Quickly slide the dough along with the parchment paper onto the baking stone. Spray water on the walls of the oven 2 or 3 times and quickly close the oven door. Spray twice more at about 30 second intervals.
- Bake for 16-18 minutes. The dough will quickly rise and begin to brown in about 8-9 minutes. The loaves should be a rich golden brown when done and reach an internal temperature of 205° using an instant read thermometer. Transfer the loaves to a wire rack and cool.
- Eat on the same day as baked or freeze, tightly wrapped. If frozen allow to thaw and refresh in a 350° F. oven for about 5 minutes.

When these rolls come out of the oven they look brown but taste wonderful. When I first used this recipe 15 years ago the instructions called for the dough to sit on the kitchen counter "overnight," hence the name Overnight Rolls. That is not a good idea because of the eggs involved. I now use the dough mode on my bread machine. I start the first stage in the bread pan outside the machine, wait 30 minutes and put the rest of the ingredients into the pan before starting the bread machine. The rolls are just as good the next day and are great for leftover turkey and ham. They are wonderful for a dinner party, and "make your own" mini sandwiches. Because this is such an easy recipe it is fun to experiment with different flours and adding herbs such as rosemary or basil.

Julie W. Snyder

California Overnight Rolls

Makes 36 rolls

1 cup cold milk
1/2 cup sugar
1 tablespoon yeast, instant preferred but not quick-rise
2 eggs, beaten
1/2 cup margarine or butter, melted and cooled
4 cups all-purpose flour

- Line a cookie sheet with parchment paper.
- In the bowl of a heavy-duty mixer combine cold milk and 1/2 cup sugar. Mix gently to dissolve the sugar. Sprinkle the yeast over the mixture in the mixing bowl and allow to sit for 30 minutes to proof the yeast.
- After the 30 minutes has elapsed, add eggs, margarine or butter and flour. Mix gently until the flour has been incorporated. The dough will be somewhat sticky.
- Cover and allow to rise until the dough has doubled in size or is finished in a bread machine on the dough mode.
- Punch down the dough and, on a floured surface, divide the dough into thirds. Roll each third into a circle. If the dough is springy, don't be concerned.
- Using a pizza-cutting wheel, divide the circle into twelve pie shaped pieces. Roll each piece starting at the large end towards the small end. It is fun to curve the edges of the roll to look like a mini croissant.
- Place on the parchment lined cookie sheet. Cover the pan of rolls with another sheet of parchment paper and place in a cold oven with the oven light turned on. Allow to rise until doubled in size.
- Preheat the oven to 425° F. Note: use an oven thermometer to determine the correct oven temperature. Do not rely on the oven temperature light going out to accurately indicate the oven's temperature.
- Remove parchment paper from the rolls and place them on the top oven shelf.
- Bake for 7 minutes.
- Remove the rolls from the oven and rub a stick of margarine or butter lightly over the tops of the rolls while they are very hot.
- Cool on a wire rack.

Fig and Fennel Bread ♥

Makes 2 12 inch loaves

1 1/4 cups warm water
1 tablespoon sugar
2 1/4 teaspoons yeast
3 cups bread flour
1 cup rye flour
2 tablespoons fennel seeds
1 tablespoon salt
1 (8 ounce) package dried Calimyrna figs, chopped, divided

- Mix the warm water with the sugar and yeast in a small bowl. Let it stand until the mixture bubbles, about 10 minutes.
- Combine bread flour, rye flour, fennel seeds, salt and 3/4 cup of the chopped figs in large bowl of a heavy-duty mixer with dough hook. Mix at slowest speed and gradually add the yeast mixture, mixing until all the flour has been incorporated. You may mix by hand, stirring vigorously with a wooden spoon until the dough comes together.
- Knead with the dough hook until the dough is smooth and elastic. To knead by hand, transfer dough to a floured work surface and knead until smooth and elastic, about five minutes.
- Place the dough in an oiled bowl and turn to coat. Cover with plastic wrap, then a kitchen towel and let dough rise in a warm place until doubled in volume, about one hour.
- Preheat oven to 375° F.
- Turn dough out onto a floured work surface and knead gently until deflated.
- Knead in the remaining 3/4 cup of chopped figs. Cut the dough in half and shape each piece into a 12 inch long loaf.
- Brush a rimmed baking sheet with oil and transfer the loaves to the sheet at least 3 inches apart. Cover with plastic wrap and then a kitchen towel and let rise in a warm area until almost doubled in volume, about 35 minutes.
- Bake bread until crust is golden and loaves sound hollow when tapped on the bottom, about 45 minutes. Cool on a wire rack.

This bread is great served with cheese or toasted for breakfast with butter, honey or orange marmalade. I adapted this recipe from one on the Epicurious Web site. It is similar to a bread served at Clarke's Restaurant in London.
It is helpful to work with this dough on a well-floured surface with well-floured hands.

Jim Terry

Yummy Sweet Rolls

Makes 2 1/2 dozen rolls

Rolls:
1 cup sour cream, scalded
1/2 cup melted butter
1/2 cup sugar
1 teaspoon salt
2 packages dry yeast
1/2 cup warm water, 105 to 115° F.
2 eggs, beaten
4 cups all-purpose flour
Filling:
16 ounces cream cheese, room temperature
3/4 cup sugar
1 egg
2 teaspoons vanilla extract
1/2 teaspoon salt
Glaze:
2 cups powdered sugar, sifted
1/4 cup milk
2 teaspoons vanilla extract

Our family first had these at Christmas in 1980. We have had them every Christmas and Easter since. Now our grandchildren have declared them a MUST for holiday breakfasts. They also freeze well. They are great with crisp apple-wood smoked bacon or sausage.

Joyce Mason

- Combine scalded sour cream, melted butter, sugar and salt and mix well.
- Dissolve yeast in warm water in large mixing bowl.
- Stir in sour cream mixture and then eggs.
- Stir in flour. The dough will be soft.
- Cover bowl tightly and chill at least 8 hours or over night.
- Grease a large baking sheet.
- Combine all filling ingredients and process with mixer until well blended. Set aside.
- Divide dough into 4 portions. Turn each on floured surface and knead 4-6 times. Roll each to 12 by 8 inch rectangle.
- Spread 1/4 of the filling over each rectangle, leaving 1/2-inch margin on edges. Roll up jellyroll fashion, beginning at long side. Pinch edge and ends to seal.
- Cut each roll into 1 1/2 inch slices.
- Place slices, cut side down, 2 inches apart on greased baking sheet. Cover and let rise in warm place for 1 1/2 hours or until doubled in bulk.
- Preheat oven to 375° F.
- Bake in preheated oven for 12 minutes or until golden brown.
- Combine all glaze ingredients and mix well. Drizzle over warm rolls.

Soups and Salads

Soups and Salads

Soups

Bean and Lamb Shank Soup, 85
Beet Soup, 93 ♥
Bouillabaisse, 88 ♥
Carrot Soup with Bacon, 89
Chilled Cucumber Soup with Crab 84
Cream of Black Bean Soup, 81 ♥
Cream of Zucchini Soup, 86
Gazpacho, 86 ♥
Gingered Peach Soup, 90
Italian Sausage Soup, 90
Jewish Cabbage Soup, 83
Nancy's Potato and Leek Soup, 95
New England Baked Fish Chowder, 91
Pasta Fagioli, 82
Sandy's Honeydew and Cantaloupe Soup, 94
Sopa de Lima, 82 ♥
Soupe au Pistou, 94 ♥
Spiced Carrot Soup, 84 ♥
Strawberry Soup, 91
Vegetable Lentil Soup, 87
Yellow and Red Tomato Soups, 92 ♥

Salads

Arugula and Escarole Salad, 96
Black Bean, Orzo, and Tomato Salad with Garlic Dressing, 105 ♥
Blue Cheese Dressing, 106
Caesar Salad, 100 ♥
Chicken Salad Fit for a Queen, 99
Clare's Salad, 98 ♥
Cobb Pasta Salad, 97
Cranberry Spinach Salad, 97 ♥
Curried Chicken Salad, 104
Greek Salad, 103
Green Salad with Roasted Cherries, Nuts and St. Marcellin, 102
Layered Chicken Salad, 101
Lightly Dilled Potato Salad, 106
Mustard Salad Dressing, 99 ♥
Prizewinner Potato Salad, 103
Rice Salad, 96
Spinach and Pear Salad with Prosciutto, 100

♥ Heart Healthy

Cream of Black Bean Soup

Serves 6

2 cups dry black beans
2-3 tablespoons olive oil
1 1/2 medium onions, finely chopped
1 stalk celery finely chopped
1 carrot, finely chopped
3 tablespoons minced garlic
1 tablespoon cumin
1-3 tablespoons Sambal Oelek*
3 tablespoons Dijon mustard
1 bay leaf
2 1/2 cups water
1 1/2 tablespoons red wine vinegar
1 1/2 tablespoons soy sauce or tamari
1 1/2 tablespoons Worcestershire sauce
1 1/2 tablespoons lemon juice
Crème fraîche or condensed skim milk for garnish at
  serving time

- Soak the beans overnight in water to cover. In the morning pour off any remaining water, rinse the beans and drain.
- Over medium-low heat, sauté all vegetables in olive oil until soft. Avoid overly browning the onions.
- Add the cumin and 1 tablespoon of the Sambal Oelek. Add beans, mustard, bay leaf and water. Bring to a simmer and cook for 30 minutes.
- Taste and add more Sambal Oelek if desired.
- Cook for 1 1/2 hours more.
- Remove the bay leaf and puree the soup in a food processor or use an immersion blender.
- Return the soup to the pot and stir in the vinegar, soy sauce, Worcestershire sauce and lemon juice. Bring to a simmer and thin with water to thickness desired.
- Serve hot with a dollop of crème fraîche.

*Sambal Oelek is a hot pepper sauce that adds a special flavor to this soup. Use according to your taste. It is available in local oriental or specialty grocers.

This recipe came from a small restaurant in Victoria, British Columbia. It is even better the second day and gets rave notices.

Margaret George

Sopa de Lima (Lime Soup)   ♥

Serves 8

3 chicken cutlets
8 cups chicken broth
1 medium onion, quartered
1 tablespoon minced garlic
6-10 black peppercorns
1 tablespoon oil
1/2 cup chopped onion
2 Jalapeño chilies, topped and chopped
1 (14 ounce) can diced tomatoes
1/2 cup fresh lime juice
1/2 of one lime
1/3 cup chopped cilantro

- In a soup pot combine chicken, broth, onion, garlic, and peppercorns.
- Bring to just below a boil. Cover and simmer for 20 minutes. Cool, strain and set aside.
- Shred the chicken and set aside.
- Wipe out the pot and warm the oil. Gently sauté the onion and jalapeños until tender.
- Add tomatoes and bring to a boil.
- Add lime juice. Squeeze juice from 1/2 a lime and add to pot with the half lime.
- Simmer 20 minutes. Remove the lime half.
- Add the shredded chicken and simmer for 10 minutes.
- Stir in cilantro and serve.

This soup is always a hit! It is an excellent starter for a Mexican dinner. Accompany it with <u>crisp</u> tortilla chips. Tostitos Lime flavored are great. Avocado slices and lime wedges are optional.

Nancy Foster

Pasta Fagioli

Serves 6

1/2 tablespoon olive oil
1 medium onion, chopped
3 cloves garlic, minced
1 1/2 pounds Italian sausage, casing removed, cut into 1 inch pieces
2 (19-ounce) cans cannellini beans or white kidney beans
2 (14-ounce) cans chicken broth
1 (28-ounce) can Italian tomatoes
1/2 cup small pasta such as ditalini
6 ounces chopped fresh spinach

This is our son's favorite soup. The recipe comes from his wife, our Irish daughter-in-law, who had this soup ready for us when we arrived at their home after a long trip. It is a great hearty soup for a crowd, best served during cold weather.

Albina Giardino

Continued on the next page.

Pasta Fagioli *continued*

- Heat olive oil in a large pot and sauté onions and garlic until soft.
- Add sausage and brown.
- When sausage is cooked, add beans, chicken broth and tomatoes. Simmer for 20 to 30 minutes.
- Add pasta and simmer for 8 minutes or until pasta is done.
- Add chopped spinach, simmer for 1 to 2 minutes and serve hot.

Jewish Cabbage Soup

Serves 6

1 medium head green cabbage, shredded
2 medium onions, chopped
4 tablespoons butter
2 tablespoons flour
2 teaspoons salt
4 cups water
2 cups tomato juice, or V-8 juice
1/2 teaspoon black pepper
2 tablespoons sugar
1 teaspoon caraway seed
1 cup sour cream

- Gently cook cabbage and onion in butter over moderate to low heat for 15 minutes.
- Sprinkle with flour and salt. Stir well.
- Slowly add water and juice, pepper, sugar and caraway seeds.
- Cook, uncovered over very low heat about 1 hour.
- Serve the soup hot topped with sour cream.

This recipe is adapted from THE ART OF VEGETARIAN COOKERY by Betty Wason. It can be made ahead and refrigerated.

Margaret Chapman

Spiced Carrot Soup ♥

Serves 8

1/2 tablespoon butter
1/2 tablespoon olive oil
1 large onion, coarsely chopped, about 1 1/2 cups
1 pound carrots, coarsely chopped
1/2 cup coarsely chopped celery
1 small baking potato, about 6 ounces, peeled and coarsely
   chopped
5 cups low-salt chicken broth
1 1/2 teaspoons ground cumin
1 teaspoon sweet paprika
1/4 teaspoon cayenne pepper
1 cup low-fat buttermilk or plain yogurt
Salt and freshly ground pepper to taste
2 tablespoons coarsely chopped flat-leaf parsley

- Melt the butter with the oil in a large saucepan. Sauté the
  onion until soft. Add the carrots, celery, potato, broth, cumin,
  paprika and cayenne pepper and bring to a boil. Cover and
  simmer until vegetables are tender, about 25 minutes.
- Puree the soup in batches in a blender or food processor and
  return it to the pot.
- Stir in the buttermilk or yogurt and season to taste.
- If serving cold, chill in the refrigerator for several hours or
  overnight. If serving warm, reheat gently.
- Ladle into bowls and sprinkle with parsley.

Karen Vernon

*I have served this
soup at many
summer luncheons
and as a first course
for dinner parties.
It goes well with a
vegetable salad or
simply serve it with
a potato roll.*

Jean Green

Chilled Cucumber Soup with Crab

Makes 6 cups

4 cucumbers, about 2 1/4 pounds, peeled, seeded, chopped
2 cups plain yogurt
3/4 cup sour cream
1/2 cup chopped green onions, white and pale green parts
1/4 cup chopped fresh dill
1 clove garlic, peeled and minced
2 tablespoons olive oil
1 tablespoon lemon juice
1 teaspoon Dijon mustard
6 ounces shelled, cooked crabmeat

Continued on next page

Chilled Cucumber Soup With Crab *continued*

- In a blender or food processor, in batches if necessary, process cucumbers, yogurt, sour cream, green onions, dill, garlic, olive oil, lemon juice and mustard until smooth.
- Add salt and pepper to taste.
- Transfer to a bowl, cover, and chill until cold, at least 2 hours and up to 6 hours.
- Ladle chilled soup evenly into bowls.
- Top each serving with about 1/4 cup crab.

Bean and Lamb Shank Soup

Serves 4-6

1 pound dried baby lima beans
1/2 pound lamb shank
1 tablespoon olive oil
3 cloves garlic, diced
4 cups chicken broth
4 cups water
3/4 cup finely chopped onion
3/4 cup finely diced carrots
1/2 cup chopped celery
2 tablespoons butter
Salt and pepper to taste

This is a hearty and delicious soup for winter.

Barbara Goodman

- Soak beans overnight in enough water to cover 4 inches above the beans.
- The next day drain the beans and set aside.
- In a large pot, heat the oil and brown the lamb shank well on all sides.
- Add the beans, garlic, chicken broth and water to the lamb shank.
- Bring the soup to a boil, lower the heat and simmer 1 1/2 hours, partly covered, stirring occasionally.
- Add the onion, carrots, and celery and cook 30 minutes longer.
- Remove the lamb shank from the pot. When cool enough to handle, remove the meat from the bones, cut into bite-sized pieces and return to the soup.
- Swirl in 2 tablespoons butter plus salt and pepper to taste.

Gazpacho   ♥

Serves 6-8

Fewer of the vegetables can be pureed and more used as garnish, depending on how chunky you like gazpacho.

A friend supplied me with this recipe after she served it on a hot day. She added several ice cubes to each bowl, making it extra refreshing. Serve with crusty bread.

Anne Bodner

2 pounds ripe tomatoes, peeled, seeded and chopped
1 cup coarsely chopped sweet onion
1 1/2 cups coarsely chopped green pepper
1 1/2 cucumbers, peeled, seeded and coarsely chopped
3 cloves garlic, minced
1 1/2 teaspoons salt
1/2 teaspoon freshly ground pepper
1/3 cup olive oil
1/3 cup red wine vinegar
1 cup ice water
Garnish:
1/2 cup finely diced sweet onion
1/2 cup finely diced green pepper
1/2 cup peeled, seeded, and finely diced cucumber

1 cup ice water as needed

- Puree all ingredients except the garnish in a food processor.
- Mix with ice water and chill for 3-hours to overnight.
- Dice the onion, pepper and cucumber. Mix well and set aside.
- Adjust the soup to the desired consistency with up to an additional cup of ice water.
- Mix in diced vegetables.
- Serve in chilled bowls.

Cream of Zucchini Soup

Serves 4-6

This soup freezes well. Do not add the soymilk and sour cream until ready to serve.

Elaine Landriau

7 cups zucchini in 1 inch cubes
1 cup coarsely chopped onions
1 cup chicken or vegetable stock
1 1/2 teaspoons salt
3 twists of fresh ground pepper
Pinch of celery seed
6 fresh basil leaves coarsely chopped or 1/2 teaspoon dried
Add just before serving:
1 cup unflavored soymilk
1/4 cup sour cream
Fresh chives snipped

Continued on next page

Cream of Zucchini Soup *continued*

- Scrub, but do not peel, zucchini. Remove the ends, quarter lengthwise, and run your knife down the length of each piece to remove most of the seeds. Line up the pieces and cross cut to create chunks. Measure 7 cups. Place in a large kettle.
- Add onions, broth and spices to the pot. Simmer 15 minutes or until all vegetables are very tender when tested with a fork.
- Remove from the heat and let cool slightly. Puree with an immersion blender or, in batches in a regular blender or food processor.
- Return the soup to the pot and whisk in soymilk and sour cream.
- Heat to serving temperature but do not allow to boil. Ladle into serving bowls and snip about 3/4 teaspoon of chives on top of each serving.

Vegetable Lentil Soup

Serves 8-10

2 medium sized carrots, diced
2 medium sized celery stalks, diced
1 medium sized onion, diced
1 garlic clove, minced, optional
2 tablespoons olive or salad oil
2 (14 1/2-ounce) cans Italian-style stewed tomatoes with juices
1 cup dry lentils
2 (13-ounce) cans chicken broth
3/4 pounds small red potatoes, in 1/2 inch dice
2 cups water
1 (14-ounce) package smoked beef sausage, in 1 inch slices, optional
2 cups shredded, sharp cheddar cheese, optional

- In a 3-quart pot over medium heat, cook carrots, celery and onion in the olive oil until tender.
- Add garlic and cook for one minute.
- Stir in tomatoes, lentils, chicken broth, potatoes and 2 cups water. Bring to a boil, reduce heat, cover and simmer about 45 minutes.
- Add sausage, if using, and simmer 10 minutes.
- Serve in soup bowls topped with shredded cheese.

I never do this recipe the same way twice. Sometimes I'll add more stewed tomatoes. Sometimes I use the shredded cheese and / or the sausage, sometimes not. I will often add more celery or onion if I have it on hand. I may vary the amount of chicken broth and water to achieve the taste and thickness I desire. It's a wonderful, adaptable main course cold weather entrée. Serve with breadsticks and green salad.

Suzanne Connolly

Bouillabaisse ♥

Serves 8

Soup Base:
1/3 cup olive oil
4 medium onions, chopped
4 green peppers, sliced
4 medium potatoes, sliced
2 cloves garlic, minced
2 bay leaves
Pinch each of thyme, saffron and salt
1/2 cup tomato paste
1 quart clam juice or fish bouillon
1 quart water
Seafood:
1 pound shrimp, peeled and deveined
1 pound scallops
2 pounds firm white fish, such as cod or grouper, in bite size pieces
1 dozen clams in shells
1/2 cup white wine
Dash of Tabasco sauce to taste
Garnish:
Chopped parsley

The soup base can be made a day ahead. Be careful not to overcook the fish and seafood.

Ina Gross

- In large pot over medium-low heat, sauté onions, peppers, potatoes, and garlic in oil for 15 minutes.
- Add bay leaves, thyme, saffron, salt, tomato paste, clam juice or fish broth and water. Stir to combine and simmer for 20 minutes.
- Add fish, shrimp, scallops and clams. Mix gently, bring just to a boil, reduce the heat and cook for 10 minutes, or until clams open.
- Add wine and a dash of Tabasco. Simmer a minute or two.
- Add salt and pepper to taste.
- Serve immediately, with a sprinkling of chopped parsley and a good, crusty bread.

Carrot Soup with Bacon

Serves 6-8

2 slices smoky bacon, chopped
1 small onion, chopped, about 1/2 cup
1/4 cup long-grain white rice
6 cups canned, fat free, low salt chicken broth
4 cups sliced carrots, about 6 large
1/2 teaspoon sugar
Pinch of ground nutmeg
1/4 cup whipping cream
Fresh Italian parsley, finely chopped for garnish

- Cook the bacon in a large, heavy saucepan over medium heat until crisp and brown. Transfer bacon to a paper towel to drain.
- Add onion to drippings in pan. Sauté until beginning to soften, about 3-4 minutes.
- Add rice and stir well to coat with bacon fat.
- Add broth, carrots, sugar and nutmeg and bring to a boil.
- Reduce heat to very low, cover and simmer until carrots and rice are tender, about 20 minutes. Allow soup to cool for 15 minutes or more.
- Puree soup using an immersion blender or in batches in a food processor or blender until very smooth. Return the soup to the pan.
- When ready to serve, mix in the cream and heat the soup. Season with salt and pepper.
- Ladle soup into bowls and sprinkle with bacon and parsley.

This colorful soup is smooth and rich. It is delicious as a first course or, with a salad and some good crusty bread, makes a meal. You can make the soup ahead and refrigerate for 4 days or freeze for 3-4 months, but do not add the cream until ready to serve. If frozen you may need to cook more bacon for the garnish.

Barbara Terry

Italian Sausage Soup

This is a good way to use up all that summer zucchini! A hearty soup like this is wonderful accompanied by a good Italian bread.

Ann Chas

Serves 6-8

1 to 1 1/2 pounds sweet Italian sausage
1 large onion, sliced
1 tablespoon butter or margarine
6 cups water
1 tablespoon beef bouillon granules or 3 bouillon cubes
1 (28-ounce) can crushed tomatoes
1/4 green pepper, diced
1/4 teaspoon dried oregano
1 tablespoon chopped fresh basil, or 1/4 teaspoon dried
2 small zucchini, cubed
2 ounces linguine in 2-inch pieces
2 tablespoons Parmesan cheese

- In a large skillet sauté the sausages until fully cooked. Pierce in several places, drain and cool. Cut into ½-inch rounds.
- In a large, heavy saucepan sauté onion in butter or margarine.
- Add water, bouillon granules or cubes, tomatoes, green pepper, oregano and basil. Bring to a full boil.
- Add sausage, zucchini, linguine and cheese.
- Lower heat, cover and simmer for 10 minutes, stirring occasionally, until pasta is al dente.
- Ladle soup into deep bowls.

Gingered Peach Soup

This is a delightful first course for a summer meal. If the peaches are really ripe, the skin can be peeled off using a sharp paring knife. If they are less ripe, cut a small cross in the bottom of each peach, blanch in boiling water for 20 seconds, remove and plunge into a bowl of ice water. The skins will slip right off.

Cynthia Jones

Serves 4 cups

1 1/2 pounds very ripe fresh peaches
2 tablespoons plus 1 teaspoon fresh lemon juice
1 1/2 cups buttermilk
2/3 cup apple juice
1/2 teaspoon peeled, grated fresh ginger
Scant 1 teaspoon kosher salt
1 teaspoon honey

- Peel and pit the peaches, rubbing them with 2 tablespoons lemon juice as needed to prevent discoloration.
- In a food processor, puree the peaches. Scrape the peach puree into a medium size bowl.
- Stir in remaining ingredients. Refrigerate until chilled.
- Ladle into bowls and top each serving with a geranium leaf, rose petal or peach slice.

Strawberry Soup

Serves 6-8

1 quart fresh strawberries, cleaned and hulled or
  1 (16-ounce) package frozen whole berries
1 cup sour cream
1 cup light cream
1/4 cup sugar
1 tablespoon light rum or 1 teaspoon rum flavoring

- Puree the strawberries in a blender or food processor.
- Add the sour cream, light cream, sugar and rum. Blend until smooth.
- Chill several hours, preferably overnight.
- Garnish with fresh strawberries.

This is a refreshing and light summer soup. It is particularly good when strawberries are in season. It is adapted from The Junior League Centennial Cook Book.

Doris Dunlap

New England Baked Fish Chowder

Serves 4

2 pounds chowder fish: scrod, haddock, cod or pollock
3 medium potatoes, cubed
3 onions, chopped
4 tablespoons butter
1/2 cup white wine
1 large bay leaf
1 1/2 teaspoons salt
1 clove garlic, chopped
4 whole cloves
1/4 teaspoon dill seeds
1/4 teaspoon pepper
2 cups boiling water
2 cups light cream or half & half, gently heated
Chopped fresh dill, chives or parsley for garnish

- Preheat oven to 375° F.
- Cut fish into big bite sized pieces and place into a 4 quart ovenproof baking dish with the rest of the ingredients except the cream. Stir gently to mix.
- Bake, covered, for 1 hour in the preheated oven.
- Before serving, add the heated cream and stir gently to avoid breaking up the pieces of fish.
- Garnish with chopped fresh dill, chives or parsley.

To make it more heart healthy, reduce the salt to 1 teaspoon and use whole milk, or even 1% milk, but don't skimp on the wine. The better the wine, the better the chowder. It can be put together early in the day with cold water. After 1 hour baking it can be cooled and frozen, adding the cream after reheating when time to serve. Serve with more of the white wine, a good green salad and loaf of French bread and you have an elegant meal.

Marilyn Worth

Yellow and Red Tomato Soups ♥

Serves 4

2 large, ripe yellow tomatoes
2 large, ripe red tomatoes
2 teaspoons white vinegar, divided
2 teaspoons fresh ginger, minced, divided
4 dashes Tabasco, divided
2 teaspoons minced garlic, divided
Salt to taste
2 tablespoons olive oil, divided
2 chicken bouillon cubes, divided
2 teaspoons fresh dill, minced, divided
2 teaspoons cumin, divided

- Preheat oven to 300° F.
- Place the tomatoes on a baking sheet and roast for 10 minutes. Remove from the oven, cool, remove peel, core and seed.
- Coarsely chop the tomatoes, keeping the colors separate.
- Make each soup separately. To make the yellow soup: in a blender, or food processor, combine the yellow tomatoes and 1 teaspoon each of the garlic, dill, cumin, vinegar, minced ginger and one bouillon cube. Season with salt and 2 dashes of Tabasco. Puree until smooth. With the blender running, add one tablespoon oil and blend until incorporated. Transfer to a small pitcher with a lip so it can be poured easily, cover and chill.
- To make the red soup, in a blender combine the red tomatoes and 1 teaspoon each of the garlic, dill, cumin, vinegar, minced ginger and one bouillon cube. Season with salt and 2 dashes of Tabasco. Puree until smooth. With the blender running, add one tablespoon oil and blend until incorporated. Transfer to a small pitcher with a lip so it can be poured easily, cover and chill.
- The soups can be prepared up to one day before serving and stored in the refrigerator. Remove from the refrigerator 15 minutes before serving.

To Serve:
- From opposite sides, simultaneously pour both soups into individual martini glasses to form a half and half pattern. The soup may be served warm, cold or at room temperature.

Anonymous

Beet Soup ♥

Serves 4

2 pounds small beets trimmed and scrubbed. Do not peel.
3 tablespoons olive oil, divided
1 tablespoon unsalted butter
1 small leek, white and light green parts only, coarsely chopped
3 shallots, coarsely chopped
1/3 cup fresh Anaheim green chili pepper, seeds and stem removed, coarsely chopped
2 tablespoons dark brown sugar
1 teaspoon freshly ground black pepper
3 1/2 tablespoons powdered ginger
Tabasco to taste
1 cup orange juice
3 cups low sodium vegetable or chicken stock
2 cups water
Crème fraîche, for garnish, optional

- Preheat oven to 350° F.
- Place a large sheet of aluminum foil on a cookie sheet.
- Place beets in a bowl, coat with 1 tablespoon olive oil and spoon onto the foil. Fold edges of foil over to make a pouch and seal tightly. Bake in preheated oven for one hour. A knife should pierce the beets with ease. Let beets cool, then peel and cut into quarters.
- Melt butter and remaining oil over medium heat in a large skillet.
- Add leeks, shallots and chili pepper and sauté, stirring occasionally, for 4 to 5 minutes until softened.
- Add brown sugar, black pepper, ginger, and a dash of Tabasco, the orange juice, vegetable stock, beets and 2 cups of water.
- Bring to a simmer and cook for 10 minutes. Let cool.
- Puree soup in batches in a food processor or with an immersion blender. If soup is too thick, thin with more orange juice.
- Add more powdered ginger if desired.
- Serve the hot soup with a dollop of crème fraîche, if desired. It is good cold too!

Ralph Peterson

Soupe au Pistou ♥

Serves 8-10

This is a great soup to have on hand during the holidays when there are lots of hungry mouths to feed. The pesto is an exciting addition to any plain vegetable soup.

Lilyan Levine

2 quarts chicken stock
3 medium potatoes, peeled and cut into 1 inch pieces
1/2 pound green beans
3 carrots, sliced
1 onion, chopped
1 teaspoon salt
1/4 teaspoon pepper
1/2 pound zucchini, sliced
1 (16-ounce) can large white beans, drained
4 cloves garlic, mashed
1 (6-ounce) can tomato paste
1 teaspoon fresh basil, chopped
1/2 cup freshly grated Parmesan cheese
1/2 cup chopped fresh parsley
1/4 cup olive oil

- Combine broth, potatoes, green beans, carrots, onion, salt and pepper in large kettle. Bring to a boil and simmer 10 minutes.
- Add the zucchini and white beans and simmer 10 minutes longer or until vegetables are tender.
- Mix garlic, tomato paste, basil, cheese and parsley with a wire whisk. Gradually beat in oil, a teaspoonful at a time, until the mixture resembles a thick sauce.
- Just before serving, stir the sauce into the hot soup.

Sandy's Honeydew and Cantaloupe Soup

8 small servings

This delicious soup came from my sister, Sandy, who lives in Reno, Nevada. She enjoys patio entertaining and this soup is a refreshing and light meal starter.

Rosie Batcheller

1/2 very ripe honeydew melon
2 teaspoons fresh lime juice
1/4 cup ginger ale
1/4 cup mint leaves
Pinch of salt
1 cup very ripe cantaloupe, diced
1/3 cup plain yogurt or crème fraiche
2 tablespoons honey
1 teaspoon lemon juice

Continued on next page

Sandy's Honeydew and Cantaloupe Soup *continued*

- In a food processor or blender puree honeydew melon, lime juice, ginger ale, mint leaves and salt. Transfer honeydew mixture to bowl and refrigerate for several hours.
- Rinse food processor or blender and process cantaloupe, yogurt or crème fraiche, honey and lemon juice.
- Transfer cantaloupe mixture to a separate bowl and refrigerate for several hours.
- To serve ladle honeydew mixture into soup bowls.
- Ladle cantaloupe mixture into the center of the honeydew mixture and use a knife tip to swirl the cantaloupe mixture throughout the honeydew mixture.

Nancy's Potato Leek Soup

Serves 6

2 1/2 cups finely chopped leeks
1 small onion, finely chopped
3 tablespoons butter
1 teaspoon olive oil
1/2 cup grated carrot
Salt and pepper to taste
3 small cans chicken broth
9 medium potatoes, peeled and cubed
1 tablespoon chopped fresh basil or 1 teaspoon dried
10 shakes cayenne pepper sauce
Nutmeg, two dashes or so
1 cup half & half
Fresh chives, chopped for garnish

- Place chopped leeks and onion in a large pan with butter and olive oil and sauté until soft.
- Add the carrots and salt and pepper and simmer for another 1-2 minutes.
- Add the chicken broth, potatoes and basil. Season again with salt and pepper to taste.
- Bring to a boil, reduce heat and cook until the potatoes are done, about 20 minutes.
- Stir in the cayenne pepper sauce and nutmeg. Continue to simmer for another 2 or 3 minutes.
- With a potato masher, mash the mixture to eliminate large pieces, but do not over process. Season again to taste.
- Add half and half and heat thoroughly.
- Garnish with fresh, chopped chives.
- Serve hot.

The carrots make this soup a rich, golden color, unusual for a leek and potato soup. The pepper sauce gives it a unique zing.

Nancy Keadey

Arugula and Escarole Salad with Figs

Serves 6

2 large bunches arugula, about 3 cups, loosely packed
1 medium head escarole, about 6 cups, loosely packed
1/3 cup port wine
1/2 teaspoon sugar
4 ounces dried figs, stems removed, 6 large or 12 small
2 tablespoons balsamic vinegar
2 medium shallots or 1/4 small red onion, minced
1/4 teaspoon salt
1/4 teaspoon ground black pepper
1/4 cup extra-virgin olive oil
1/4 pound blue cheese, crumbled

- Wash, dry, and tear arugula and escarole into bite size pieces.
- Bring port, sugar and figs to boil in medium saucepan over high heat. Cover pan, reduce heat to low and simmer until figs are very soft but not mushy, about 15 minutes.
- Reserving liquid, remove figs with slotted spoon, and when cool enough to handle, trim stems, quarter and set aside.
- Whisk vinegar, shallots, salt and pepper into the reserved port; gradually whisk in oil
- Return the figs to the dressing and reheat over medium heat, stirring occasionally until warm but not steaming.
- Toss greens and warm dressing to coat in large mixing bowl.
- Divide dressed greens among 6 serving plates, sprinkle with blue cheese and serve immediately.

The flavors of both the greens and the dressing are bold, a consideration when pairing with an entrée.

Norma Berry

Rice Salad

Serves 10-12

2 cups rice
4 tablespoons butter, softened
1 cup golden raisins
1/4 cup olive oil
2/3 cup orange juice
8 scallions, sliced
Vidalia Onion Vinaigrette, Oak Hill Farms preferred

- Boil rice until fluffy. Cool until tepid.
- Add butter, raisins, olive oil, orange juice and scallions and mix well
- Sprinkle in the vinaigrette to taste.

The vinaigrette can be purchased in the produce department of most grocery stores. You may have to add a little more olive oil if mixture seems too dry. Serve at room temperature.

Zina Quinn

Cobb Pasta Salad

Serves 4-6

1 pound wagon wheel or bow tie pasta
2-3 cups cooked chicken cut into bite-size pieces
10 ounces bacon, fried and crumbled
4 cups of several kinds of lettuce. Can include spinach
1 (4-ounce) package crumbled blue cheese
Optional: sunflower seeds, black olives, or diced tomatoes
Dressing:
1 teaspoon Dijon mustard
1/4 cup red wine vinegar
1 cup olive oil
1/2 teaspoon freshly ground black pepper
1 teaspoon sugar or honey
Garlic to taste

- Combine ingredients in a jar, shake well and set aside.
- Cook pasta until al dente. Drain, rinse and drain again.
- In a large salad bowl combine cooked pasta, chicken, bacon, lettuce, blue cheese, dressing and optional ingredients. Toss gently and serve.

This is a great recipe and can be set in the middle of the table for everyone to help themselves. A loaf of sourdough or French bread goes very nicely. The dressing and bacon can be prepared ahead of time. I have used leftover turkey in place of chicken.

Mary Stuneck

Cranberry Spinach Salad

Serves 4

6 ounces salad spinach
1 (6-ounce) can mandarin oranges, drained
1/2 cup sweetened dried cranberries
1 red onion, thinly sliced, as desired
1/4 cup toasted, sliced almonds
Dressing:
1/2 cup honey
1/2 cup fresh lime juice
2 tablespoons Dijon mustard

- Whisk together dressing ingredients and set aside.
- Wash spinach, dry thoroughly and divide among 4 salad plates.
- Top greens with mandarin oranges and cranberries.
- Add sliced red onion, if desired.
- Top with dressing and garnish with almonds.

This is a colorful and delicious salad and the dressing is fat free. It is lovely with fowl, fish or pork. Also blends nicely with many vegetarian entrees.

Karen Marshall

Clare's Salad ♥

Serves 6

Salad:
1/2 cup sliced almonds
2 tablespoons sugar
3-4 drops water
1/2 head iceberg lettuce, coarsely chopped
1/2 head romaine lettuce, torn into bite sized pieces
1 cup chopped celery
2 green onions, chopped
2 oranges, segmented, with all white pith removed
Dressing:
1/2 teaspoon salt
Dash pepper
1/4 cup olive oil
1 tablespoon fresh parsley, chopped
2 tablespoons sugar
2 tablespoons red raspberry vinegar
Dash Tabasco sauce

This was my mother's recipe and I find that everyone likes the combination of the almonds and orange segments. I often make a double batch of the almonds, keep them in an airtight jar, and use them on multiple salads during the week. They will keep up to two weeks. Sometimes I use a can of Mandarin oranges if I don't have the real thing on hand.

Janet Lorant

- In a large frying pan sprayed with olive oil or cooking spray, caramelize the sliced almonds with the sugar and water over medium heat. Cook until the sugar dissolves and the nuts are brown, stirring constantly.
- Remove from the heat and spread the almonds on a linen dishtowel to cool. When cool, remove from the towel and place in an airtight container until ready to use. The almonds may stick to the towel, but will come off with a little effort.
- Combine all the dressing ingredients and shake or whisk until well blended and emulsified. Set it aside until ready to use.
- Just before serving toss the lettuces, celery and onion and oranges together in a salad bowl. Pour the dressing over the salad and toss to coat all ingredients. Place the dressed salad on individual plates and divide the caramelized almond slices among them to top the salads.

Spinach and Pear Salad with Prosciutto *continued*

- In a large saucepan, sauté onion in olive oil on medium-low heat until golden, 30-45 minutes.
- Add wine, mustard, salt and pepper to taste, and vinegar.
- Taste dressing; add Splenda or sugar to taste. Keep the dressing warm.
- Brush a cookie sheet with oil and arrange prosciutto in single layer. Toast in preheated oven for 7-8 minutes until edges are crisp. Cut crosswise into 1/4-inch strips and let cool on paper towels.
- Quarter pears, peel and cut into 1/8-inch slices.
- Put pears, spinach and warm onion sauce in a salad bowl and toss.
- Divide among 4 plates and garnish with prosciutto strips.

Layered Chicken Salad

Serves 8

Suzanne's Red Dressing:
1 teaspoon grated onion
1/2 teaspoon salt
1/2 cup sugar or artificial sweetener
1/2 cup catsup
1/4 cup vinegar
1 cup olive oil
Salad Layers:
One head of green lettuce, torn into bite-size pieces
4 cooked chicken breasts, cut into bite-size pieces
2 tomatoes, roughly chopped
1 onion, roughly chopped
1/2 cup sliced black olives
1 can kidney beans, drained
1 packet taco seasoning
1 pound grated Cheddar cheese
1/2 bag crushed Fritos

My sister, Suzanne, has made this for years usually bringing it to family picnics. It is a favorite of both the kids and adults. We often substitute tomato juice for the ketchup when making the dressing.

Janet Lorant

- Combine dressing ingredients and mix well to dissolve sugar or sweetener. Set aside.
- Layer the salad ingredients in the order listed up to and including the cheddar cheese.
- Pour the dressing over the salad or serve it on the side.
- Sprinkle crushed Fritos over the top and serve.

Green Salad with Roasted Cherries, Nuts, and Saint Marcellin

Serves 4

24 walnuts halves
16 ripe, sweet cherries such as Bing
1/4 cup extra virgin olive oil
Few splashes of Kirsch
1 tablespoon red wine vinegar
Salt to taste
2 wheels Saint-Marcellin cheese, 3 ounces each, room
** temperature**
4-5 ounces mixed young lettuces, washed and dried
4 slices, chewy rustic style bread, toasted

- Preheat oven to 325° F.
- Roast the nuts on a baking sheet about 10-15 minutes. Remove from oven. Increase oven temperature to 400° F.
- Coarsely chop the nuts.
- Toss the cherries with a few drops of olive oil and season with a few drops of kirsch and a pinch of salt. If you cannot find fresh cherries, substitute dried cherries that have been plumped first by soaking in warm water for 20 minutes.
- Make the dressing by combining the oil, vinegar, and salt. Add another few drops of kirsch and season to taste.
- Place parchment paper on a sheet pan with sides. Place the cheese on the paper and the cherries to one side.
- Roast in preheated oven until the fruit is near to bursting and the cheese is beginning to slump, about 6 minutes.
- Combine the lettuces and 2/3 of the walnuts in a medium bowl and dress very lightly with the vinaigrette. Arrange the greens on plates.
- Garnish with the warm cherries and place 1/2 of a warm cheese wheel next to each salad. Sprinkle remaining nuts over the top of the salad.
- Serve with toasted bread.
  This recipe is adapted from THE ZUNI CAFÉ COOKBOOK by Judy Rogers.

Anonymous

Prizewinner Potato Salad

Serves 10-12

2 pounds white potatoes
1/2 cup mayonnaise
1/2 cup sour cream
2 tablespoons horseradish
1 tablespoon chopped parsley
1/2 teaspoon salt
1/2 teaspoon pepper
4 eggs, hardboiled and chopped
3 slices bacon, cooked and crumbled or bacon bits
2 green onions, sliced very thin
1/2 cup finely chopped celery

- Peel and cook potatoes. Drain, cool and cut into 1-inch cubes.
- In large bowl, whisk mayonnaise, sour cream, horseradish, parsley, salt and pepper until smooth.
- Stir in potatoes and remaining ingredients until well combined.
- Refrigerate for several hours to blend flavors.

The horseradish and bacon make this a very flavorful potato salad. It makes a great summer lunch or is delicious as an accompaniment to grilled foods.

Ralph Allen

Greek Salad

Serves 4-6

1 large head Romaine lettuce, washed, dried and torn
1/2 cup cucumber, thinly sliced
2 tomatoes, sliced or quartered
1/2 cup Greek oil-cured black olives or plain black olives
1 jar marinated artichoke hearts, drained
1/4 pound feta cheese, crumbled
1/2 teaspoon dried oregano leaves
3 tablespoons lemon juice
6 tablespoons olive oil
Salt and pepper

- Arrange bed of lettuce on an attractive serving platter.
- Scatter cucumbers, tomatoes, olives, artichokes and feta over the lettuce.
- Sprinkle all with oregano, lemon juice and oil. Pass salt and pepper.

This salad always receives raves and looks very pretty.

Margaret Chapman

Curried Chicken Salad

Makes 6 generous 1 cup servings

Salad:
1 package rice pilaf, I use 703 Near East River Pilaf
2 cups cooked chicken breast, cubed
2 medium red apples, peeled, cored and cubed
1/2 cup raisins
Dressing:
3/4 cup mayonnaise
1/2 cup orange marmalade
1/4 cup dairy sour cream
2-3 teaspoons fresh lemon juice
1 1/2 teaspoons curry powder

Salad greens
Toasted, slivered almonds

- Prepare rice according to directions on the package, using oil since the salad is chilled.
- Place the cooked pilaf in a large bowl, cover and chill.
- Combine rice pilaf, chicken, apples, and raisins, tossing to combine. Pour the dressing over the chicken mixture. Stir gently to coat evenly.
- Serve the salad on greens and garnish with almonds.

I have been serving this chicken salad for years and have never failed to receive many compliments. It's a lovely lunch selection, perhaps served with fresh homemade rolls and grapes.

Karen Marshall

Black Bean, Orzo and Tomato Salad
with Garlic Dressing ♥

Serves 6

1 cup orzo
1 1/2 teaspoons salt, divided
2 (19-ounce) cans black beans, drained and rinsed
1 1/2 cups diced tomatoes
1/2 cup chopped sweet red onions
1 1/2 tablespoons Dijon mustard
3 tablespoons red wine vinegar
1 tablespoon minced garlic
1/4 teaspoon crushed red pepper
6 tablespoons olive oil
2 tablespoons chopped fresh parsley
3 tablespoons chopped fresh basil, plus several sprigs for
  garnish.

- Bring 2 quarts water to boil. Add orzo and 1 teaspoon salt. Reduce to simmer and cook until orzo is just tender, 8 to 10 minutes. Drain well and place in a non-reactive mixing bowl.
- Add beans, tomatoes and onions. Mix well.
- In a separate bowl, whisk together mustard, vinegar, garlic, red pepper flakes and 1/2 teaspoon salt. Gradually whisk in olive oil.
- Pour dressing over the salad and toss to mix.
- Cover and refrigerate.
- Bring to room temperature 30 minutes before serving.
- When ready to serve, add chopped parsley and basil to salad and mix well.
- Mound salad on serving platter or in large shallow bowl.
- Garnish with basil.

This is a delicious and attractive salad for a family picnic. I found the recipe in a newspaper. It is easy to prepare and looks great in a large, colorful bowl. It can be a whole meal in itself.

Sam Mason

Lightly Dilled Potato Salad

Serves 12-14

2 tablespoons corn oil
1 tablespoon apple cider vinegar
4 pounds small red potatoes, cooked and quartered
1 cup reduced calorie mayonnaise
1 cup plain low fat yogurt
1 tablespoon Dijon mustard
1 cup minced red onion
1/2 cup minced fresh dill
Salt and pepper to taste

- In a large bowl, sprinkle corn oil and vinegar over potatoes. Toss lightly to coat.
- Combine mayonnaise, yogurt and mustard.
- Add mayonnaise mixture with onion, dill and salt and pepper to the potatoes. Toss to coat well.
- Cover and chill.

This was the winner of a Best Potato Salad contest that 10,000 people entered. The grand prize of $5,000 went to Maureen Bevelaqua of Muttontown, NY. This keeps well for several days in the refrigerator.

Beverly Long

Blue Cheese Dressing

Serves 12

1 cup Hellman's mayonnaise
4 tablespoons vegetable oil, olive oil or combination
1 tablespoon cider vinegar
1 teaspoon Worcestershire sauce
1 clove garlic, crushed in a garlic press
4 ounces blue cheese
1/2-3/4 cups sour cream
Salt and pepper to taste

- Whisk together oil and mayonnaise until well blended. Add remaining ingredients and mix well.

This salad dressing is always popular. The recipe has been passed on many, many times. Sometimes I use Maytag blue cheese but more often Danish blue. I use a variety of mixed greens, sometimes adding avocado. The dressing is substantial enough that no other additions to the greens are necessary.

Shirley Perry

Fish

and

Shellfish

Fish and Shellfish

Fish

Cashew Crusted Triggerfish with Confederate Caviar, Fried Green
Tomatoes and Lime Riesling Sauce, 114
Gravlax, 110
Green Sauce for Fish, 110
Grilled Salmon Salad with Vegetable Balsamic Dressing, 107 ♥
Pan Roasted King Salmon with Grilled Radicchio on Creamed Corn, 112
Poached Salmon, 111 ♥
Salmon Croquettes, 116
Shallot Crusted Halibut, 109
Swordfish Kabobs, 113 ♥
Tuna Tonnato, 108

Shellfish

Cioppino, 121
Cornmeal Crusted Shrimp with Leeks and Bacon, 120
Crab au Gratin, 119
Crawfish Étouffée, 124
Fruits de Mer, 122 ♥
Maryland Crab Cakes with Aioli Sauce, 125
Paella Catalan, 126
Seared Scallops with Leeks and Carrots, 120
Shrimp Artichoke Casserole, 123
Shrimp Bourbon, 122
Shrimp with Pernod, 128
Shrimp with Tomatoes and Feta Cheese, 118
Shrimp, Red Pepper and Asparagus with Spicy Asian Sauce, 117 ♥
True Grits and Shrimp, 127

♥ Heart Healthy

Grilled Salmon Salad with Vegetable Balsamic Dressing ♥

Serves 6

1/2-cup olive oil
6 tablespoons fresh lime juice
6 8-ounce salmon filets, 1 inch thick
Dressing:
3/4 cup olive oil
3 small tomatoes, peeled, seeded, chopped, about 1/2 cup
1 small carrot cut in matchstick sized pieces
1 small zucchini cut in matchstick sized pieces
1/4 cup chopped fresh Italian parsley
1/4 cup balsamic vinegar
1 tablespoon minced fresh basil
1 tablespoon minced fresh tarragon
Salt and pepper to taste

10 cups mixed baby greens
2 heads Belgian endive, sliced crosswise

- Mix 1/2 cup oil and lime juice in small bowl.
- Place salmon in dish large enough to hold filets in single layer. Pour marinade over, cover, and refrigerate 2 hours, turning once.

Dressing:
- Combine oil, tomatoes, carrot, zucchini, parsley, vinegar, basil and tarragon, salt and pepper to taste. Dressing can be prepared 2 hours ahead. Cover and let stand at room temperature.

- Prepare grill, medium-high heat, or preheat broiler.
- Grill salmon until just cooked through, about 4 minutes per side.
- Toss greens and endive with enough vegetable dressing to coat. Divide among 6 plates.
- Place salmon on top of greens.
- Spoon additional vegetable dressing over salmon and serve.

This is a wonderful summer supper. The combination of the warm salmon and crisp greens makes a very interesting meal. Serve with warm crusty bread.

Susanne Hotte

Tuna Tonnato

Serves: 8

Mayonnaise:
1 egg
1 egg yolk
4 teaspoons Dijon mustard
2 1/2 tablespoons fresh lemon juice
1/2 cup olive oil
1/2 cup corn oil
Tuna sauce:
1/2 cup canned tuna, drained
1 1/2 tablespoons capers, drained
4 anchovy fillets, drained
1 tablespoon lemon juice
1/3 cup olive oil
2 teaspoons lemon zest
Salt and pepper to taste
Marinade:
1/3 cup olive oil
1/3 cup lemon juice
1/2 teaspoon black pepper
Fish:
8 tuna steaks, 1 inch thick, about 6 ounces each
Garnish:
2 tablespoons chopped parsley
1 1/2 tablespoons capers, drained
1 tablespoon lemon zest

This is a delightful dish for a summer dinner party; so cool, and less expensive than the classic Veal Tonnato.
Works very well for a summer buffet. The sauce can be made in advance.

Cynthia Jones

- Prepare mayonnaise: place egg, egg yolk, mustard and lemon juice in a food processor and process for 15 seconds. With motor running, pour both oils slowly through the feed tube and process until mayonnaise thickens. Cover and refrigerate if you are making in advance.
- Prepare tuna sauce: combine tuna, capers, anchovies, lemon juice and oil in a food processor and process about 1 minute.
- Fold tuna sauce into the mayonnaise; add lemon zest, salt and pepper. Cover and refrigerate for at least 4 hours. Can be made one day ahead.
- Day of serving: mix the olive oil, lemon juice, and black pepper in a shallow dish just large enough to hold all the tuna steaks in a single layer.
- Add the steaks, coat with marinade, cover and refrigerate for 30 minutes, turning once.
- Preheat broiler.

Continued on next page

Tuna Tonnato *continued*

- Remove tuna steaks from marinade and place on broiling pan. Broil 4 inches from heat for 3-4 minutes per side. Do not overcook. Set aside and cool to room temperature.
- Arrange the cooled tuna steaks on serving platter or on individual plates.
- Spread tuna-mayonnaise sauce on top of each steak. Sprinkle with parsley, capers and lemon zest.

Shallot-Crusted Halibut

Serves 4

1 1/2 tablespoons olive oil
4 large shallots, minced
2 tablespoons snipped fresh chives
2 tablespoons chopped flat leaf parsley
2 teaspoons chopped fresh thyme
3 tablespoons butter, melted
1 cup dried breadcrumbs, made from crusty Italian bread
2 teaspoons fresh lime juice
Salt and freshly ground black pepper to taste
4 (6-ounce) halibut fillets, about 1 inch thick

- Preheat the oven to 400° F.
- Heat the oil in a heavy skillet over medium heat; add the shallots and the herbs and cook, stirring, until softened but not browned. Transfer to a bowl.
- In the same skillet, melt the butter over medium heat. Add the breadcrumbs and cook, stirring, until crisp and golden, about 5 minutes.
- Add the crumbs, lime juice, salt and pepper to the shallot mixture. Toss to blend.
- Season halibut on both sides with salt and pepper.
- Put fish into a buttered baking dish and spread breadcrumb mixture on top.
- Bake for 20 minutes in the preheated oven or until the fish is just opaque throughout.

Gillian Cell

Gravlax

Serves 30 as part of a buffet

1 4-pound fresh salmon filet
1/4 cup Kosher or any other coarse salt
1 teaspoon each cracked pepper, black and white
1/4 cup brown sugar
Zest of 1 lemon, lime and orange
Juice from 1 lemon, 1 lime and 1 orange
2 or more tablespoons Grand Marnier or other orange
**   flavored liqueur**
1/2 cup sour cream

- Cut the filet in half lengthwise.
- Mix salt, pepper, sugar, zests, and juices together and add enough Grand Marnier so that the mixture is the consistency of beach sand.
- Put half the marinade on the first half filet that is skin side down. Put the remaining half filet on top with the skin side up. Cover with the rest of the marinade. Weight with a heavy object, cover tightly and marinate, refrigerated, for 1 day.
- To serve, slice very thinly on the bias, but not through the skin.
- Serve covered with lemon, lime and orange zests.
- Boil down the juices, mix with sour cream and serve as a sauce.

This is different and delicious and is an attractive dish for a party buffet.

Vaughn Owen

Green Sauce for Fish

Serves 2

1 cup fresh parsley or cilantro
3 green onions
1 cup fresh dill sprigs
1 tablespoon capers, drained
3 cloves garlic
4 tablespoons lemon juice
1/4 cup sour cream
1/4 cup mayonnaise
Salt, pepper, sugar to taste

- In a food processor pulse the parsley or cilantro, green onion and dill until minced. Add the capers and garlic and pulse again. Add the lemon juice, sour cream and mayonnaise and pulse to mix. Add salt, pepper and sugar to taste.

This recipe came from my mother, who used to serve it with poached shad or salmon. The sauce is delicious and fresh tasting. It is great with fish and can be used with cold meats or poultry as well.

Reg Lorant

Poached Salmon

Serves 4

4-5 serving pieces skinless salmon

2 cups water or 1 cup water and one cup white wine
1/2 cup sliced onion
2-3 thin lemon slices and 1 tablespoon lemon juice
2 bay leaves
8 peppercorns
1 teaspoon salt
1 teaspoon dry dill weed

1 1/2 tablespoons flour
1/4 cup water

- Combine water or water and wine, onion, lemon slices and juice, bay leaves, peppercorns, salt and dill weed in a saucepan. Bring to a boil and boil for 5 minutes. Cool slightly and strain.
- In a large skillet pour poaching liquid over salmon. Bring to boil, reduce heat and simmer for about 8 minutes. Do not overcook.
- Drain the fish and keep warm, reserving the poaching liquid.
- Pour the reserved liquid into a saucepan, bring to a boil and reduce to 1 cup.
- Dissolve the flour in the water, add a little of the reduced poaching liquid and pour the mixture into the remaining poaching liquid, stirring until it bubbles and thickens.
- Correct the seasoning and add some freshly ground black pepper. Serve the sauce with the fish.

You may enhance the basic flavors of the sauce by adding a teaspoon each of horseradish and Dijon mustard. One or two tablespoons of sour cream or a pat of butter will enrich the mixture. If I don't have wine, I add a chicken bouillon cube and adjust the salt.

Stacy Koehler

Pan Roasted King Salmon with Grilled Radicchio on Creamed Corn

Serves 4

For the radicchio:
1/2 cup fresh lemon juice
1/2 cup sugar
1/3 cup olive oil
1 small garlic clove, chopped
2 heads radicchio, quartered
Salt and pepper

For the creamed corn:
1 tablespoon unsalted butter
1 jalapeño pepper, minced
1/2 red bell pepper, diced
1/2 white onion, diced
1 teaspoon minced garlic
1 teaspoon minced shallots
Corn kernels from 2 fresh ears of corn
1 tablespoon granulated sugar
1/4 cup heavy cream
Juice of one lemon
Salt and pepper

For the salmon:
2 tablespoons olive oil
4 salmon filets, 6 ounces each
Salt and pepper
3 tablespoons unsalted butter
3 sprigs fresh thyme, leaves only

Shane Ingram
Executive Chef and
co-owner, Four
Square Restaurant,
Durham, NC

Former Chef
Fearrington House
Restaurant

The radicchio:
- Whisk together the lemon juice, sugar, oil, and garlic.
- Pour over the quartered radicchio.
- Allow to sit at room temperature for one hour. Drain very well.
- Grill over medium heat. Be careful not to burn the radicchio.
- Season to taste with salt and pepper.

The creamed corn:
- Sauté jalapeño, bell pepper, onion, garlic and shallots in butter. Cook over moderate heat for one minute.
- Add the corn kernels and sauté for 2 minutes.
- Sprinkle with the sugar and allow the mixture to caramelize slightly, stirring, about 2 minutes.
- Add cream and cook until the mixture begins to thicken.
- Season with lemon juice, salt and pepper. Keep warm.

Continued on the next page

**Pan Roasted King Salmon with Grilled Radicchio
on Creamed Corn** *continued*

The salmon:
- Heat the olive oil in a sauté pan over high heat.
- Season the salmon filets with salt and pepper and sear for 3 minutes on one side.
- Turn the filets over and reduce heat to medium.
- Add butter and thyme and baste the fish with the herb butter.
- Cook until the salmon is medium rare.

To serve:
- Spoon a portion of corn onto a warm plate. Place grilled radicchio on the corn and top with a salmon filet. Drizzle thyme butter from the salmon sauté pan over all.

Swordfish Kebobs

Serves 4

Two pounds swordfish filets, 1 inch thick
Marinade:
2 tablespoons soy sauce
2 tablespoons olive oil
2 teaspoons grated lime peel
1 teaspoon lime juice
1 teaspoon minced garlic
2 teaspoons spicy mustard
2 scallions, white and green parts, chopped
2 teaspoons minced fresh ginger
1/4 cup dry sherry

- Combine marinade ingredients in a large shallow dish.
- Remove skin and cut the swordfish into 1-inch squares.
- Add swordfish to marinade. Toss to coat and allow to stand, covered, at room temperature for at least 3 hours and up to 6 hours.
- Place swordfish on metal skewers or into a fish basket designed for an outdoor grill.
- Grill over white charcoal coals or on a hot gas grill for 3-4 minutes per side until slightly browned. Do not overcook.
- Serve with rice and a green salad.

This recipe cannot be duplicated using the broiler of an oven. There is something about the outdoor grilling process that makes it really come together.

Janet Lorant

Cashew-Crusted Triggerfish with Confederate Caviar, Fried Green Tomatoes and Lime Riesling Sauce

Serves 4

Confederate Caviar:
2 cups cooked or canned black-eyed peas, drained
1/2 cup roasted corn kernels
1/4 cup minced red onion
2 tablespoons chicken stock
1 cup thinly sliced okra
2 tablespoons thinly sliced green onions
2 tablespoons unsalted butter
Salt and pepper to taste

Fried Green Tomatoes:
1/2 cup flour
Salt and white pepper to taste
2 eggs, beaten
2 tablespoons cream
2 tablespoons water
1 cup dry breadcrumbs
1/4 cup finely chopped fresh basil leaves
2 tablespoons finely chopped fresh parsley leaves
2 tablespoons finely chopped fresh chives
2 tablespoons freshly grated Parmesan cheese
1 tablespoon olive oil
2 green tomatoes cut into 1/4-inch slices
3 cups peanut oil for frying

Lime Riesling Sauce:
Zest and juice of 2 limes
1/2 cup Riesling
1 shallot, coarsely chopped
1 tablespoon thinly sliced peeled fresh gingerroot
1 tablespoon heavy cream
1 1/2 cups butter, cut into cubes
Salt and white pepper to taste

Fish:
4 triggerfish or tilapia fillets
Salt and pepper to taste
1 cup flour
2 eggs, beaten
2 cups cashews, crushed

Warren Stephens
Chef-Owner
Grey Ghost
Restaurant
Southern Pines, NC

Former Chef
Fearrington House
Restaurant

Continued on the next page

Cashew-Crusted Triggerfish *Continued*

Confederate Caviar:
- Combine black-eyed peas, corn, onion and stock in a sauté pan. Bring to a simmer.
- Add okra and green onions.
- Cook just until the okra is tender, about 6 -8 minutes.
- Stir in butter and season with salt and pepper. Set aside.

Fried Green Tomatoes:
- In a shallow pan combine flour, salt and white pepper.
- Stir together eggs, cream and water in another shallow pan.
- Combine breadcrumbs, basil, parsley, chives, cheese, olive oil, salt and pepper in a third shallow pan.
- Dredge the tomato slices in the flour. Dip into the egg mixture and coat with the crumb mixture. Place on a baking sheet. The tomatoes may be prepared to this point and refrigerated or frozen for later use.
- Heat the oil in a large heavy pan to 375° F.
- Fry the tomato slices a few at a time until browned on both sides. Drain on paper towels. Keep warm.

Lime Riesling Butter Sauce:
- Combine the lime zest, lime juice, wine, shallot and gingerroot in a saucepan.
- Cook until the mixture is reduced by 90 percent.
- Add the cream and cook for 1 minute. Set aside.
- Cook fish now and complete sauce while fish is cooking.
- Complete sauce by reducing the heat to very low and adding the butter a few pieces at a time. Stir to melt completely after each addition. Season with salt and white pepper.
- Strain the sauce into a bowl and keep warm.

Fish:
- Preheat oven to 350° F.
- Season fish with salt and pepper.
- Dredge fish in flour; dip in eggs and coat with cashews.
- Place the fish on a parchment-lined or buttered baking sheet.
- Bake for 12-14 minutes or until the fish flakes easily.

To Serve:
- Spoon 1/4 cup Lime Riesling Butter Sauce onto each plate.
- Place 2 Fried Green Tomato slices over the sauce.
- Top with a fish fillet. Spoon Confederate Caviar over the fish.

Salmon Croquettes

Serves 2

Croquettes:
1 (16-ounce) can of salmon
1 tablespoon onion, grated
1 egg, beaten
2 tablespoons breadcrumbs
1 tablespoon chopped fresh parsley
Salt and pepper
Coating Mixture:
1 egg, beaten
1/2 cup seasoned breadcrumbs
1/2 cup flour
1 teaspoon salt
1/4 teaspoon pepper
1/2 teaspoon paprika
Dash of garlic powder

Oil for frying, corn or peanut

- Remove the skin and bones from the salmon and discard.
- Mash the salmon and mix with the onion, egg, breadcrumbs, parsley, salt and pepper.
- Form 4 croquettes.
- Combine breadcrumbs, flour, salt and pepper, paprika, and garlic powder. Mix well.
- Dip each croquette first in beaten egg, and then in the breadcrumb mixture,
- Pour the oil 1 inch deep in a 12-inch skillet. When hot, gently place the croquettes in the pan. Fry until deep brown, turning once. Drain well on brown paper.

This economy dish is just delicious. The croquettes may be prepared early in the day, refrigerated and fried before serving or they can be fried early, drained and served at room temperature. Serve hot with creamed spinach and baked potatoes or at room temperature on a roll with a thick slice of tomato.

Lilyan Levine

Shrimp, Red Pepper, and Asparagus with Spicy Asian Sauce ♥

Serves 6

Sauce:
1 cup dry white wine
2 tablespoons oyster sauce
1 tablespoon hoisin sauce
1 tablespoon tomato paste
1 tablespoon Braggs Amino Acid or soy sauce
1-2 teaspoons garlic-chili sauce
2 tablespoons chunky peanut butter
Shrimp:
1 tablespoon oil
1 tablespoon grated fresh ginger
1 tablespoon minced garlic
2 pounds shrimp, peeled and deveined
2 bunches asparagus, chopped into 1-inch pieces
2 red peppers, chopped into 1-inch pieces
1 tablespoon cornstarch mixed with 2 tablespoons water to thicken sauce at end of cooking preparation
Finely chopped parsley for garnish

Sauce:
- Combine all sauce ingredients. Break up peanut butter with a fork. The sauce can be made two or three hours ahead.

Shrimp:
- In a large sauté pan or wok, sauté ginger and garlic in oil for a minute or two. Add shrimp, cover, and simmer for five or six minutes until just pink, stirring frequently. Remove from pan and set aside.
- Add asparagus and red pepper with the prepared sauce to the pan and simmer approximately five minutes until tender, but still crisp. Return shrimp to pan and reheat.
- If desired, thicken the sauce with a little of the cornstarch-water mixture.
- Serve over rice and garnish with minced parsley.

This dish is the result of tweaking a bland Cantonese recipe. The ingredients for the sauce are available in the Asian section of a supermarket. Serve over white or yellow rice that has been shaped in a ramekin. Two cups raw rice plus 1 teaspoon turmeric yields six cups cooked yellow rice. Ramekins can be made a day ahead or in the morning and heated in the microwave. Invert ramekin with rice on middle of plate, surround with shrimp mixture, and sprinkle minced parsley over rice.

Maggie Gaudet

Shrimp with Tomatoes and Feta Cheese

Serves 4-5

1 tablespoon butter
1 teaspoon minced garlic
1/4 cup finely chopped onion
2 cups chopped, peeled tomatoes, about 2 pounds
2 tablespoons finely chopped fresh basil
1 teaspoon Dijon style mustard
1 teaspoon sugar
1/4 cup dry white wine
1/4 cup parsley, minced
1 tablespoon lemon juice
1/2 teaspoon salt
Freshly ground black pepper
3/4 pound large shrimp, peeled and deveined
2 tablespoons crumbled feta cheese
2 tablespoons minced parsley, for garnish

- Preheat oven to 450° F.
- In large skillet, melt butter on low heat. Add garlic and onions and sauté until wilted, about 5 minutes.
- Add tomatoes, basil, mustard and sugar; mix well to blend and cook over medium heat until sauce is thick, stirring occasionally.
- Add wine, parsley, lemon juice, salt and pepper; mix well.
- Add shrimp, stirring frequently for 3-4 minutes, just until opaque. Take care not to overcook or shrimp will toughen during final cooking.
- Remove from heat and transfer to an open au gratin dish. If preparing in advance, cool, then cover with plastic wrap and refrigerate until one hour before serving.
- Allow casserole to come to room temperature and sprinkle with feta cheese.
- Bake for 10 minutes or until bubbly and cheese is melted. Run under broiler briefly to brown.
- Sprinkle with parsley.
- Serve with or over rice.

This may be partially prepared 12 hours in advance. I acquired the recipe 25 years ago from a Boston, MA college club dinner.

Carole O'Loughlin

Crab au Gratin

Serves 4

3 tablespoons unsalted butter
1/4 cup finely chopped scallions, or shallots
1 tablespoon finely chopped parsley
1 1/2 tablespoons flour
1 cup sour cream
1/2 cup milk
Tabasco to taste
1 teaspoon freshly ground black pepper
2 tablespoons lemon juice
2 tablespoons dry sherry
1 pound jumbo lump crab
1 1/2 cups Cheddar cheese, finely shredded

- Preheat oven to 350° F.
- In skillet over moderate heat, melt butter and sauté the scallions or shallots and parsley until soft, 2-3 minutes.
- Blend in flour, sour cream and milk and mix until smooth and cook until beginning to bubble.
- Remove from the heat and add a dash of Tabasco, the black pepper, lemon juice and sherry.
- Gently break up lumps of crabmeat and place in a baking dish.
- Pour sour cream sauce over the crabmeat and fold gently to combine.
- Fold in cheese to mix with the crabmeat and bake in the preheated oven for 30 minutes or until cheese has melted and crabmeat is bubbling.

It is essential to use fresh, jumbo, lump crabmeat. You may use either blue or stone crab. This is a rich and rewarding dish and worth every penny that fresh crabmeat may cost.

Ralph Peterson

Seared Scallops with Leeks and Carrots ♥

Serves 4

2 teaspoons butter
4 medium carrots, peeled and cut into 2-inch matchsticks
Salt and white pepper to taste
3 medium leeks, washed, trimmed and cut into 2-inch
   matchsticks
1/4 cup white wine or dry vermouth
2 teaspoons butter
1 pound large sea scallops, dried on paper towels
1 lemon cut in 4 wedges for serving

- Melt 2 teaspoons of butter in a saucepan over moderate heat.
- Add the carrots, toss them in the butter, and sprinkle lightly with salt. Cover the pan and lower the heat.
- Cook carrots, shaking the pan once or twice for 3 minutes.
- Add leeks and toss the vegetables together over medium heat for 1 minute. Add the white wine or vermouth.
- Season with salt and pepper, cover, and cook for 6 minutes.
- Melt the remaining 2 teaspoons butter in a frying pan over moderately high heat.
- Place the scallops in the pan in a single layer. Increase the heat to high and cook the scallops for 2-3 minutes or until the underside is deeply brown.
- Turn and cook for 2 minutes more.
- For serving, turn the carrots and leeks onto a heated platter or individual plates and place the scallops on top.
- Garnish with lemon wedges.

This dish came from the Boston Globe. It is a very nice and simple winter dish. Serve with couscous, a good choice with the addition of some raisins and pine nuts.

Carol and Nick Gillham

Cornmeal Crusted Shrimp with Leeks and Bacon

Serves 2

4 strips bacon
2 leeks, thinly sliced, including some of the light green part
2 cloves garlic, minced
3/4 pound large shrimp, shelled and deveined
Cornmeal for dredging
2 tablespoons olive oil
2 ounces dry vermouth
4 ounces half & half or evaporated skim milk
1 tablespoon Dijon mustard

Continued on next page

Cornmeal Crusted Shrimp with Leeks and Bacon *continued*

- In large skillet, cook the bacon until crisp. Remove the bacon and drain on paper towels. Crumble the bacon when cool and reserve.
- In the bacon fat, sauté leeks and garlic until soft and slightly brown. Remove from skillet and reserve with the bacon.
- Dredge the shrimp in cornmeal. Heat olive oil in the same pan and cook the shrimp for 1-2 minutes. Add vermouth and simmer for 1 minute.
- Return the leek, garlic and bacon mixture to the pan and add half and half or evaporated skim milk. Heat through but do not bring to a boil.
- Remove from heat and whisk in Dijon mustard.
- Serve with rice.

I enjoyed this dish at Catskill Rose, Mount Tremper, NY, a delightful restaurant in the central Catskills of New York State. Chef Peter told me the ingredients and I experimented until duplication was a success!

Jack Gill

Cioppino

Serves 4-6

2 medium onions, chopped
4 cloves garlic, chopped
2 1/2 cups parsley sprigs, chopped
1/4 cup olive oil
1/2 cup white wine
1 (28-ounce) can plum tomatoes undrained, chopped
2 cups water
1 (6-ounce) can tomato paste
1 teaspoon pepper
1/2 teaspoon thyme
1/2 pound hot sausage
1/2 pound scallops
1/2 pound shrimp
1/2 pound crabmeat

- Cook onions, garlic and parsley in olive oil for 5 minutes.
- Add wine and boil 1 minute.
- Add tomatoes with juice, water, tomato paste and spices. Bring to a boil, reduce heat and simmer for 20 minutes.
- Crumble sausage and sauté over medium heat for about 10 minutes. Add to soup and simmer for 45 minutes.
- Add the seafood and simmer for 5-10 additional minutes.

I often add small chunks of white fish. Serve with crusty bread and a green salad. I received this recipe from Lois Pederson, Sun City, AZ.

Beverly Long

Shrimp Bourbon

Serves: 8

2 tablespoons butter
2 large shallots, chopped
2 garlic cloves, minced
1 cup chicken broth
1/2 cup bourbon
1 cup half & half
1/2 teaspoon red pepper
1 pound fettuccini, cooked and hot
2 pounds medium sized fresh shrimp, peeled and deveined
Parmesan cheese, optional

- Over medium heat melt the butter in a large pan. Add shallots and garlic and sauté 3 minutes.
- Stir in the chicken broth and bourbon, half & half and red pepper. Cook, stirring, 5 minutes or until slightly thickened.
- Cook fettuccini in boiling water until al dente. Drain.
- Add the shrimp to the sauce and cook 3 minutes.
- Serve shrimp and sauce over pasta.
- Sprinkle with Parmesan cheese if desired.

Serve with a tossed salad and a nice wine.

Wilhelmina De Graaf Hanrath

Fruits de Mer ♥

Serves 4

1/4 cup olive oil
1 cup finely chopped onions
2 cloves garlic, minced
1/4 teaspoon dried red pepper, optional
1 1/2 cups fresh or canned tomatoes, peeled and diced
1 1/2 cups dry white wine
1 teaspoon dried oregano
Salt and pepper to taste
2 pounds fresh mussels, debearded and cleaned
1/2 pound shrimp, shelled and deveined
1/2 pound sea scallops, salmon or other firm-textured fish
  cut into bite-size pieces

- In a large, preferably cast iron kettle, heat the olive oil and add the onions and garlic. Stir and cook until wilted.
- Add the red pepper, tomatoes, wine and oregano. Add salt and pepper to taste. Cover and cook 10 minutes.
- Add the scallops or fish, shrimp and mussels. Cover and cook about 10 minutes or until the mussels open. Serve with rice.

This is an adaptation of a recipe in Pierre Franey's 60 Minute Gourmet cookbook.

Eric Goodman

Shrimp Artichoke Casserole

Serves 4-5

4 1/2 tablespoons butter, melted
4 1/2 tablespoons flour
3/4 cup milk
3/4 cup whipping cream
Salt and freshly ground pepper to taste
1 (20-ounce) can artichoke hearts or 1 package frozen
   artichoke hearts, cooked
1 pound fresh shrimp, shelled, deveined and cooked
Topping:
2 tablespoons butter
1/4 pound fresh mushrooms, sliced
1/4 cup dry sherry
1 tablespoon Worcestershire sauce
1/4 cup freshly grated Parmesan cheese
Paprika

- Preheat oven to 375° F.
- Add the butter to a saucepan over medium heat. Stir in the flour and cook 1 minute, stirring.
- Add the milk and cream, stirring constantly. When thick and smooth, season with salt and pepper and set aside.
- Arrange artichokes in a buttered 2-quart baking dish.
- Scatter the shrimp over the artichokes.
- In a small skillet cook the mushrooms in the butter until soft and spread over shrimp.
- Add the sherry and Worcestershire sauce to the cream sauce, stir to mix and pour over the artichoke-shrimp mixture.
- Sprinkle the cheese and paprika over the dish and bake in the preheated oven for 20 minutes.

The flavor of this dish improves if made the day before and refrigerated before baking. Serve over rice.

Suzanne North

Crawfish Étouffée

Serves: 4-6

2 onions, chopped
1/2 cup butter
4 bay leaves
4 cloves garlic, crushed
Dried red pepper to taste
2-3 tablespoons paprika
Zest and juice of 1 lemon
1 pound crawfish
1/2 cup chopped parsley
10 green onions, chopped
2 cloves garlic, chopped
1 tablespoon Worcestershire sauce
5 tablespoons Madeira wine
1 or 2 dashes Tabasco, to taste
Cooked rice
Lemon wedges for garnish

This is Elizabeth William's recipe, collected in Crowley, LA. The dish freezes well. Good with a ripe tomato salad.

Beverly Long

- Brown the onions in the butter
- Add bay leaves, garlic, red pepper, paprika, lemon juice and zest and crawfish and simmer over low heat for 10-15 minutes.
- Add the parsley, green onions, garlic, and Worcestershire sauce and cook an additional 15 minutes.
- Add Madeira wine and a dash or 2 of Tabasco. Simmer 2 minutes.
- Remove bay leaves before serving.
- Serve over rice with lemon wedges

Maryland Crab Cakes with Aioli Sauce

Serves: 4

Crab cakes:
1 egg
2 tablespoons mayonnaise
1/2 teaspoon dry mustard
1/2 teaspoon pepper
2 teaspoons Old Bay seasoning
2 teaspoons Worcestershire sauce
Dash of Tabasco
1 pound back fin crabmeat
1/3 cup saltine cracker crumbs
1/4 pound butter
2 tablespoons vegetable oil
Cornmeal for coating
Basil Aioli Sauce:
3/4 cup mayonnaise
1/3 cup fresh basil, finely chopped
1 tablespoon lemon juice
1 1/2 teaspoons minced garlic
1 1/2 teaspoons lemon zest

Crab cakes:
- In the bowl of a food processor mix egg, mayonnaise, mustard, pepper, Old Bay, Worcestershire and Tabasco. Process until foamy. Pour into a large bowl.
- Gently mix the crabmeat with the mayonnaise mixture. Add the cracker crumbs and gently form into patties. You should have 8 crab cakes.
- Refrigerate the crab cakes for at least 2 hours.
- Melt the butter and oil in a large skillet. Dip the crab cakes in cornmeal and fry until golden brown, turning so that both sides brown evenly, about 5 minutes on each side.
- Serve immediately with Basil Aioli sauce.

Basil Aioli Sauce:
- Mix all ingredients and serve as a sauce for crab cakes.

The recipe for these crab cakes was given to me by the chef of a famous Maryland Eastern Shore restaurant. They have never failed to gather praise. They may be kept warm for a short time in a warm oven. Be careful not to keep them warm too long for they can dry out.

The Basil Aioli Sauce can be made a day or two ahead. It is good with many fish dishes.

Peggy Quinn

Paella Catalan

Serves 4

1/4 cup olive oil
4 pieces chicken, cook's choice, skinless and boneless
1 clove garlic, crushed
1 onion, peeled and chopped
1/4 pound cooked ham, in thin strips or chorizo, sliced
1 cup medium grained or Paella rice
12 large uncooked shrimp, peeled and deveined
1/2 pound white fish, your choice, thick pieces, cut into large cubes
1 (4-ounce) jar pimentos, drained and chopped
12 large mussels
1 cup green peas cooked, or1 small package frozen peas
1/8 teaspoon saffron, soaked in 3 tablespoons hot water for 30 minutes
2 1/2 cups chicken stock or water
Salt and pepper

- Heat oil in paella pan or deep skillet and fry chicken over moderate heat until brown on all sides. Remove to a plate.
- Add garlic and onion. Sauté until onion is transparent.
- Add ham or chorizo and rice. Stir until rice kernels turn white.
- Gather shrimp, fish, pimento and mussels so they are ready to use.
- Scrub mussels under running water.
- Arrange all these ingredients on the rice.
- Add chicken and peas.
- Push mussels deep into the rice.
- Lay shrimp on top.
- Add saffron and soaking liquid to stock or water and pour over ingredients in paella pan.
- Bring to a boil, reduce heat and simmer, uncovered, until all ingredients are cooked and liquid is absorbed, about 20 minutes.
- Discard any mussels that do not open.
- Present the beautiful paella at the table for your guests to admire. Enjoy.

Guests love this dish! It is a one dish meal, easy to prepare and there is a WOW factor. This recipe is from a "Serendipity Cooker" I first introduced to W T Grant Stores when I was a buyer back in the early 1970's. The cooker had several components including a paella pan. I first made the paella in 1983 and have revised the original recipe to suit my taste. Chorizo may be added if you desire.

John Webster

True Grits And Shrimp

Serves 4

6 medium thick slices apple wood smoked bacon
4 cups water
1 cup quick grits
2 tablespoons butter
1 teaspoon salt
3/4 cup freshly grated sharp Cheddar cheese
3/4 cup freshly grated Parmesan cheese
Pinch white pepper
Pinch cayenne pepper
Pinch freshly grated nutmeg
2 tablespoons butter
1 1/4 pounds shrimp, peeled and deveined
8 ounces fresh mushrooms, sliced
1 cup chopped green onions
2 1/2 teaspoons minced garlic
4 teaspoons freshly squeezed lemon juice
1/4 cup dry white wine
Hot pepper sauce to taste
1/4 cup chopped fresh parsley
Salt and black pepper

- Cook the bacon in a large skillet until crisp. Drain, crumble and set aside. Pour off all but 1 tablespoon of the drippings and reserve the pan to cook the shrimp.
- Bring water to a boil in a heavy saucepan.
- Add grits, butter and salt and whisk to mix well.
- Lower heat to medium and cook 10 minutes, stirring often.
- Lower heat to maintain the grits at a slow bubble for about 20 minutes more. Stir often to be sure the mixture is NOT LUMPY. The texture should appear creamy, but not dry.
- Stir in Cheddar and Parmesan cheeses, white pepper, cayenne and nutmeg. Keep warm.
- Add butter to the reserved skillet and heat over medium-high.
- Add shrimp, mushrooms, green onions and garlic. Sauté until the shrimp turns pink.
- Add lemon juice, wine, pepper sauce, parsley, salt and pepper to taste and stir to combine.
- Serve grits into individual warm bowls. Lightly stir the shrimp mixture into the grits.
- Sprinkle crumbled bacon over the shrimp and serve immediately.

The secret to good grits is to start off with boiling water and stir until mixed, using the whisk often. I use smooth and creamy Quaker Brand grits. Be sure the grits are stirred evenly over the bottom of the pan. Keeping the heat down after the initial cooking helps prevent lumpy grits.

A nice light salad with fresh strawberries or mandarin oranges goes nicely with this.

Joyce Mason

The anise flavor of Pernod complements the flavors of shrimp very well. Guests love this dish. Serve crusty French bread to dip in the sauce. The basic recipe may be altered to add other seafood or finely diced vegetables. Scallions or onions may be substituted for the shallots or a bit of finely diced cooked smoky bacon or ham might be added. One might add more aromatics such as onions and more cream and Pernod to have more sauce, as in a 'pan stew', or, you could use less cream and Pernod and dice the shrimp to make a spread for topping crisp hot toasts. Create your pleasure!

Barbara Terry

Shrimp with Pernod

Serves 4 for cocktails or 3 as a first course

2-3 large cloves garlic, finely minced
2-3 tablespoons extra virgin olive oil, or unsalted butter
2 teaspoons minced shallots
2 dozen medium shrimp, shelled and deveined
1/4 teaspoon salt
1/8 teaspoon red pepper flakes
2 tablespoons Pernod or other anise flavored liquor
3-4 tablespoons heavy cream
1/4-1/2 cup fresh bread crumbs, optional

- Over low heat warm the garlic in the olive oil for 3-5 minutes. Do not allow the garlic to brown. Cool the garlic in the pan and reserve.
- When ready to serve, warm the garlic and oil over low heat, add the shallots and simmer very gently 2-3 minutes, to release the flavors but do not brown.
- Add the shrimp and cook slowly just until the shrimp are beginning to turn pink.
- Remove the shrimp and set aside, leaving most of the garlic/shallot mixture in the pan.
- Add the salt, red pepper flakes and Pernod and quickly bring to a boil for 30 seconds to 1 minute, releasing the alcohol.
- Add the cream and simmer until the mixture begins to thicken. Taste and add a spoonful of Pernod or a bit more cream to achieve the taste and consistency you prefer.
- Remove pan from the heat. Taste and add more Pernod or cream as desired, boiling briefly to integrate flavors.
- Taste again and adjust salt/pepper as needed.
- Add the shrimp and warm gently in the sauce.
- The dish may be served in a bowl with cocktail picks or the mixture may be placed in small, ovenproof ramekins with the breadcrumbs on top and baked for 5-8 minutes in a 425° F. oven. Alternatively, you might sauté the breadcrumbs in butter or olive oil and sprinkle on the shrimp just before warming in the oven.

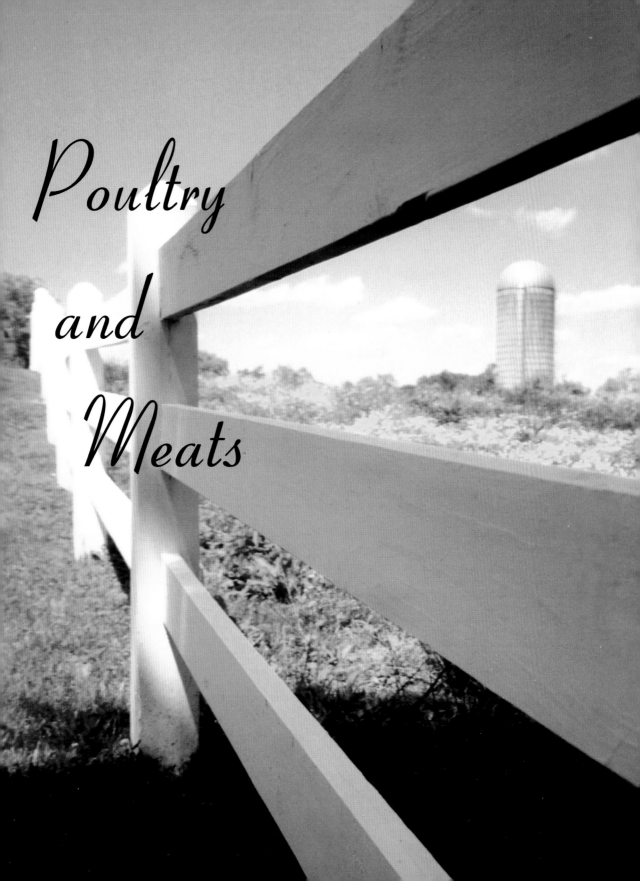

Poultry

and

Meats

Poultry and Meats

Poultry

Chicken Breasts with Grapes and Raisins, 139
Chicken in Orange Cream, 140
Chicken Kabobs for Kids, 137 ♥
Chicken Picata, 131
Chicken Tetrazzini, 133
Chicken with Nuts and Hoisin Sauce, 130 ♥
Coq au Vin, 134
Curried Chicken or Lamb, 152
Easy Couscous with Chicken 138
Grilled Duck Breast with Cherries, 136
North End Hunter's Stew, 130
Rolled Chicken Breasts with Pancetta and Sage, 129
Turkey Thyme Loaf, 135
White Bean Chicken Chili, 132 ♥

Meat

Armenian Eggplant, 164
Baked Mustard Corned Beef, 170
Baton Rouge Sweet'n Sour Pork Loin, 151
Beef Burgundy, 148
Beef Tenderloin with Mushrooms and Sherry, 158
Black Bean Chili with Jalapeño, 155
Bourbon Beef, 140
Chasen's Chili, 156
Conny Tozer's Pork Tenderloin, 167
Curried Lamb or Chicken, 152
Elegant Filet Mignon, 141

Estouffade of Beef with Apricots, Almonds and Raisins, 160
Fennel Scented Rack of Lamb, 159
Flank Steak on Baguettes, 158
Grilled Pork Roast with Port-Cranberry Sauce, 152
Ham Loaf, 161
Herb Stuffed Flank Steak, 145
Lamb Shanks Braised with White Beans, 162
Moussaka, 146
Osso Buco, 150
Pan Fried Pork Chops on Creamy Shrimp Hominy, 168
Party Beef Ragout, 147
Polpette with Marinara Sauce, 144
Pork with Apple Rye Stuffing, 163
Pot Roast Piquant, 170
Ragout Bolognese with Pappardelle, 171
Roast Leg of Lamb with Ginger, 156
Rosemary Lamb Shanks, 154
Sauerbraten Meatloaf with Ginger Sauce, 165
Tuscan Style Pork Loin, 142
Veal Casserole, 166
Veal Scaloppini with Mushrooms and Cheese, 157
Veal Scallops with Tarragon, 153

♥ Heart Healthy

Rolled Chicken Breasts with Pancetta and Sage

Serves 2

1 whole skinless chicken breast
6 1/8-inch thick strips of pancetta, each 2 inches x 1/2 inch,
   divided
6 fresh sage leaves, each torn in half, divided
Freshly ground pepper
Salt, preferably sea salt
2 tablespoons vegetable oil
1 tablespoon butter
1/2 cup white wine

- Preheat oven to 350° F.
- Lightly pound the chicken breast and cut in half.
- Place two strips of pancetta and 4 sage leaf halves on each breast half. Season with salt and pepper. Roll breasts up the long way and close with one or two toothpicks.
- Add vegetable oil and butter to ovenproof sauté pan over medium-high heat.
- After the foam subsides, add the remaining 4 sage leaf halves and the rolled breast halves.
- Brown thoroughly 5-10 minutes, taking care to turn them once or twice and then sprinkle with salt and pepper.
- Add the wine and boil briskly for 20-30 seconds.
- Remove from heat, place the remaining two strips of pancetta on the breasts, cover and place in the oven for about 15 minutes or longer for thicker breasts.
- Remove from the oven, remove breasts to a warm plate and keep warm.
- Return the pan to a surface burner, bring sauce to a boil and reduce the sauce to a thickness that nicely covers each serving.
- Serve on warm plates.

Serve the chicken with polenta to which butter and Parmesan cheese have been added. You might mold the hot polenta in a small glass bowl and invert it onto a serving plate. Topped with butter-browned sage leaves it makes an attractive accompaniment. You can cool the polenta completely, slice in 1/2-inch slices and sauté or grill. This goes well with greens such as rapini or kale braised with olive oil and garlic.

This recipe is easily expanded to four or six servings. Do not ask your pancetta supplier to slice it since it will not slice thinly at room temperature. Buy a large chunk of pancetta and store it in the freezer. Remove for about 10 minutes before slicing. The dimensions of the pieces are not critical.

Francis A. DiGiano

North End Hunter's Stew

Serves 4

8 chicken thighs with bone and skin, rinsed and dried
1/2 cup flour
Salt and pepper
1/4 cup olive oil
1/4 pound pancetta, coarsely chopped
4 cloves garlic, minced
1 large onion, minced, about 1 cup
2 tablespoons dried rosemary, crumble before adding
1 cup dry Marsala wine
1 (24-ounce) can Muir Glen fire-roasted diced tomatoes

- Combine the flour with salt and pepper in a plastic bag. Place the chicken in the bag and shake to coat.
- Sauté the chicken in olive oil in a large Dutch oven or skillet until brown on all sides, about 5-10 minutes. Brown in batches if necessary. Remove the chicken to a plate.
- Wipe excess fat from the pan with a paper towel and add pancetta, garlic, onion, and rosemary. Sauté for about 5 minutes, stirring occasionally.
- Add the wine and boil to reduce for about 5-7 minutes. Add the tomatoes, and salt and pepper to taste. Stir until well blended.
- Return the chicken to the pot and simmer, covered, for one hour.

This recipe comes from a Northern Italian cooking class I took in Boston. Serve over pasta or gnocchi or over garlic bread with a side salad. Rabbit or a whole chicken may be substituted which gives white meat fans a chance. Replace pancetta with Canadian bacon for a lower fat dish. The Muir Glen fire-roasted tomatoes add additional smoky flavor. It is actually better made a day ahead as the flavors meld. The recipe is easily doubled and freezes very well.

Patricia Nenninger

Chicken with Nuts and Hoisin Sauce ♥

Serves 2-4

2 boneless, skinless chicken breast halves in 1-inch cubes
1 teaspoon cornstarch
1 tablespoon dry sherry or sake
2 tablespoons cooking oil
8 ounces mushroom slices
1/2 cup bamboo shoots, drained
6 water chestnuts, drained and sliced
2 tablespoons Hoisin sauce
1/2 cup cashew nuts, unsalted

Continued on next page

Chicken with Nuts and Hoisin Sauce *continued*

- Toss the chicken with the cornstarch. Sprinkle with the sherry and toss again.
- Marinate in the refrigerator 4 or more hours.
- Heat oil in wok, or large skillet, and stir-fry chicken 2-5 minutes.
- Add vegetables and stir-fry 1-3 minutes.
- Add Hoisin Sauce and mix well.
- At the last moment, stir in the cashews.

Serve with rice. Hoisin sauce is now available in most supermarkets in oriental food section. This dish goes well with egg drop soup and spinach salad. A colorful garnish steps up the eye appeal.

Nancy Foster

Chicken Picata

Serves 4

4 chicken breasts halves, boned and skinned
1 large egg
3 tablespoons lemon juice, divided
1/4 cup flour
1/8 teaspoon garlic powder
1/8 teaspoon paprika
1/4 cup butter or olive oil
2 teaspoons chicken bouillon granules dissolved in 1/2 cup boiling water

- Beat the egg with 1 tablespoon of the lemon juice and pour onto a plate.
- Combine flour, garlic powder and paprika on a separate plate.
- Heat the butter or oil in a large skillet over medium-high heat.
- Dip the chicken breast pieces in the egg mixture and then in the flour mixture, shaking off any excess flour.
- Quickly brown the chicken in the hot skillet, about 2 minutes per side.
- Add the bouillon water with the remaining lemon juice to the skillet. Cover and simmer for 20 minutes on very low heat.
- Remove chicken pieces to a warm platter.
- Pour the liquid in the skillet over the chicken and serve on a platter with thin slices of lemon on top of the chicken.
- You may strain the sauce if you like.

This dish is always a winner! It is quick and easy. I serve it with pasta and a marinara sauce or a rice pilaf.

Linda Taft

White Bean Chicken Chili ♥

Serves 6-8

Homemade cornbread is terrific with this soup.

Julie Snyder

For the Beans:
1 pound dried white navy beans
1 sweet red pepper, diced
1 medium Spanish onion, diced
2 tablespoons olive oil
7 cups chicken stock, homemade or canned
2 cloves garlic, diced
1 tablespoon ground cumin
1 tablespoon chili powder
3 plum tomatoes, chopped
1 tablespoon salt, or to taste
Pepper to taste

For the Chicken:
3 whole chicken breasts
2 tablespoons olive oil
1 teaspoon chili powder
1 teaspoon ground cumin
1 tablespoon diced garlic
2 tablespoons chopped fresh cilantro leaves
Salsa and sour cream for topping
Chopped fresh cilantro for garnish

For the beans:
- Soak the beans overnight in water to cover. Drain.
- Over low heat, stir peppers and onions in olive oil for 1 minute.
- Add beans and sauté over medium heat for 5 minutes, stirring.
- Add stock, garlic, cumin, and chili powder.
- Simmer, uncovered until beans are soft, about 1 1/2 hours, adding more broth as necessary.
- Stir in tomatoes about 20 minutes before beans are done.
- Season to taste with salt and pepper.

For the chicken:
- Preheat oven to 350° F.
- Flatten chicken.
- Rub chicken with oil and season with chili powder, cumin, garlic and the 2 tablespoons cilantro.
- Roast in preheated oven about 30 minutes; do not to overcook.
- Cool slightly and slice in thin slices diagonally.
- To serve, place a generous portion of beans in large flat soup bowl. Top with the sliced chicken. Top with salsa and sour cream and garnish with cilantro.

Chicken Tetrazzini

Serves 8

6 tablespoons butter, divided
2 tablespoons flour
1/4 teaspoon paprika
1/2 teaspoon salt
1/4 teaspoon pepper
2 cups chicken broth
1/4 cup sherry
1 cup heavy cream
2 whole chicken breasts, cooked and sliced lengthwise into
  thirds
1/2-3/4 pound thin spaghetti
1/2 pound fresh mushrooms, sliced
1 tablespoon lemon juice
1/3 cup grated Parmesan cheese

- Heat 3 tablespoons butter in skillet.
- Remove from heat and stir in flour, paprika, salt, and pepper.
- Slowly stir in chicken broth and sherry.
- Return to heat and simmer, stirring until thick.
- Add cream, mixing well. Pour over chicken and refrigerate.
- Cook spaghetti 6 minutes in boiling salted water until tender.
- Drain and pour into large baking dish.
- In medium skillet, sauté mushrooms in 3 tablespoons butter until soft.
- Add lemon juice and season to taste with salt and pepper.
- Toss the mushroom mixture with the cooked spaghetti and refrigerate overnight.
- One hour before serving, preheat oven to 400°F.
- Stir sauce and chicken and pour over spaghetti and toss.
- Sprinkle with grated Parmesan cheese and paprika.
- Bake 25 minutes or until hot.

Barbara Hunt

Coq au Vin

Serves 4-6

This is a classic French country dish. Serve with noodles, rice or crusty bread. It is even better if made a few days ahead and kept in the refrigerator with everything in one container. It freezes very well. We usually make at least a double recipe and freeze some.

Eric Goodman

4 ounces salt pork or thick bacon, finely chopped
1 4-pound chicken, cut into 8 pieces
Salt and pepper to taste
1/2 pound mushrooms, sliced
1 cup chopped onions
1/2 cup sliced carrots
1/2 cup pearl onions, canned or fresh. If fresh, drop in boiling water for 1 minute and pinch off skins.
3 tablespoons all purpose flour
3 cups dry red wine
1 cup chicken stock
2 tablespoons tomato paste
2 bay leaves
1/2 teaspoon dried thyme
1/2 teaspoon dried oregano

- In a large, heavy Dutch oven sauté the salt pork or bacon over medium heat until browned. Remove to a plate.
- Season the chicken with salt and pepper and sauté in batches in the Dutch oven until deep golden brown on all sides, about 10-15 minutes. Remove the chicken to a plate.
- When all the chicken is browned, remove it and pour off all but 4 tablespoons of the fat from the pan. You may remove the fat and substitute olive oil if desired.
- Add the mushrooms and cook until they give up their moisture. Add onions, carrots and pearl onions. Cook, stirring occasionally, until the vegetables are tender, about 10 minutes.
- Stir in the flour and reduce the heat to low. Cook, stirring constantly, until the roux begins to turn light brown, about 5 minutes. Add a little oil if necessary.
- Into the roux pour the wine, chicken stock, tomato paste, bay leaves, thyme and oregano and stir to combine. Increase the heat to high and bring the sauce to a boil, stirring constantly.
- Return the chicken, bacon or salt pork and any juices to the pan. Return the sauce to a boil and reduce the heat until the liquid barely simmers. Cover and cook 30-40 minutes until the chicken juices are clear when pricked with a fork.
- Remove everything but the liquid to a plate or bowl. Bring the sauce to a boil over high heat, stirring constantly until it is thick and lightly coats a wooden spoon.
- Serve the chicken on plates or in shallow bowls and cover with sauce.

Turkey Thyme Loaf

Serves 8

1 1/4 pounds ground turkey
1/2 cup plain dried bread crumbs
1/4 cup sliced green onions
1/2 cup chopped celery
1/2 cup peeled and diced Granny Smith apples
1 egg, beaten
1 tablespoon fresh thyme leaves or 3/4 teaspoon dried
2 teaspoons chopped fresh sage or 1/2 teaspoon dried
1 teaspoon salt
1/2 teaspoon pepper
For Serving:
lettuce leaves
fresh thyme leaves and apple slices for garnish
Glaze:
3 tablespoons Dijon mustard
2 tablespoons brown sugar
3 tablespoons lemon juice

This recipe was submitted to the Raleigh News & Observer in 1997, and won a first place for Rosemarie Berger, Jamestown, N.C.

Karen McGrain

- Preheat oven to 350° F.
- Prepare an 8 x 4-inch loaf pan with cooking spray.
- In a large bowl mix together all loaf ingredients except lettuce and garnish.
- Press into the prepared pan.
- Bake in preheated oven for 55 minutes. Drain any accumulated fat and let stand 5 minutes.
- Combine glaze ingredients in a small saucepan, heat until sugar melts and mixture is smooth.
- Slice turkey loaf and arrange on a lettuce-lined serving platter; drizzle with glaze. Garnish as desired with fresh thyme and apple slices.

Grilled Duck Breast with Cherries

Serves 2

1 whole duck
2 tablespoons butter or oil
1 cup roughly chopped onions
1 cup roughly chopped celery
1 cup roughly chopped carrots
1 bay leaf crushed
1 sprig fresh thyme or 1 teaspoon dried
3 whole black peppercorns
5 cups water
1/2 cup dried cherries
1/2 cup freshly squeezed orange juice
1 cup plum wine
1 cup dry red wine
Salt and pepper

Cory Mattson
Executive Chef
Fearrington House
Restaurant

- Preheat oven to 425° F.
- Remove duck breasts with skin from the carcass and refrigerate, tightly covered.
- Roast the remainder of the carcass with legs until very dark brown and overcooked. Remove carcass from pan.
- Allow the carcass to rest until cool enough to handle and shred the leg and thigh meat with a fork and refrigerate, covered.
- Pour fat from roasting pan. Add 1 cup water, bring to a boil and scrape browned bits from the bottom of the pan. Reserve.
- In a large stockpot, melt butter or oil. Add vegetables and herbs and sauté over medium heat until tender.
- Add the carcass, water and reserved pan juices. Bring to a boil. Simmer 4-6 hours. Add more water as necessary.
- Allow the stock to cool, strain and refrigerate overnight.
- Remove fat from the stock.
- In a heavy saucepan bring stock to a boil and reduce the liquid to about one cup. Set aside.
- Soak cherries in orange juice for 30 minutes to 1 hour.
- In a medium saucepan, combine the plum wine and red wine and simmer until reduced to 1/2 cup.
- Combine reduced stock and wine and simmer for 10 minutes.
- Add the cherry-orange juice mixture and simmer until the sauce is slightly thickened and coats a spoon. Set aside.

Continued on next page

Grilled Duck Breast *continued*

- If using a grill, prepare it now.
- Warm the shredded meat in a small saucepan and keep warm.
- Warm the sauce and keep warm.
- Season duck breasts on both sides with salt and pepper.
- Heat a cast iron skillet over high heat until just beginning to smoke. Lower heat to medium and cook duck breasts, skin side down, until skin is very brown and crisp, about 5-8 minutes.
- Finish cooking the breasts on the grill to medium rare, 115° F. internal temperature. Alternatively, the breasts may be finished in the pan if desired.
- To serve, place half the shredded duck meat on a warm serving plate. Season lightly with salt and pepper. Slice the breast meat and spread over the leg meat. Taste the sauce and season to taste. Spoon sauce over the meat.
- The duck may be served atop cooked julienne vegetables or cooked greens such as chard or spinach.

Chicken Kabobs for Kids　♥

Serves 6-7

2 pounds boneless chicken breasts
1/2 cup olive oil
1/4 cup minced fresh basil
3 tablespoons fresh lemon juice
2 teaspoons minced garlic
1 tablespoon soy sauce
1/2 teaspoon grated lemon zest
1 teaspoon salt

- Mix all ingredients except the chicken in a zip lock bag.
- Add chicken, turning to coat. Close bag and refrigerate overnight, turning occasionally.
- Drain and dry the chicken breasts and grill over medium heat, turning at least twice. Be certain the chicken is cooked all the way through.
- Allow chicken to cool enough to handle. Cut into cubes and thread onto wooden skewers with chunks of yellow peppers, fresh pineapple, cherry tomatoes or any other colorful vegetables.
- Serve warm or at room temperature.

Anonymous

Easy Couscous and Chicken

Serves 4-6

Chicken
2 tablespoons butter or margarine
3 pounds boneless, skinless chicken thighs
1/2 teaspoon cumin
1 tablespoon grated fresh ginger or 1 teaspoon, ground
1/2 teaspoon turmeric
1/4 teaspoon saffron, optional
2 teaspoons finely chopped garlic
Salt and pepper to taste
4 cups rich chicken broth
1 leek, halved lengthwise, and cut into one-inch pieces
1 cup drained, canned tomatoes, cut into quarters
1 medium onion, cut into quarters
2 ribs celery, sliced into one-inch lengths
3 small carrots, scraped and sliced into one-inch lengths
1 red or green sweet pepper cut into two inch pieces
2 medium white turnips, peeled and cut into quarters
2 small zucchini cut into one-inch slices
1 (14-ounce) can chickpeas, drained and rinsed
Couscous
3 cups broth from the cooked chicken
1 1/2 cups quick-cooking couscous
Hot Sauce (Optional)
Purchase Harissa or make your own hot sauce by mixing:
2 tablespoons dried hot red-pepper flakes
3 tablespoons water
1 tablespoon olive oil
1/2 teaspoon ground coriander.

This is a modified version of a recipe published by Pierre Franey at least twenty years ago in The New York Times. The chicken can be made through the simmering step and before adding the vegetables, up to a day ahead. Serve with a salad and crusty bread

Anne Bodner

- Heat the butter in a skillet that has a lid and add the chicken, turning it to coat with the butter.
- Sprinkle the chicken with cumin, ginger, turmeric, saffron, garlic, salt and pepper.
- Cook, stirring, until chicken starts to lose its raw color.
- Add the chicken broth, leek, tomatoes and onions. Bring to a boil and simmer, covered, for 20 minutes.
- Add celery, carrots and sweet pepper and cook 5 minutes.
- Add turnips and cook 5 minutes.
- Add the zucchini and chickpeas, salt and pepper to taste and cook 5 minutes, for a total of 35-40 minutes.

Continued on the next page

Easy Couscous and Chicken *continued*

- Drain the chicken mixture; reserve 3 cups of the liquid for preparing the couscous. Return the remaining broth, along with the chicken-vegetable mix to the skillet and set aside.
- Using the three cups of reserved liquid, prepare the couscous as directed on the package.
- To serve, warm the chicken mixture, spoon a generous portion of couscous into shallow soup bowls and serve the chicken and vegetables, along with broth, either on top or along side the couscous. Supply hot sauce to those who want it.

Chicken Breast with Grapes and Raisins

Serves 8

4 whole boneless, skinless chicken breasts, cut into halves
2 teaspoons salt
1 lemon sliced very thin, ends discarded
1/4 cup white wine vinegar
1/2 cup water
1/4 cup raisins
1/4 cup sugar
1 cup white wine
2 tablespoons flour
3 tablespoons butter
1/2 cup white grapes halved lengthwise
Chopped fresh parsley for garnish, optional

Serve with parsley noodles or rice and green peas.

John Karvazy

- Simmer chicken in salted water to cover until just cooked through, about 15 minutes. Remove from heat, cover and let stand 15 minutes. Drain and reserve the broth.
- Place chicken breasts on a platter and keep warm
- Simmer the lemon slices in vinegar and the 1/2 cup water in a separate pan for 30 minutes. Drain and discard the liquid. Place the lemon slices on the chicken breasts.
- Cook the raisins and sugar in the wine until the raisins become plump, about 5 minutes.
- In a separate saucepan blend the flour in the butter over low heat for 2-3 minutes, stirring constantly. Slowly add 1 cup of the reserved broth and stir or whisk the mixture until it is smooth and thickened.
- Add the raisin-wine mixture and the grapes. Mix well.
- Add salt and pepper to taste. Pour the sauce over the chicken.
- Garnish with optional parsley if desired.

Chicken in Orange Cream

Serves 4

1 ounce salted butter
4 skinless, boneless chicken breasts
1 medium onion, chopped
2 tablespoons flour
1/2 pint orange juice
5 ounces sour cream
1 tablespoon orange marmalade, preferably Rough Cut
    Marmalade
1/2 teaspoon dried marjoram
Wedges of orange and fresh parsley to garnish

This recipe comes from the United Kingdom.

Shirley Griffin

- Melt butter in a non-stick skillet and brown chicken on both sides. Remove and place in a casserole dish.
- In the same pan, sauté the onion until soft.
- Stir in flour and cook for 1 minute, stirring constantly. Gradually blend in the orange juice. Bring to a boil and stir until thickened. Stir in all of the remaining ingredients and pour over the chicken.
- Cover and bake at 350° F. for 45 minutes or until chicken is tender.
- Garnish with orange wedges and parsley.

Bourbon Beef

Serves 8-10

1 flank steak, 2 1/2 to 3 pounds
1 cup ketchup
5 tablespoons Worcestershire sauce
6 tablespoons steak sauce
3/4 cup chutney
3/4 cup chili sauce
1/2 teaspoon hot pepper sauce
1/2 cup bourbon

Continued on next page

Bourbon Beef *continued*

- Preheat oven to 350° F.
- Combine ketchup, Worcestershire sauce, steak sauce, chutney, chili sauce, hot pepper sauce and bourbon in a saucepan and heat to a boil.
- Grill the flank steak for 6-8 minutes for medium rare and 2 minutes more for medium.
- Slice the steak thinly and place in an ovenproof dish.
- Pour the sauce over the steak and bake for 30 minutes in the preheated oven.
- You may also simmer the dish on top of the stove.

This is another great recipe from my son in Pennsylvania who has his own diner. The sauce can be made ahead and stored in the refrigerator. This is good for serving a large group.

Robert Holmgren

Elegant Filet Mignon

Serves 2

1 tablespoon butter
2 (6-ounce) filet mignon steaks, each about 1 inch thick
2/3 cup canned beef broth
1/4 cup brandy
2 teaspoons chopped fresh rosemary, or 1/2 teaspoon dried
Blue cheese, crumbled, about 3 ounces

- Melt butter in heavy, medium skillet over medium-high heat.
- Season the steaks with salt and pepper.
- Add the steaks to skillet and sauté until cooked to desired doneness, about 4 minutes per side for medium rare. Transfer steaks to a plate and keep warm.
- Add broth, brandy and rosemary to skillet and boil until sauce is reduced to about 1/3 cup, scraping up browned bits, about 5 minutes.
- Spoon sauce over steaks and top with crumbled blue cheese.

Peg Perlman

Tuscan Style Roast Pork Loin

Serves 6-8

Brining the roast
2 cups kosher salt or 1 cup table salt
2 cups packed dark brown sugar
10 large cloves garlic, peeled and lightly crushed
5 6-inch sprigs fresh rosemary
**1 bone-in, center cut 4 pound pork loin roast with chine
    bone cracked, preferably from the rib end, bones
    removed and reserved   See NOTE below.**
Garlic-Rosemary paste
**8-10 cloves garlic, minced to a paste, about 1 1/2
    tablespoons**
1 1/2 tablespoons finely chopped fresh rosemary leaves
1 teaspoon ground black pepper
1 tablespoon extra virgin olive oil
1/8 teaspoon kosher salt

1 cup dry white wine, for the roast
Sauce
1 teaspoon ground black pepper
1 medium-large shallot, minced, about 3 tablespoons
1 1/2 teaspoons minced fresh rosemary leaves
1 3/4 cups homemade or canned low-sodium chicken broth
2 tablespoons unsalted butter, softened
For brining the Roast:
*   Dissolve the salt and brown sugar in 1 1/2 quarts hot water in
    a large stockpot.
*   Stir in garlic and rosemary sprigs.
*   Add 2 1/2 quarts cold water and submerge the meat and bones.
*   Refrigerate for 3 hours.
*   Rinse meat and ribs under cold water and dry thoroughly.
For the Paste:
*   While the roast brines, mix garlic, rosemary, pepper, olive oil
    and salt in a small bowl to form a paste; set aside.
Roasting the Meat:
*   Preheat oven to 325° F. Adjust oven rack to middle position.
*   Heat a heavy bottomed 12-inch skillet over medium heat.
*   Place the roast, fat side down, in the skillet and brown well,
    about 8 minutes.
*   Transfer roast, brown side up, to a roasting pan and set aside.

*This recipe is
adapted from
ITALIAN
CLASSICS by the
Editors of Cook's
Illustrated
Magazine*

Norma Berry

Continued on next page

Tuscan Style Roast Pork Loin *continued*

- Pour off the fat from the skillet and add the wine. Increase heat to high, bring to a boil and scrape with a wooden spoon to loosen the browned bits. Set aside.
- Make a lengthwise incision in the pork loin to open it up and spread it flat like butterfly wings. Rub 1/3 of the garlic-rosemary paste in an even layer on one side of the cut leaving 1/2 inch bare on each end. Spread the remaining paste mixture evenly along the bones from where the meat was cut, leaving 1/2 inch bare on each end.
- Use about 7 lengths of twine to tie the meat back onto the bones. Sprinkle the browned side of the roast with pepper.
- Pour wine mixture from the skillet into the roasting pan.
- Roast, basting the loin with the pan drippings every 20 minutes, until the center of the loin registers 135° F., about 65 to 80 minutes. Do not overcook. If the wine evaporates, add about 1/2 cup water to roasting pan to prevent scorching.
- Transfer roast to a carving board, Tent loosely with foil. Let stand until center of loin registers 15° F., about 15 minutes.

For the Sauce:

- While the roast rests, spoon off most of the fat from the roasting pan and place the pan over two burners at high heat. Add shallot and 1 1/2 teaspoons rosemary. Using a wooden spoon, scrape up browned bits and boil until liquid in the pan is reduced by half and shallot has softened, about 2 minutes.
- Add chicken stock and cook, stirring occasionally, until reduced by half, about 8 minutes. Add any accumulated juices from the roast and cook one minute longer. Remove from heat and whisk in butter. Strain the jus into a gravy boat.
- Cut twine on roast and remove meat from the bones. Set meat, browned side up, on a board and cut in 1/4 inch slices.
- Serve immediately, passing the jus separately.

NOTE: Preparing a bone-in pork roast

- Ask your butcher to separate the meat from the bones in one piece, retaining the bones.
- If boning the roast yourself, position the loin so the rib bones are perpendicular to the cutting board. Using a sharp knife, start from the far end, working toward you and separate the meat from the rib bones by pressing the knife along the rib bones.
- Use a series of small, easy strokes to cut along the bones, following the rib bones along the curve to the backbone until the meat is free of the bones. You will have a compact eye of the loin, with a small flap attached to the side.

Polpette with Marinara Sauce

Serves 6

Marinara Sauce:
1 cup chopped Vidalia or other sweet onion
2 cloves garlic, minced
3 tablespoons olive oil
2 (#2) cans tomatoes, Cento San Marzano, preferred,
    processed in a blender or food processor
1 (8-ounce) can tomato sauce
1 (6-ounce) can tomato paste
1 cup water
2 tablespoons chopped fresh basil, or 2 teaspoons dried
2 tablespoons minced flat leaf parsley
2 teaspoons salt
1/4 teaspoon freshly ground black pepper
1 teaspoon dried oregano
1 teaspoon fennel seeds, do not use ground fennel
1 teaspoon Worcestershire sauce
4 dashes Tabasco sauce
Sugar as needed

These meatballs can also be served hot, without the sauce, with vegetables and a salad.

Bernice Restivo

- Sauté onion and garlic in olive oil for 2-3 minutes.
- Add all other ingredients and bring to a simmer. Taste and add tiny amounts of sugar if the sauce tastes too acidic. You should never need more than 1 teaspoon at the most!
- Simmer over low heat for at least 1 hour.

Polpette (Meatballs)
5 slices stale, sliced white bread, crusts removed
1/2 pound ground pork
1 pound ground beef
3 eggs, may reduce to 2 if desired, lightly beaten
3 tablespoons Locatelli Peccorino Romano cheese, grated
1 clove garlic, minced
1/2 cup chopped sweet onion
2 tablespoons chopped parsley
Salt and pepper to taste
Flour for dredging
6 tablespoons olive oil or less

Continued on next page

Polpette with Marinara Sauce *continued*

- Soak bread in water 5 minutes; squeeze dry and add to a large bowl with the meat, eggs, cheese, garlic, onion, parsley, salt and pepper. Mix thoroughly. Shape into balls about the size of a small egg.
- Roll in flour and fry in hot olive oil for about 10 minutes or until golden brown.
- Add to the Marinara Sauce above and serve with your favorite pasta.

Herbed Stuffed Flank Steak

Serves 6

1 2-pound flank steak
2 tablespoons butter
1/2 large onion, chopped
1 clove garlic, minced
1/2 cup chopped mushrooms
1/4 cup chopped fresh parsley
1 1/2 cups soft bread cubes
1/2 teaspoon oregano
1/2 teaspoon basil
1/2 teaspoon salt
Freshly ground black pepper to taste
1 egg, slightly beaten
1 tablespoon olive oil
1/2 cup bouillon
1 cup dry white wine.

- Preheat oven to 350° F.
- Score steak lightly on both sides.
- In a skillet, heat the butter. Add the onion and garlic and cook until lightly browned.
- Add mushrooms and cook 3 minutes.
- Remove pan from the heat. Add parsley, bread cubes, herbs, salt, pepper and egg. Mix well.
- Spread the stuffing mixture on the steak. Roll lengthwise, as for a jellyroll, and tie with string at 2-inch intervals.
- In a heavy Dutch oven brown the meat well in the olive oil.
- Add the bouillon and wine, cover and bake for two hours.
- To serve, cut into one-inch slices and serve with pan juices.

The meat can be stuffed early in the day and refrigerated until ready to cook. This is a recipe adapted from the NEW YORK TIMES COOKBOOK.

Ethel D. Cunningham

Moussaka

Serves 10-12

4 medium eggplants
4 tablespoons butter
2 pounds ground beef
3 medium onions, chopped
2 tablespoons tomato paste
1/4 cup chopped parsley
1/2 cup red wine
Salt and pepper
1/2 cup water
Dash of cinnamon
2 large eggs, beaten
1/2 cup sharp cheddar, grated
1/2 cup breadcrumbs
Sauce:
6 tablespoons butter
6 tablespoons flour
3 cups hot milk
Salt & pepper to taste
Dash of nutmeg
4 egg yolks, beaten

Oil for broiling eggplant
Oil and breadcrumbs for preparation of dish

Grated cheddar cheese, enough to sprinkle over entire dish

- Remove 1/2-inch strips of peel lengthwise from eggplants, leaving 1/2-inch peel between strips. Cut into 1/2-inch slices, sprinkle with salt and let stand between two heavy plates.
- Melt the butter and sauté meat and onions until browned.
- Add tomato paste, parsley, wine, salt and pepper to taste, water. Simmer until liquid is absorbed. Cool.
- Stir in cinnamon, eggs, cheese and the breadcrumbs.

Sauce:
- Cook flour in 6 tablespoons butter over medium heat, stirring.
- Slowly add milk, stirring until thick and smooth.
- Add salt, pepper and nutmeg.
- Add half the egg yolk mixture to the hot sauce and stir. Add remaining egg mixture to sauce and cook over low heat for 2 minutes, stirring constantly.

Continued on next page

Guests love this dish. It may seem complicated but if you have all the ingredients ready to use, it flows right along. The meat mixture can be prepared a day in advance and reheated before using.

Jane Gribbin

Moussaka *continued*

- Preheat the broiler.
- Brush eggplant slices with oil and brown under broiler.
- Preheat oven to 350° F.
- Grease an ovenproof casserole and sprinkle with breadcrumbs. Alternate layers of eggplant slices and meat. Continue until all eggplant and meat is used, ending with a layer of eggplant.
- Cover with sauce and sprinkle with cheddar.
- Bake in preheated oven for 1 hour.

Party Beef Ragout

Serves 8-10

3 tablespoons cooking oil
4 tablespoons flour
1 1/4 teaspoons salt
Black pepper
3 1/2 pounds chuck steak, cut into 2-inch cubes
1 (10.5-ounce) can beef bouillon
1/2 cup water
1/2 teaspoon ginger
1/2 teaspoon oregano
2 large onions, about 1/2 pound, cut into eighths
1 (16-ounce) can whole berry cranberry sauce
1/4 cup dry sherry
2 tablespoons brown sugar, packed

- Heat oil in a large Dutch oven.
- Mix flour, salt and pepper together and lightly coat meat with flour mixture.
- Brown the meat well in batches. Remove any excess fat.
- Add the bouillon, water, ginger, oregano and onions. Bring to a boil. Reduce heat, cover and simmer for 1 1/2 hours.
- Combine the cranberry sauce and sherry and heat to boiling. Add brown sugar and boil for 1 minute. Set aside.
- After the meat has simmered until tender, add cranberry sauce mixture and heat together.

The addition of cranberries and brown sugar gives this dish an interesting and delicious flavor. Prepare the ragout the day before serving. The flavor improves with age. Serve with rice or noodles. It freezes well.

Julie Smith

Beef Burgundy

Serves 6

6 ounces salt pork, trimmed of rind, rind reserved, salt
    pork cut into1/4x1/4x1-inch long pieces
10 sprigs parsley, torn into pieces
6 sprigs fresh thyme
2 medium onions, coarsely chopped
2 medium carrots, coarsely chopped
1 head garlic, cloves separated and crushed but unpeeled
2 bay leaves, crumbled
1/2 teaspoon black peppercorns
1/2 ounce dry porcini mushrooms rinsed
4 to 4 1/2 pounds chuck roast, trimmed of fat and silver
    skin, cut into 1 1/2-inch cubes
4 tablespoons unsalted butter
1/3 cup all-purpose flour
1 3/4 cups chicken broth
1 cup water
2 tablespoons tomato paste
1 bottle burgundy or pinot noir, divided
Onion & mushroom garnish
1 bag frozen pearl onions
1 tablespoon unsalted butter
1 tablespoon sugar
1/2 teaspoon salt
1/2 cup water
10 ounces button mushrooms, halved if medium, quartered
    if large
3 tablespoons brandy
Minced parsley for garnish

- Preheat oven to 300° F.
- Bring salt pork, reserved rind and 3 cups water to boil over
  high heat. Boil 2 minutes and drain well and set aside.
- Cut two 22-inch lengths of cheesecloth; lay out criss-cross on
  the counter. Wrap parsley, thyme, onions, carrots, garlic, bay
  leaves, peppercorns, porcini mushrooms and blanched salt
  pork rind in cheesecloth, bundle and tie closed with twine.
  Trim off excess cheesecloth and place the bundle in a Dutch
  oven.
- Cook salt pork in large skillet until brown and crisp; add to the
  Dutch oven. Pour off most fat from the skillet and reserve.

Continued on next page

*To make ahead,
complete through
the oven step and
refrigerate. To
serve, remove fat,
reheat and proceed
with the rest of the
recipe. This dish
requires some
lengthy preparation
but is wonderful to
serve and well
worth the effort. It
is always a hit,
especially on a cold
winter's night with
crispy French
bread.*

Florence Johnson

Beef Burgundy *continued*

- Season beef with salt and pepper. Working in batches, over high heat, brown the meat well, adding reserved fat as needed. Transfer the browned meat to the Dutch oven.
- Return the skillet to high heat and add butter. When foamy, whisk in flour and cook stirring, until the color of peanut butter. Stir in chicken broth and water. Cook, stirring frequently, until thick. Whisk in tomato paste and transfer the mixture to the Dutch oven.
- Add 3 cups wine to the Dutch oven and stir to combine. Bring to a boil and cook, covered, in the preheated oven until meat is tender, about 1 1/2-3 hours.
- Remove the pot from oven. Using tongs, transfer vegetable bundle to a sieve set over the Dutch oven. Press out all juices, then discard bundle.
- With a slotted spoon, remove beef to large bowl. Bring liquid in the Dutch oven to a boil. Simmer briskly, stirring often to reduce liquid to about 3 cups. It should be the consistency of heavy cream.
- While the sauce is reducing, bring pearl onions, butter, sugar, salt and 1/2 cup water to boil in medium skillet over high heat. Cover, reduce heat to medium and simmer, shaking pan occasionally until all liquid is evaporated. Add mushrooms and cook uncovered until vegetables are brown and glazed.
- When liquid in the Dutch oven is reduced, stir in remaining wine and brandy. Season to taste. Stir in meat, mushrooms and onions. Heat through about 5-8 minutes.
- Sprinkle with minced parsley and serve with boiled or mashed potatoes.

Osso Buco

Serves 6

1 (4-ounce) piece of prosciutto
3 medium carrots, peeled
2 medium ribs celery
1 large red onion, peeled
1 clove garlic, peeled
10 sprigs Italian parsley, leaves only
6 veal shanks, 2 inches thick
1/4-1/2 cup olive oil
About 1/2 cup flour
Salt and freshly ground pepper
1 cup dry white wine
1 (14-ounce) can Italian tomatoes, chopped, reserve the
  juice
1 to 2 cups chicken or beef broth
1 pound frozen tiny peas
Gremolata:
15 sprigs Italian parsley, leaves only, finely chopped
1 tablespoon grated lemon peel
1 teaspoon chopped garlic

This is good for a company meal. The flavor is enhanced by making it up to 1 to 2 days in advance and refrigerating until the day of serving. Allow enough time in the oven to reheat meat thoroughly and cook the peas. Remove from refrigerator at least 1 hour in advance of reheating. Serve with polenta or risotto Milanese and a salad.

Judie Burke

- Preheat oven to 350° F.
- Cut prosciutto into very small pieces and set aside.
- Chop together carrots, celery, onion, garlic and parsley leaves in a food processor, or by hand.
- Tie each veal shank with a string to hold it together.
- In large skillet, sauté prosciutto in olive oil for 4 minutes.
- Season the veal shanks with salt and pepper and lightly flour them. Brown on each side in pan with the prosciutto.
- Remove shanks, add chopped vegetables and more olive oil if necessary, and cook 5-8 minutes until soft.
- Add the wine and evaporate for 10 minutes, then add tomatoes and their juice.
- Put veal shanks in a deep baking dish large enough to hold them. Add vegetable mixture and enough broth to cover.
- Cover and cook in preheated oven for 45 minutes to 1 hour.
- Remove the veal shanks to an ovenproof serving dish and put the sauce in a blender or food processor and puree. Be careful to put a towel on the top of the blender to avoid burning yourself. Pour the sauce over the shanks. The dish may be refrigerated or frozen at this point.
- When ready to serve, preheat the oven to 350° F. and bring the veal to room temperature.

Continued on next page

Osso Buco *continued*

- Mix the gremolata ingredients together and set aside.
- Place the dish of shanks in the preheated oven and heat until bubbling.
- Spread the peas over the dish and return to the oven for an additional 10-15 minutes.
- Sprinkle each portion with the gremolata at the time of serving.

Baton Rouge Sweet'n Sour Pork Loin

Serves 8

4 pounds boneless pork loin
1/4 cup chopped fresh rosemary
1 cup dry white wine
Glaze:
1/2 cup honey
1/2 cup ketchup or salsa
1/2 cup soy sauce
3-5 cloves garlic, chopped
Rub:
1 envelope dry onion soup mix
1/2 teaspoon salt
1/2 teaspoon pepper
1/2 teaspoon onion powder
1/4 cup chopped fresh rosemary, divided

- Preheat oven to 250° F. Prepare heavy pan with cooking spray.
- Prepare the glaze by mixing all ingredients together in small container and set aside.
- Rub the dry onion soup mix over the pork roast. Add additional salt and pepper and onion powder as desired. Sprinkle with 1/2 the fresh rosemary.
- Place the pork loin in the prepared roasting pan. Pour wine over the roast, cover and bake for 30 minutes per pound.
- Pour glaze over the roast and baste thoroughly. Raise the oven temperature to 300° F. and bake, covered, for 1 more hour.
- Reduce oven temperature to 250° F., baste with glaze, and sprinkle remaining rosemary over roast. Bake, covered, for 1 more hour for a total of 4 hours cooking time.
- Remove the roast from the oven and allow it to rest for 15 or 20 minutes before slicing.
- Pour pan gravy into a dish and serve with the roast.

The Cajuns love this dish. Enjoy!

Beverly Long

Curried Lamb or Chicken

Serve 4

1 tablespoon butter or oil
1 large Granny Smith apple, pared, cored and sliced
1 large onion, sliced
1 tablespoon good curry powder, or to taste
1 tablespoon flour
2 cups chicken stock
Salt to taste
2 tomatoes seeded, cut in wedges
2 tablespoons chutney
1 tablespoon golden raisins, optional
8-10 slices cooked lamb or chicken
Condiments of choice

This is a tasty way to use leftover lamb or chicken. Guests love it.

Consi Scott

- Preheat oven to 325° F.
- Sauté apple and onion in butter or oil until golden.
- Add curry, stir and simmer 3-4 minutes. Remove from heat, stir in flour and cook 2 minutes. Add stock, bring to a boil, stirring, add salt and simmer 10 minutes.
- Add tomatoes, chutney and raisins, and simmer 10 minutes or longer until sauce is fairly thick.
- Put meat in a baking dish, pour sauce over meat, shake to mix.
- Bake in preheated oven until hot, about 20-25 minutes.
- Serve with rice and bowls of chutney, golden raisins, unsalted peanuts, candied ginger, pickled pineapple, minced green onions or other condiments of your choice.

Grilled Pork Roast with Port-Cranberry Sauce

Serves 6

1 cup olive oil
1/4 cup white wine
1 teaspoon salt
2 teaspoons black pepper
1 tablespoon minced garlic
2 teaspoons dried thyme
1 (750 ml) bottle tawny port
1 tablespoon minced onion
2 cups heavy cream
1/2 cup dried cranberries
3 1/2 pounds pork tenderloin or 1 rolled loin roast

If using tenderloins, prepare sauce in advance as they cook a relatively short time. If using a rolled roast you can prepare the sauce while the meat is grilling. The meat can also be grilled or roasted on a spit.

Michael Cotter

Continued on next page

Grilled Pork Roast with Port-Cranberry Sauce *continued*

- Whisk together oil, white wine, salt, pepper, garlic and thyme. Pour marinade over pork and refrigerate, covered, overnight.
- On the day of serving, boil port until it is reduced to 1 cup. Add onions and cream and boil until the mixture is reduced by half. Add the cranberries and simmer 3-5 minutes until softened. Season with salt and pepper and keep warm, covered.
- Drain pork, discarding the marinade. Dry the meat thoroughly and grill until the internal temperature is 155-160° F. Serve the pork with the sauce.

Veal Scallops with Tarragon

Serves 4

4 veal scallops, about 4-5 ounces each
Salt and freshly ground pepper
1 tablespoon butter or margarine
2 tablespoons brandy
1 cup chicken or beef broth
1 tablespoon fresh tarragon, chopped
Fresh tarragon sprigs to garnish

- Place veal scallops between two sheets of waxed paper. Pound with the flat side of a meat mallet or roll with a rolling pin to flatten to about 1/4 inch thick. Season with salt and pepper.
- Melt butter in a large frying pan over medium-high heat until sizzling but not brown.
- Cook the scallops for 1 1/2-2 minutes, turning once. Transfer to a serving platter and cover loosely to keep warm.
- Add brandy to the pan. Pour in the broth and bring to a boil. Add the tarragon and continue boiling until the liquid is reduced by half.
- Return veal to the pan with any accumulated juices and heat through. Serve immediately, garnished with tarragon sprigs.

This is a delicious recipe for veal. Serve it with broccolini and au gratin potatoes. The veal is also good for two people with leftovers for lunch. It is very tasty and heart-healthy. It makes great sandwiches the next day. These thin slices of veal need little cooking and the sauce is made very quickly as well. Great for couples cooking.

Janet Daly

Rosemary Lamb Shanks

Serves 6

2 tablespoons olive oil
Salt and pepper
6 (12-14 ounce) lamb shanks, trimmed
2 carrots, 1/4-inch diagonal slices
2 celery stalks, 1/4-inch diagonal slices
1 large onion, thinly sliced
2 garlic cloves, chopped
2 cups dry red wine
1 cup canned beef broth
1 cup canned low salt chicken broth
2 tablespoons chopped fresh rosemary or 2 teaspoons dried
2 bay leaves
2 teaspoons cornstarch
Rosemary sprigs for garnish

The recipe can be made with three shanks, keeping all other ingredients the same. Made with eight shanks, use 1 1/2 times the rest of the recipe.

Amelia Carew

- Preheat oven to 375° F.
- Heat oil in a large, heavy Dutch oven over medium-high heat.
- Season the lamb shanks with salt and pepper. Working in batches, add the lamb to the Dutch oven and brown on all sides, about 8 minutes per batch. Transfer the lamb to a plate.
- Add the carrots, celery, onion and garlic to the pan. Sauté until light brown, about 4 minutes. Add 1 3/4 cups of the wine and bring to a boil, scraping up any brown bits, about 2 minutes. Add beef and chicken broth, rosemary and bay leaves. Return the lamb to the Dutch oven and bring the mixture to a simmer.
- Cover and cook in the preheated oven until lamb is very tender, about 1 1/2 hours.
- Transfer the lamb shanks to a platter and tent with foil. Strain the cooking liquid, reserving the vegetables. Discard the bay leaves.
- The lamb and sauce can be refrigerated at this point so that the fat can be removed easily.
- Return the liquid to the Dutch oven. Boil until reduced to 1 1/2 cups. Mix the remaining 1/4 cup of wine with the cornstarch and add it to the cooking liquid. Simmer until thickened, stirring frequently, about 5 minutes.
- Return the lamb and vegetables to the pan. Simmer until heated through. Season to taste with salt and pepper.
- Arrange the lamb and vegetables on a platter, spoon the sauce over and garnish with fresh rosemary sprigs.

Black Bean Chili with Jalapeño

Serves 6

2 tablespoons olive oil
1 1/4 pounds boneless beef chuck, trimmed, cut into
  3/4-inch cubes
Salt and pepper
1 large onion
8 large garlic cloves, coarsely chopped
1 1/2 pounds ground beef
1/4 cup chili powder
2 tablespoons paprika
1 tablespoon jalapeño chile, seeded and chopped
1 1/2 teaspoons ground cumin
3/4 teaspoon ground coriander
1 cup dry red wine
2 (14-ounce) cans low-salt chicken broth
1/2 cup tomato sauce
3 tablespoons hot chili sauce
2 tablespoons tomato paste
2 (15-ounce) cans black beans, drained

The chili can be made one day ahead. Cool, cover and refrigerate.

Barbara Snotherly

- Heat the oil in a large, heavy pot over medium-high heat.
- Sprinkle the beef cubes with salt and pepper. Sauté in the oil until browned on all sides, about 8 minutes. You may need to brown the meat in batches. Using a slotted spoon, transfer the meat to a medium bowl.
- Add onion and garlic to the same pot. Reduce the heat to medium and sauté until tender, about 5 minutes.
- Add the ground beef and sauté until cooked through and almost all of the liquid has evaporated, about 15 minutes.
- Stir in the chili powder, paprika, jalapeno, cumin and coriander.
- Add the wine and simmer until almost all the liquid evaporates, stirring occasionally, 3-5 minutes.
- Add the chicken broth, tomato sauce, chili sauce, and tomato paste. Bring to a boil.
- Return the beef cubes to the pot. Over medium-low heat simmer the chili, uncovered, until beef cubes are tender and liquid thickens, about 45 minutes.
- Stir in black beans and cook until heated through, about 15 minutes. Season to taste with salt and pepper.

Chasen's Chili

Serves 8-10

1/2 pound pinto beans
5 cups canned tomatoes, chopped, including juice
1 1/2 tablespoons olive oil
1 pound green bell peppers, seeded and chopped
1 1/2 pounds onions, coarsely chopped
2 garlic cloves, crushed, about 1 1/2 teaspoons
1/2 cup chopped fresh parsley
2 1/2 pounds beef chuck, coarsely ground
1 pound pork, coarsely ground
1/3 cup chili powder, yes, 1/3 cup
1 tablespoon salt
1 1/2 teaspoons pepper
1 1/2 teaspoons ground cumin

- Soak the beans overnight in water to cover. Drain and cover with fresh water. Simmer until tender but not mushy. Drain, return to the pot, add tomatoes and simmer 5 minutes.
- In a large skillet sauté the peppers, onion, garlic, and parsley in the oil until tender.
- In a separate skillet, sauté ground meats until cooked through.
- Combine the meats with the onion-pepper mixture and add the chili powder, stirring well. Cook 10 minutes.
- Combine the meat-vegetable mixture with the bean-tomato mixture and add the salt, pepper and cumin.
- Cover and simmer 1 hour. Uncover, simmer 30 minutes more.

This chili is from the now closed Chasen's Restaurant in Los Angeles, where they charged $25 a bowl in 1985. Liz Taylor and Richard Burton had it flown to them all over the world! The preparation of this dish must be done in the sequence listed. I tried streamlining the process and the chili powder was overwhelming – I don't know why. It is not especially hot if you follow the procedure.
Serve with beer or wine, crusty bread and some "yummers"

Nancy Foster

Roast Leg of Lamb with Ginger

Serves 6

1 leg of lamb, oven ready
2 cloves garlic
Ground ginger
Flour
Salt and pepper to taste
1 lemon, thinly sliced

- Preheat oven to 450° F.
- Make 4 incisions in "X" shape, one in each corner of lamb.

Continued on the next page

Roast Leg of Lamb with Ginger *continued*

- Halve the cloves of garlic and insert 1/2 in each incision.
- Spread ground ginger on entire surface of lamb with fingers.
- Salt and pepper the lamb and dust lightly with flour.
- Place lemon slices in a pattern on the surface of the lamb.
- Reduce oven temperature to 350° F. and roast lamb for 20-25 minutes per pound for medium to rare, 155-165°; 30 minutes per pound for well done, 170-180°.
- Remove lamb from the oven and allow to rest 15 minutes.
- Skim some of the fat from the pan and add flour, stirring and cook for 2 minutes. Slowly add sufficient water to achieve the desired gravy consistency, stirring constantly. Season with salt and pepper to taste.

The pan drippings make the MOST delicious gravy. Be sure to make enough gravy to add to left over ground lamb in a Shepherd's Pie. To use this recipe on a boned leg of lamb, cooking times would have to be adjusted.

Jane Gribbin

Veal Scaloppini with Mushrooms and Cheese

Serves 4

1 pound mushrooms, cleaned and sliced
5 tablespoons butter, separated
1/2 cup flour
Freshly ground black pepper
1 3/4 pounds veal scaloppini, pounded
2 3/4 tablespoons olive oil, separated
2 tablespoons chopped fresh rosemary
1/3 pound Jarlsberg or Leerdammer cheese, sliced

- Preheat oven to 250° F.
- Line cookie sheet with oiled aluminum foil.
- Sauté mushrooms in 1 tablespoon butter. Set aside.
- Place flour on a plate, add pepper generously and mix.
- Dredge the veal in the flour mixture.
- In large skillet, heat 2 tablespoons each, butter and oil to bubbling. Sauté the veal briefly in batches, turning once. Veal should be golden along edges. Do not crowd the veal.
- Reheat mushrooms.
- Place veal on prepared cookie sheet and keep warm in preheated oven. Sauté remaining veal.
- Remove veal from oven and set the oven to low broil.
- Spread mushrooms over veal and sprinkle with rosemary.
- Cover with cheese. Broil until cheese begins to color.
- Serve immediately.

This is delicious with a green salad and crusty French or Italian bread slices dressed with olive oil.

Whitney Irwin

Flank Steak on Baguettes

Teenagers love this. Serve with Cole Slaw.

Anne Bodner

Serves 6-8

1 2-3 pound flank steak, at least 3/4 inch thick, trimmed
1/3 cup dry sherry or wine
1/3 cup soy sauce
3 tablespoons sesame or vegetable oil
2 cloves garlic, minced
1 teaspoon wine vinegar
2 teaspoons brown sugar
1 teaspoon grated fresh ginger or 1/2 teaspoon ground
3 large loaves French bread or 6-8 small baguettes
Dijon-style mustard and softened butter, for serving

- Combine all ingredients except bread, mustard and butter in a plastic bag, closing it securely to prevent leaking.
- Refrigerate several hours or overnight, turning the bag several times to redistribute the marinade.
- Allow the steak and marinade to come to room temperature.
- Prepare the grill or broiler.
- Remove meat from marinade. Reserve liquid. Place meat on a hot grill or under a preheated broiler. Cook eight minutes per side, basting occasionally with the marinade.
- Allow meat to cool 10-15 minutes. Slice thinly across the grain.
- Serve at room temperature or cold on sliced French bread, spread with the mustard and/or butter.

Beef Tenderloin with Mushrooms and Sherry

This is a family recipe. Pork tenderloin may be substituted. To prevent pork from drying out, brown first to seal in juices.

Carole O'Loughlin

Serves 8

5 pound beef tenderloin
5 tablespoons butter
1 pound mushrooms, sliced
1 cup sherry
Salt and pepper to taste

- Preheat oven to 400° F.
- Place meat in shallow baking pan. Roast for 30 minutes.
- Heat butter in skillet over moderately low heat.
- Add mushrooms and sauté until tender. Spoon mushrooms around meat; pour sherry over all and season generously with salt and pepper.
- Reduce oven temperature to 375° F. Roast 20 minutes more to 140° for rare or 160° for medium rare. Baste frequently.

Fennel Scented Rack of Lamb

Serves 4

1 8-rib rack of lamb, oven ready
Salt and pepper
Fennel Butter
6 tablespoons butter, room temperature
3 tablespoons fennel seeds, crushed in a mortar, spice-
    grinder or food processor
3 garlic cloves, minced
2 tablespoons Dijon mustard
1 1/2 tablespoons soy sauce
1 tablespoon coarsely ground black pepper
1 1/2 teaspoons dried rosemary, crushed
Fresh Thyme Oil
2 tablespoons finely chopped fresh thyme
1 1/2 tablespoons garlic, minced
1/2 cup extra virgin olive oil

1 cup fresh breadcrumbs

- Mix fennel butter ingredients in a medium bowl. Cover and refrigerate overnight. Bring to room temperature before using.
- Combine thyme oil ingredients, stir and refrigerate overnight.
- Trim most of the fat off the rack of lamb and French the bones for at least 1 1/2 inches.
- Spread 2-3 tablespoons thyme oil over all surfaces of the lamb and season generously with salt and pepper.
- Set the lamb, meat side up, in an oiled roasting pan. Allow to marinate for 1 hour.
- Preheat oven to 500° F.
- Roast the lamb for 10 minutes.
- Remove from the oven and coat generously with fennel butter.
- Reduce oven temperature to 400° F. and roast for 10 minutes.
- Remove lamb from the oven and spread with a small amount of fennel butter. Sprinkle breadcrumbs over all and drizzle with a tablespoon of thyme oil.
- Roast for 7 minutes more.
- Remove lamb from the oven and begin testing for doneness. It will be done to a rosy rare at 125° F. on an instant read thermometer. Roast longer to desired doneness
- Allow the rack to rest at room temperature for 15 minutes before carving.

The fennel butter provides unique flavors especially suited for lamb. The chops may be served hot or at room temperature. A sauce might be made with red wine, broth and some of the fennel butter.
The recipe is a variation of one in Bon Appetit.

Barbara Terry

Estouffade of Beef with Apricots, Almonds and Raisins

Serves 8

1/2 pound dried apricots
1 1/2 cups boiling water
4 1/2 pounds boneless beef shanks OR 3 pounds sirloin tip
  roast, cut into 1 1/2-inch cubes
Salt and freshly ground pepper
1/2 teaspoon cinnamon
1/2 cup olive oil, divided
2 large onions, finely chopped
3 cloves garlic, finely minced
2 teaspoons ground cumin
1 teaspoon ground coriander
1/4 teaspoon ground cloves
1/2 cup dry white wine
2 cups canned, crushed tomatoes with liquid
2 1/2 cups beef stock or canned broth
2 bay leaves
1 cup golden raisins
Garnish:
1 cup slivered, blanched almonds
2 tablespoons finely chopped flat leaf parsley

- In a medium bowl, soak the dried apricots in the boiling water until plumped, about 30 minutes. Drain and reserve.
- In a large bowl, toss the beef cubes with 1 teaspoon of salt, 1 teaspoon pepper and the cinnamon.
- In a large, heavy skillet, heat 4 tablespoons olive oil until almost smoking. Add half the beef cubes and cook over high heat, turning, until well browned on all sides, 8 to 10 minutes.
- Transfer the beef to a large plate.
- Add 1 more tablespoon of the oil and brown the remaining beef. Remove the browned beef to the plate.
- Add the remaining 3 tablespoons oil to the pan.
- Add onions and cook 10 minutes over medium heat until softened, scraping up any browned bits from the pan.
- Add the garlic, cumin, coriander and cloves and cook, stirring, until the spices are aromatic, about 3 minutes.
- Add the white wine and cook until almost all the liquid is evaporated, about 2 minutes.
- Stir in crushed tomatoes with their liquid and the beef stock.
- Add the apricots to the pan, reserving 8 for garnish. Simmer the sauce for 2 minutes

Continued on next page

This is a good dish to freeze or to have for a large group. It is very good served over Mrs. Weiss' Kluski noodles. To freeze the estouffade, let cool completely and refrigerate until cold. Transfer to plastic containers, covering the beef cubes with sauce. Press plastic wrap against the surface of the sauce, seal the containers and freeze for up to one month. To reheat, allow to thaw in the refrigerator for 24 hours. Remove the plastic wrap, transfer to an enameled cast-iron casserole and warm over low heat, stirring occasionally.

Jewel Hoogstoel

Estouffade of Beef with Apricots, Almonds and Raisins

continued

- Working in batches, puree the sauce in a food processor until smooth, about 20 seconds.
- Transfer the puree to an enameled cast-iron casserole.
- Add the beef and bay leaves and bring to a simmer over moderate heat. Cover and cook over low heat, stirring occasionally, for 1 3/4 hours.
- Uncover and simmer for 15 minutes.
- Add the raisins and simmer until the meat is very tender and the sauce is thick, about 15 minutes longer.
- Discard the bay leaves and season with salt and pepper.

Garnish:
- Preheat oven to 350° F.
- Toast almonds on baking sheet a few minutes until browned lightly.
- Slice reserved apricots.
- Garnish estouffade with apricots, almonds and parsley.

Ham Loaf

Sauce:
1 can tomato soup
1 teaspoon dry mustard
1 cup brown sugar
1/2 cup water
1/2 cup vinegar
Loaf:
2 pounds lean, cured ham
2 pounds lean, fresh pork
2 cups graham cracker crumbs
3 eggs, beaten
3/4 cup evaporated milk

- Combine all sauce ingredients and mix well.
- Preheat oven to 325° F.
- Grind the two meats together twice or have your butcher do this.
- Mix together graham cracker crumbs, beaten eggs and milk.
- Add meat and mix thoroughly.
- Shape into one large or two smaller loaves.
- Pour the sauce over the loaf and bake in preheated oven for two hours, basting with the sauce occasionally.

I received this recipe from my sister-in-law. It was an old family recipe from several generations back. It is a great favorite of my grandson, Brooks. Good hot or cold.

Dortha Hall

Lamb Shanks Braised with White Beans

Serves 4

1 cup dried navy or great northern beans
1 1/2 tablespoons extra virgin olive oil
4 lamb shanks, about 1/2-3/4 pounds each
1 medium onion, diced
2 medium carrots, diced
1 stalk celery, diced
4 garlic cloves, minced
1 cup dry red wine
1 cup chicken broth
1 cup tomatoes, peeled, seeded and chopped
2 tablespoons tomato paste
1/2 teaspoon dried thyme
1/2 bay leaf
Salt and pepper
1 1/2 tablespoons lemon zest
1 1/2 tablespoons chopped fresh parsley

We have served this dish to several excellent cooks who gave rave notices. Enjoy.

Michael Cotter

- Sort the beans, discarding stones or broken beans. Rinse the beans, drain and soak overnight covered with water by 3 inches. If you are in a hurry, you may place the beans in a pot with water to cover. Bring to a boil and cook 1 minute. Remove from heat and cover. Let stand 1 hour and proceed with the recipe.
- Heat olive oil in a Dutch oven over medium heat. Add the shanks in batches so they do not touch, and brown on all sides, 10-12 minutes. Transfer to a plate.
- In the Dutch oven, sauté onion, carrot, celery, stirring occasionally, until tender, 6-8 minutes. Add the garlic and cook, stirring, 1-2 minutes.
- Drain and rinse the beans and add to the pot along with the wine, broth, tomatoes, tomato paste, thyme and bay leaf. Stir to mix.
- Add the lamb shanks, bring to a simmer, and reduce heat to low. Cover and simmer until beans are tender and meat is nearly falling off the bone, 3-4 hours. Season with salt and pepper to taste and discard the bay leaf.
- Transfer lamb shanks and beans to individual bowls or plates and garnish with lemon zest and parsley.

Pork with Apple-Rye Stuffing

Serves 4

2 1/2 tablespoons butter, divided
1 1/2 cups diced red onion
1/2 cup dried cranberries
2 Granny Smith apples, peeled and cut into 1/4-inch dice
2 Granny Smith apples, peeled and sliced 1/4-inch thick
3 tablespoons chopped fresh sage, divided
1 1/2 teaspoons salt, divided
1 teaspoon pepper, divided
1/2 cup apple brandy or cider, divided
6 slices toasted seeded rye bread, diced
1 1/2 teaspoons canola oil
4 boneless center cut pork loin chops, 3/4-inch thick or
   10-12 slices of pork tenderloin, 3/4-inch thick
1/2 cup heavy cream
1 tablespoon grainy mustard

- Preheat oven to 350° F.
- Butter a 1 1/2-quart baking dish.
- In a non-stick skillet melt 2 tablespoons of the butter and add onion and cranberries. Sauté 4 minutes.
- Add diced apple, 2 tablespoons of the sage, 1 teaspoon of the salt, and 1/2 teaspoon of the pepper. Sauté 2 minutes.
- Add 1/4 cup of the brandy or cider and cook 30 seconds.
- Add bread, stir 30 seconds or until all bread is moist. Spoon the mixture into the baking dish, cover and put in the oven to warm thoroughly while preparing the pork.
- Wipe the skillet with a paper towel. Heat oil and remaining 1/2 tablespoon of the butter in the skillet over high heat.
- Add the pork and brown 1 minute per side. Reduce heat to medium, cover and cook 4 minutes. Turn the pork, cover and cook 4 more minutes, 3 minutes if using tenderloins. Remove the pork and keep warm.
- To the drippings in the skillet add the sliced apples and raise the heat to high. Sauté 2 minutes until crisp-tender. Add remaining 1/4 cup brandy or cider and boil 30 seconds.
- Add the cream, mustard and remaining tablespoon of the sage. Boil 2 minutes until thickened. Add remaining 1/2 teaspoon each of salt and pepper.
- Transfer the pork to serving plates, top with the apple slices and sauce. Serve with the stuffing.

Joan Angevine

Armenian Eggplant

Serves 6

1 large or 2 small eggplants, unpeeled, ends trimmed and
  sliced 1/4 inch thick or less
2 tablespoons cooking oil
1 small green pepper, finely chopped
2 onions, finely chopped
1 or 2 cloves garlic, minced, optional
2 pounds ground round beef or lean lamb
1/2 cup chopped parsley
Salt and pepper to taste
1/2 teaspoon allspice
1 cup canned tomato sauce
1 large tomato, cored and cut into thin slices
2 tablespoons butter or margarine

*This is adapted
from a Pierre
Franey recipe
published in The
New York Times
about 30 years ago.
It has been a
favorite with my
family and guests
ever since. Serve
with a salad and
crusty bread to sop
up the juices.*

Anne Bodner

- Preheat oven to 400° F.
- Heat oil in heavy skillet and cook green pepper and onion at
  moderate heat until wilted.
- Add garlic if using and sauté briefly.
- Add meat, breaking up lumps with a spoon. Cook until the
  meat loses its color.
- Add parsley, salt and pepper, and allspice. Add the tomato
  sauce, mix, and then pour the mixture into a colander placed
  on a mixing bowl and allow to drain. Reserve the liquid.
- Arrange the eggplant slices, overlapping, in the bottom of a
  rectangular baking dish, about 9x13 inches.
- Pour in the reserved liquid from the drained meat mixture and
  place the dish in the oven for ten minutes.
- Remove the dish and reduce the oven to 375° F.
- Spoon the meat mixture over the eggplant. Arrange the
  tomato slices on top. Dot the butter over the top.
- Bake for 30 minutes.

Sauerbraten Meat Loaf with Ginger Sauce

Serves 6

Meat Loaf:
1 pound ground chuck
3/4 cup soft breadcrumbs
1 egg, beaten
1/2 cup finely chopped carrot
1/2 cup finely chopped onion
1/4 cup water
3 tablespoons gingersnap crumbs
1 tablespoon lemon juice
1/4 teaspoon salt
1/4 teaspoon pepper
Sauce:
1 cup water
2 tablespoons lemon juice
1/4 cup gingersnap crumbs
2 tablespoons brown sugar
2 tablespoons raisins
1 teaspoon beef-flavored bouillon granules

This recipe is a variation on one from an old COOKING LIGHT annual book.

Betty Lu Long

- Preheat oven to 350° F.
Meatloaf:
- Combine meat loaf ingredients and stir well to combine. Shape into 8 x 4-inch loaf.
- Place on a rack in a pan coated with cooking spray.
- Bake in preheated oven for one hour.
Sauce:
- Combine sauce ingredients and cook over medium heat for 10 minutes or until thickened, stirring occasionally.
- Place meat loaf on serving platter. Spoon sauce evenly over the meat loaf. Serve warm.

Veal Casserole

Serves 6

2 1/2 -3 pounds veal cutlet cut into cubes
3 tablespoons butter
1 tablespoon olive oil
2 tablespoons chopped onion
1 clove garlic, chopped
2 tablespoons flour
1 cup chicken broth
1 cup dry white wine, more if necessary
4 large tomatoes, peeled or 1 (16-ounce) can tomatoes,
**   drained**
Juice of 1 lemon
Salt and pepper to taste

1 pound mushrooms, sliced
2 tablespoons butter

- Preheat oven to 350° F.
- In a large, heavy skillet over medium-high heat, brown veal cubes in batches in 3 tablespoons butter and the olive oil. Avoid crowding meat in the pan. When browned, place veal in a baking dish.
- Reduce heat to medium-low and sauté onion and garlic in the same skillet, adding more oil if necessary.
- Add flour and cook for 2 minutes, stirring. Add the chicken broth, 1/4 cup of the wine, tomatoes, lemon juice, and salt and pepper to taste.
- Pour mixture over veal and simmer, covered, for 1 1/2 hours. Add remaining wine as necessary.
- Sauté the mushrooms in two tablespoons butter and spread over the meat. Cook an additional 30 minutes.

This dish is best if made a day ahead and refrigerated overnight so that the flavors have a chance to blend and "marry." If you intend to make it ahead, bring to room temperature and add the sautéed mushrooms just before reheating. It can be frozen successfully without the mushrooms. It is always well received. Serve with buttered noodles and a tossed salad.

Rosemary Giess

Conny Tozer's Pork Tenderloin

2 or 3 pork tenderloins

Marinade:
1/2 cup soy sauce
1/4 cup chopped green onions
2 cloves garlic, minced
1/2 teaspoon pepper
1/4 cup sesame seeds
1 teaspoon ginger
Sauce:
1/2 cup sour cream
1/3 cup mayonnaise
1 teaspoon chopped green onion
1 1/2 teaspoons vinegar
Dash of salt
1/2-1 teaspoon horseradish sauce, to taste

Pork:
- Mix all marinade ingredients and pour over the meat. Cover and marinate all day in the refrigerator, turning once in a while.
- Preheat oven to 325° F.
- Drain and dry the tenderloins, discarding the marinade.
- Roast tenderloins in preheated oven for about 45 minutes or an internal temperature of 160°F. Check often so as not to overcook.
- As an alternative, cook them for 20 to 30 minutes on an outside grill.

Sauce:
- Combine sauce ingredients and stir well. Refrigerate for several hours before serving to heighten flavors.
- Serve the sauce in a sauceboat.

This recipe comes from Connie Tozer, a former resident of Fearrington. My family and friends love it. It is the most used recipe in the box!

Jane Palkoski

Pan-Fried Pork Chops
on Creamy Shrimp Hominy

Serves 4

For Shrimp Stock:
Shrimp shells from 8 ounces fresh shrimp
10 ounces bottled clam juice
8 ounces homemade chicken stock or water

- In a 1-quart saucepan, combine the shrimp shells, clam juice and stock or water. Bring to a boil, reduce the heat to low and simmer 25 to 30 minutes.
- Strain, pressing on the shells. Cool and reserve the liquid, discarding the shells.

For the Creamy Shrimp Hominy:
1 (15-ounce) can white hominy, drained, rinsed in cold water, drained and reserved
1 cup heavy cream
3 tablespoons peanut oil
1 medium onion, cut into fine dice
4 ounces green bell pepper, seeded and cut into fine dice
2 ribs celery, cut into fine dice
1 jalapeño, seeded and minced fine or 1 teaspoon crushed red pepper flakes
2 tablespoons minced garlic
2 tablespoons fresh oregano, chopped
1 tablespoon fresh thyme leaves
1 cup canned tomatoes, seeded and chopped
1/4 cup cider vinegar
2 cups shrimp stock
8 ounces shrimp, peeled, split lengthwise, and deveined, with shells reserved for stock
Salt, black pepper and Tabasco to taste
1 bunch scallions, green tops only, sliced crosswise into rings for garnish

- In a 1-quart saucepan, combine the rinsed hominy and cream; bring to a simmer over medium heat and cook until lightly thickened, about 5 minutes. Reserve.
- In a heavy-bottomed 3-quart saucepan, heat the peanut oil over medium heat. Add the onion, green pepper and celery; cook until softened but not browned.

My mother used to prepare "smothered" pork chops and serve them with buttered hominy on the side for family suppers. This recipe was created for a Food and Wine article on comfort food; it certainly fulfills that qualification. Serve with string beans sautéed with bacon.

Ben Barker
Chef Owner
Magnolia Grill
Durham, NC

Former Chef
Fearrington House

Continued on the next page

**Pan-Fried Pork Chops
on Creamy Shrimp Hominy** *continued*

- Add the bay leaf, jalapeño, garlic, herbs and tomatoes and cook 2 minutes, stirring. Add the vinegar and shrimp stock, bring to a boil, reduce the heat and simmer gently for 15 minutes.
- Stir in the hominy cream and return to a simmer.
- Stir in the shrimp and cook 1-2 minutes, until just opaque. Season with salt, black pepper and Tabasco if desired. Keep warm.

For the pork chops
4 pork T-bone chops, 8 ounces each
1/2 cup flour
1 teaspoon salt
1 tablespoon freshly ground black pepper
1 teaspoon paprika
1/2 teaspoon cayenne pepper
1 teaspoon dried oregano
Peanut oil
1/4 cup bourbon
1/4 cup cider vinegar
1 cup white wine
Salt and pepper to taste

- Heat a heavy sauté pan over medium heat for 5 minutes.
- Combine flour, salt, black pepper, cayenne, paprika, and oregano on a shallow plate. Dry the pork chops with paper towels and lightly dredge them in the seasoned flour, shaking off the excess.
- Add peanut oil to the hot pan to a depth of 1/4 inch. Pan fry the chops for 2-3 minutes per side, until nicely browned, and remove from the pan. Pour off excess oil.
- Off the heat, deglaze the pan with the bourbon and cider vinegar. Return to the heat and bring to a boil; add wine and pork chops, bring to a simmer and cook, covered, over low heat for 8 -10 minutes, until the chops are cooked to medium. Remove the chops and keep warm. Reduce the braising juices by half, skimming the impurities from the top. Season.

To Serve:
- Divide the shrimp hominy between 4 plates or wide, shallow bowls. Place a chop on each, spoon some pan juices over the chops and sprinkle with the sliced scallion greens.

From NOT AFRAID OF FLAVOR: RECIPES FROM MAGNOLIA GRILL by Ben and Karen Barker. Photographs by Ann Parks Hawthorne. Copyright ©2000 by Ben and Karen Barker. Used by permission of Ben Barker and the University of North Carolina Press. http://www.uncpress.unc.edu

Pot Roast Piquant

Serves 6-8

3/4 cup port or sherry
1/4 cup soy sauce
2 tablespoons water
1 clove garlic, sliced
1 teaspoon powdered ginger
1/4 teaspoon oregano
1 tablespoon brown sugar
4 pounds chuck roast

- Preheat oven to 300° F.
- Combine the wine with the soy sauce, water, garlic, ginger, oregano and brown sugar and stir to dissolve sugar.
- Place the roast in a heavy pan, pour the wine mixture over the top, cover and roast in preheated oven for 4 hours. Baste occasionally.

The cold leftovers make great sandwiches.
If desired, you may add carrots during last 30 minutes of cooking time.

Suzanne Steward

Baked Mustard Corned Beef

Serves 4-6

3 pounds corned beef
2 bay leaves
6 peppercorns
Sauce:
2 tablespoons salad oil
1 tablespoon prepared brown mustard
1/3 cup brown sugar
5 tablespoons ketchup
3 tablespoons cider vinegar

- Cover corned beef with cold water. Add bay leaves and peppercorns and bring to a boil.
- Remove scum, cover and reduce heat. Simmer about 3 hours or until tender.
- Allow to cool and slice. Put slices in a shallow baking dish.
- Preheat oven to 350° F.
- Combine sauce ingredients and cook until blended, stirring. Pour over the meat.
- Cover and bake in the preheated oven until heated through. If you like more of a glaze don't cover while baking.
- Serve with buttered noodles or mashed potatoes.

The sauce recipe can be doubled for those who like lots of gravy.
The beef can be prepared one day ahead.

Dorothy Samitz

Pasta, Rice

Vegetables

and

Condiments

Pasta, Rice, Vegetables and Condiments

Pasta
Fettuccini Belvedere, 173
Lemon Pasta, 173
Ragout Bolognese with Pappardelle, 171
Spaghetti Pie with Broccoli Rabe, 174
Spinach Lasagna Rolls, 172

Rice
Green Rice, 175
Mom's Wild Rice Casserole, 176
Nutted Wild Rice, 177 ♥

Vegetables
Asparagus in Dijon Mustard Sauce with
Roasted Red Bell Pepper, 186
Bear's Corn Pudding, 185
Black Beans with Yellow Rice, 188 ♥
Boston Baked Beans, 178
Brandied Pureed Carrots, 179
Greek Style Pickled Mushrooms, 183 ♥
Green Beans with Bacon and Shallots,
187
Ingrid's Collard Greens, 181
Mexican Lasagna, 174

Peas with Scallions, 187
Puffed Potatoes, 181
Roasted Potatoes and Onions with
Balsamic Vinegar and Thyme, 189 ♥
Roasted Tomatoes, 188 ♥
Sautéed Carrots with Apricots, 186
Spinach Soufflé, 184
Sweet and Sour Onions, 182 ♥
Sweet Potato and Apple Scallop, 182
Sweet Potato and Carrot Puree, 184
Turnip Casserole, 179
Vegetarian Pie, 180
Well Dressed Asparagus, 190 ♥

Condiments
Cranberry Walnut Conserve, 193 ♥
Fig Chutney, 194 ♥
Grandma Davidson's Chili Sauce, 190 ♥
Pepper Hash, 192 ♥
Pickled Cantaloupe, 191 ♥
Sassy Cranberry Sauce, 194 ♥
Semi-Dried Tomatoes, 193 ♥
Tomato Chutney, 192 ♥

♥ Heart Healthy

Ragu Bolognese with Pappardelle

Serves 4-6

3 tablespoons olive oil
3 tablespoons butter
1 thick slice pancetta, chopped into small cubes
1 cup coarsely chopped onion
1/2 cup coarsely chopped celery
1/2 cup coarsely chopped carrots
2 cloves garlic, minced
2 tablespoons thyme
2 bay leaves
1 pound lean ground veal
1 pound lean ground pork
1/2 cup red wine
2 (14-ounce) cans beef broth
1 1/2 cups Italian tomatoes, drained and finely chopped
Salt and pepper to taste
1 tablespoon finely chopped Italian parsley
Freshly ground nutmeg
1 pound pappardelle, or other wide pasta

- Heat butter and oil in large heavy skillet or Dutch oven.
- Sauté the pancetta until it begins to brown.
- Add onion, celery, carrot and garlic and sauté until vegetables become translucent.
- Add thyme, bay leaves, veal & pork. Break up meat with fork and sauté until brown.
- Add wine, beef broth and tomatoes and bring sauce to a boil. Test for seasonings.
- Reduce heat to low, half cover the pan with lid and simmer slowly for about 3 hours, stirring occasionally, or until most of the liquid has cooked away and sauce is thick and flavorful.
- Add parsley and nutmeg and stir to combine.
- Prepare pappardelle and serve with the sauce.

This is a hearty tomato sauce and should be served on wide pasta such as pappardelle. Fettuccine may also be used but never use thin angel hair pasta. It can't hold the heavy sauce. This sauce freezes well and will keep in the refrigerator up to a week. A must try for true pasta lovers! Pancetta is unsmoked Italian bacon and may be purchased at most deli-counters.

Peggy Quinn

Spinach Lasagna Rolls

Serves 4-6

This recipe was adapted from one in the Firefighters Cookbook by John Dinero. The dish can be made ahead but does not freeze well. Serve with a green salad and crusty bread.

Betsy Ahern

1 (10-ounce) package frozen, chopped spinach
8 lasagna noodles
1 large onion chopped, about 1 1/2 cups
1 medium green pepper, chopped, about 1 cup
2 cups sliced, fresh mushrooms
2 garlic gloves, sliced
1 (15-ounce) can diced tomatoes, with juice
1 tablespoon chopped fresh basil, or 1/2 teaspoon dried basil
1 (8-ounce) can tomato sauce
1/2 teaspoon sugar
1/4 teaspoon black pepper
2 cups small curd cottage cheese
1 egg, beaten
1/8 teaspoon nutmeg
1/2 cup freshly grated Parmesan cheese plus additional for topping

- Cook spinach. Drain well and set aside.
- Cook lasagna noodles according to package directions. Drain, separate noodles onto paper towels and set aside.
- Spray a large skillet with cooking spray. Add onions, green peppers, mushrooms and garlic. Cook until tender.
- Stir in tomatoes, basil, tomato sauce, sugar and pepper. Bring to a boil, then simmer, uncovered, for 5 minutes.
- In a medium bowl stir together cottage cheese, spinach, nutmeg, egg and Parmesan cheese.
- Spoon 1 cup of the tomato-onion-mushroom sauce into a 12x7 1/2x2-inch baking dish.
- Spread 1/2 cup cheese-spinach mixture on each noodle. Roll up jellyroll fashion, beginning at the short side.
- Place rolls, seam side down in the dish. Spoon on remaining sauce. Cover with plastic wrap and refrigerate 2-24 hours.
- At cooking time, preheat oven to 375° F.
- Remove the plastic wrap, sprinkle with Parmesan cheese, cover with foil and bake in preheated oven for 60 minutes or until bubbly.
- You may bake for 45 minutes covered then uncovered for 15 minutes to brown.

Lemon Pasta

Serves 4

4 tablespoons unsalted butter
1 cup half and half
3 tablespoons freshly squeezed lemon juice
1 pound fresh egg fettuccine
2 teaspoons finely grated lemon zest
Salt and freshly ground black pepper to taste
Freshly grated Parmesan cheese to taste

- Melt butter in a deep 12-inch skillet over medium-low heat.
- Add the half & half and lemon juice and stir to combine. Remove the skillet from the heat, cover to keep warm.
- Cook the pasta until al dente, 2-3 minutes. Drain the pasta, reserving 1/2 cup of the pasta cooking liquid.
- Add the drained pasta to the skillet along with the lemon zest and 2 tablespoons of the reserved pasta cooking liquid. Toss to coat. Add more pasta liquid as needed to thin the sauce.
- Season with salt and pepper and Parmesan cheese to taste.

This is the favorite recipe of my good friend Viola Nevi Orsinger whose family is from Northern Italy. Everyone loves it.

Bernice Restivo

Fettuccini Belvedere

Serves 4

12 ounces sliced mushrooms
6 scallions, chopped
2 tablespoons unsalted butter
2 tablespoons olive oil
4 garlic cloves, minced
1/4 teaspoon crushed red pepper flakes
1 (28-ounce) can plum tomatoes, drained and chopped
1/4 cup dry white wine
1/2 cup heavy cream
1/2 teaspoon salt
2 tablespoons fresh chopped parsley
1 pound fettuccini
1/3 cup freshly grated Parmesan cheese

- Sauté mushroom and scallions in butter and oil until browned.
- Add garlic and pepper flakes and cook 2 minutes.
- Add tomatoes and wine and cook 3 minutes.
- Add cream and salt and boil 1 minute. Stir in parsley.
- Cook pasta and drain.
- Toss with sauce and sprinkle with Parmesan cheese.

This recipe was enjoyed during a visit to Belvedere, California.

Sally Johnson

Spaghetti Pie with Broccoli Rabe

Serves 6

1 bunch broccoli rabe (rapini), thick stalks trimmed,
   remainder coarsely chopped
8 ounces sweet or hot Italian sausage, removed from
   casings
1 tablespoon olive oil
1 large garlic clove, thinly sliced or minced
1/2 teaspoon kosher salt and pepper to taste
2 1/2 cups thin spaghetti, cooked
4 ounces Italian Fontina cheese cut into 1/3-inch cubes
8 large eggs, lightly beaten

*Serve with bread
and a salad.*

Helga Van Iten

- Preheat oven to 400° F.
- Cook broccoli rabe 5 minutes in boiling salted water and drain.
- Cook sausage meat in an ovenproof skillet until browned. Transfer with a slotted spoon to a large bowl.
- Add oil and garlic to the skillet and cook over moderate heat until garlic is golden, about 1 minute. Add broccoli rabe and cook, tossing, 3 minutes. Add salt and pepper to taste.
- Transfer broccoli rabe to bowl with the sausage and add the spaghetti, cheese and eggs. Toss well and spoon mixture into a baking dish, spreading to smooth the top.
- Bake in the middle of the preheated oven until the center is set, 20-25 minutes. Let the pie stand 5 minutes before cutting it into wedges to serve.

Mexican Lasagna

Serves 8

10 ounces fresh spinach, washed and picked over
2 cups fresh corn removed from the ears
2 cups shitake mushrooms, cleaned and sliced

24 corn tortillas
Vegetable oil

1 cup crème fraîche or heavy cream, not sour cream
5 cups prepared salsa

3 cups shredded Jack cheese

Continued on next page

Mexican Lasagna *continued*

- Preheat oven to 350° F.
- Barely cook spinach, corn and mushrooms individually in separate pans. Mix together.
- Heat tortillas in heavy fry pan with a hint of hot oil and drain on paper towels. Cut in half.
- Mix together crème fraîche and salsa and set aside.
- Coat bottom of lasagna pan or baking dish with salsa mixture. Add single layer of tortillas. Drizzle with 1 1/2 cups of salsa mixture. Add half the vegetable mixture. Add 1 cup Jack cheese.
- Repeat: salsa layer, tortilla layer, salsa layer and remainder of vegetable mixture.
- Top with 1 cup jack cheese, tortilla layer, a generous layer of salsa and 1 more cup jack cheese.
- Bake in the preheated oven for 25 minutes.
- You may refrigerate the dish for a day until ready to bake.

John Webster

Green Rice

Serves 8

3 cups cooked rice
1 cup cooked chopped spinach, well drained
2 eggs, well beaten
1 cup milk
1 teaspoon Worcestershire sauce
1 1/4 teaspoons salt
1/2 tablespoon grated onion
1/4 cup butter, melted
1/2 cup grated sharp cheese

- Preheat oven to 325°F.
- Toss rice and spinach together.
- Add eggs, milk, Worcestershire, salt and onion. Mix well.
- Pour into a two-quart baking dish.
- Pour butter over casserole and sprinkle cheese on top.
- Bake 30-40 minutes in the preheated oven.

Janet McCarthy

Mom's Wild Rice Casserole

Serves 6-8

1 cup wild rice
1 teaspoon salt
1 pound mushrooms, sliced
2 stalks celery, chopped
1/2 cup chopped onion
1 teaspoon salt
1/2 teaspoon pepper
1/2 stick butter (or combination of olive oil and butter)
1 tablespoon flour
1/2 cup canned chicken broth
1/2 cup light cream, milk, or chicken broth

- Preheat oven to 350° F.
- Wash rice and drain.
- Bring 2-3 quarts of water to a boil.
- Add the 1 teaspoon salt and slowly pour in the rice. Stir occasionally. When rice pops and is firm but soft, about 35-40 minutes depending on variety, drain thoroughly.
- Sauté mushrooms, celery, onions, salt and pepper in butter until soft.
- Stir flour into the vegetable-butter mixture and cook until it begins to bubble.
- Slowly add chicken broth and cream, stirring or whisking constantly until the mixture thickens and comes to a slow simmer.
- Combine rice with sauce and pour into an ovenproof casserole dish.
- Bake in preheated oven 35-40 minutes.

You may use a mixture of wild, brown, and/or white rice. Cook each rice separately and adjust cooking times accordingly. This is my mother's dish, learned at a PTA's cooking class and used for family Thanksgiving dinners.

Emily Halpern

Nutted Wild Rice   ♥

Serves 8-10

1 cup raw wild rice
5 1/2 cups defatted chicken stock
1 cup white converted rice
1 cup shelled pecan halves
Grated rind of 1 large orange
1/4 cup chopped fresh mint
4 scallions, thinly sliced
1/4 cup olive oil
1/3 cup fresh orange juice
1 1/2 teaspoons salt
Freshly ground black pepper to taste

- Put wild rice in a strainer and run under cold water. Rinse thoroughly.
- Place wild rice in a medium-size heavy saucepan. Add stock and bring to a rapid boil. Adjust heat to a gentle simmer and cook uncovered for 45 minutes.
- Check for doneness at 30 minutes. Rice should not be too soft.
- Place a thin towel inside a colander and turn rice into the colander to drain. Reserve stock for another use if desired. Transfer drained rice to a bowl.
- Cook white rice according to directions on the package.
- Toss both rices together and add pecan halves, orange rind, mint, scallions, oil and orange juice. Toss gently. Adjust seasonings to taste.
- Let mixture stand for 2 hours to allow flavors to develop.
- Serve at room temperature.

This rice can be made a day ahead or early in the day of a dinner party. It is a wonderful accompaniment for poultry as part of a holiday buffet.

Julie Snyder

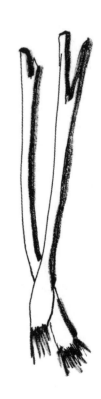

Boston Baked Beans

Serves 8

1 pound dried yellow-eyed beans, or pinto beans
12 bacon slices, about 8 ounces, cut into 1/2-inch pieces
8 cups water
1 1/3 cups chopped onion
1 cup ketchup
1/3 cup pure maple syrup
1/4 cup dry mustard
1/4 cup apple cider vinegar
2 tablespoons light molasses
2 bay leaves
1 1/2 tablespoons chopped garlic
1 teaspoon salt
1 teaspoon ground pepper

- The beans need to soak in water overnight so start this recipe at least a day ahead. Place the beans in a large bowl. Add enough water to cover by 3 inches. Let stand overnight.
- Drain beans. Rinse and drain again and set aside.
- Preheat oven to 350° F.
- In a large heavy pot cook bacon until crisp, about 8 minutes.
- Add beans, water and all remaining ingredients to the pot. Bring to a boil.
- Transfer the pot to the oven. Bake uncovered until beans are tender and liquid thickens, stirring occasionally, about 4 hours.

This is a wonderful recipe for New England baked beans. The beans can be made 1 day ahead and chilled, covered. Bring the beans to a simmer before serving.

Joan Richardson

Brandied Pureed Carrots

Serves 4

1 large or 2 medium sized bunches carrots with the tops on
1/4 cup Grand Marnier
1/4 cup dark brown sugar, packed
5-7 pieces candied ginger
1/3 teaspoon kosher salt
4 tablespoons fresh lemon juice
1/4 cup light cream, warmed
1-2 ounces butter, melted

- Cut tops from the carrots. Peel and slice.
- Add carrots to 1 cup boiling water. Carrots should just be covered. Cook over medium heat in a heavy covered pot until carrots are just fork tender. Drain thoroughly.
- Place the carrots with all remaining ingredients in a blender or food processor. Puree until smooth. Carrots should be the consistency of mashed potatoes. Reheat if necessary before serving.

This makes an elegant dish for company. It can be made the day before and reheated in the oven or microwave. Many persons who do not usually like carrots love this dish. Because it is rich it can take the place of a starch for the diet conscious.

Marietta Williams

Turnip Casserole

Serves 4-6

3 cups grated yellow turnips or rutabagas
3 tablespoons butter
3-4 teaspoons sugar
1 1/2 teaspoons salt
Freshly grated pepper to taste
3/4 cup soft breadcrumbs
2 eggs
Topping:
1 tablespoon butter, melted
1/2 cup soft breadcrumbs

- Preheat oven to 350° F. Butter a 1 1/2-quart soufflé dish.
- Combine turnips, butter, sugar, salt, pepper, 3/4 cup breadcrumbs and eggs in a food processor fitted with the steel blade. Process with on-off turns until well blended.
- Turn into the prepared dish.
- Mix melted butter and 1/2 cup breadcrumbs. Sprinkle over casserole.
- Bake in the preheated oven until the top is browned, about 35 minutes

This is an unusual casserole and I think the sugar makes all the difference. I've shared this recipe with friends and all agree that it is fabulous. This is wonderful with the Herbed Stuffed Flank Steak, page 145. It also works well with Thanksgiving fare.

Ethel D. Cunningham

Vegetarian Pie

Serves 6

Crust:
2 large potatoes peeled and cut into chunks
2 tablespoons butter
Salt and pepper
1/4 cup chopped onion
2 tablespoons canola oil, divided
1/3 pound cheese, shredded, Gruyere, Cheddar, or Swiss
Filling options:
Cooked vegetables: frozen spinach cooked with dry mustard and nutmeg; mushrooms, sliced and sautéed with onions, oregano and thyme; broccoli, chopped and sautéed with garlic; one tomato, sliced and sprinkled with basil and dill; asparagus, chopped and steamed with tarragon. You may use any combination of the above, other favorite vegetables, or cooked leftovers. Want more herbs? Use small snipped amounts of parsley, chives, etc.
Custard:
3 egg whites
1 cup milk, plain yogurt, or buttermilk
Paprika

This dish can also be served at room temperature. It always turns out and it's great.

Teddy Speser

Crust:
- Preheat oven to 375° F.
- Grease a 9 or 10 inch pie pan with canola oil.
- Boil potatoes until tender and drain. Add butter, salt and pepper, onion and mash well.
- Place mashed potatoes into the pie pan, pressing down firmly along the bottom and sides. Make a fluted edge.
- Bake 45 minutes.
- After 20 minutes lightly brush the crust with oil. You may immediately complete the recipe. It is not necessary for the crust to cool before the next step.
- Layer the cheese on top of the crust. This forms a barrier and keeps the crust crisp.

Filling:
- Layer the vegetables over the cheese.

Custard:
- Beat the egg whites with the liquid. Pour over the filling.
- Dust the top with paprika.
- Bake in 375° F. oven for 40 minutes or until firm.
- Cool for 10 minutes before slicing into wedges. Voila!

Ingrid's Collard Greens

Serves 8-10

4 pounds collard greens
1 1/2 cups finely chopped onions
1 1/2 teaspoons minced garlic
8 ounces Gwaltney center cut bacon, chopped
1 1/2 teaspoons ground nutmeg
1 1/2 tablespoons salt (This is correct!)
Freshly ground pepper
1 1/2 tablespoons apple cider vinegar
2 tablespoons honey

- Wash and drain the collard greens, remove the midribs and main veins and chop coarsely.
- In a large pot, sauté the onions and garlic with the bacon until the onions are translucent and the bacon slightly crisp.
- Over very low heat add the collard greens and simmer, covered, until the collards have cooked down to about 1/3 of the original volume, 5-10 minutes.
- Add nutmeg, salt, pepper, vinegar and honey, and, after a quick boil, cover and simmer for 1 hour.

For a vegetarian version: instead of bacon, use 3-4 tablespoons Bacos and about 2-3 tablespoons canola oil for sautéing the onions and garlic. Add the Bacos after the greens have cooked down a bit then continue as above.

Ingrid Baird

Puffed Potatoes

Serves 8

1 large onion, diced
1/3 cup butter plus 1 tablespoon, divided
8 medium boiling potatoes, peeled, cooked, mashed
1 1/2 cups grated sharp cheddar cheese
3/4 cup milk
Salt and freshly ground pepper
2 eggs, beaten

- Preheat oven to 375° F. Grease a 2-quart baking dish.
- Sauté onion in 1 tablespoon of butter until translucent.
- Combine onion and mashed potatoes with remaining butter and the cheese, milk, salt and pepper. Place into the top of a double boiler.
- Cook until cheese and butter are melted. Fold in beaten eggs.
- Turn into the prepared dish and bake in the preheated oven for 45 minutes, until potatoes are puffed and brown.
- Serve immediately.

This has been a favorite in our family for Thanksgiving dinner since 1981. This dish may be prepared in advance, leaving only the baking to be done before serving. I even do the baking in advance and reheat the next day after bringing to room temperature.

Betty Anne Cook

Sweet Potato and Apple Scallop

Serves 6

2 cups pared and cored, thinly sliced apples
3 cups boiled and peeled sweet potatoes, in 1/2-inch slices
3/4 cup brown or white sugar
Grated rind of one orange
1/4 cup melted butter
1/2 teaspoon salt
Generous dash each: ginger, nutmeg and cloves
Few drops of almond extract, optional
1/3 cup unstrained orange juice

- Preheat oven to 350° F.
- Place a layer of apples in the bottom of greased 8x10-inch baking dish and top with a layer of sweet potatoes.
- Mix sugar, orange rind, melted butter, salt and spices to a paste. Spread half the mixture over the sweet potatoes.
- Repeat layers of apple, sweet potatoes and sugar paste.
- Add a few drops of almond extract to orange juice and pour over the apples and sweet potatoes.
- Cover and bake in preheated oven for 45-50 minutes.
- Remove cover the last 20 minutes of baking. Baste with pan juices several times during baking time to improve the flavor.

I sometimes cook this dish longer, to cook down the moisture and achieve a candied coating on the top.

Liz Whaling

Sweet and Sour Onions

Serves 4

1 1/2 pounds Cipolline onions or any small white onions
1 cup white wine or water
2 tablespoons olive oil
Salt and pepper to taste
Red pepper flakes, to taste
2 tablespoons sugar
2 tablespoons balsamic vinegar
1 tablespoon honey
1 tablespoon tomato paste

This is a great recipe to serve with beef or pork. It comes from a cook in Florence, Italy and is a favorite Tuscan side dish. Cipolline onions are the small flat onions usually found in the produce section. These onions are especially good if served the day after you make them.

Peggy Quinn

Continued on next page

Sweet and Sour Onions *continued*

- Peel onions and place in a single layer in a large skillet. Cover the onions with the white wine diluted with a little water.
- Add olive oil, salt and pepper, and red pepper flakes as desired.
- Cover and boil for 10 minutes stirring occasionally.
- Remove cover; add sugar, vinegar, honey and tomato paste. Stir to mix.
- Boil to glaze the onions. Stir to prevent burning or sticking.

Greek Style Pickled Mushrooms ♥

Serves 6

1 pound evenly sized button mushrooms, or larger mushrooms halved or quartered
1 clove garlic, crushed
1 medium red onion, finely chopped
1/2 cup extra virgin olive oil
1/4 cup tarragon vinegar
1 tablespoon best quality balsamic vinegar
1 teaspoon grated lemon rind
1/2 teaspoon salt, or to taste
Freshly ground black pepper to taste
1/4 cup chopped parsley
4 tablespoons lemon zest

- Clean mushrooms with damp cloth or paper towels. Keep mushrooms dry.
- Combine garlic, onion, oil, vinegars, lemon rind and seasonings, mixing well. Pour over the mushrooms in a non-corrosive bowl. Set aside at room temperature and stir every 20 minutes until the mushrooms are glossy and slightly darkened, about 2-3 hours.
- Chill for several hours.
- To serve sprinkle with parsley and lemon zest at the last minute.

This is a great dish for vegetarian diets, the perfect picnic food or potluck treat. I developed this recipe using several Greek recipe sources. This is a "must bring" to the Blueberry Lane Road Association meeting every July on Orr's Island, Maine.

John Webster

Sweet Potato and Carrot Puree

Serves 10-12

1/2 cup sour cream
1/2 cup heavy cream
2 pounds sweet potatoes
1 pound carrots
2 1/2 cups water
2 tablespoons butter
1 tablespoon sugar
1/2 teaspoon nutmeg
Salt and pepper

This recipe can be halved. It freezes well. From the kitchen of Charity Tremblay. Serve with pork, chicken or turkey.

Barbara Tremblay

- Mix sour cream and heavy cream and leave covered at room temperature overnight.
- Preheat oven to 350° F. and grease a 1 1/2-quart baking dish.
- Cook sweet potatoes.
- Clean carrots. Cook with water and butter until tender, water is gone and carrots sizzle in butter.
- Peel sweet potatoes and mash with carrots.
- Puree potatoes and carrots with the cream mixture and the remaining ingredients.
- Transfer to the prepared baking dish. Bake in the preheated oven for 25 minutes.

Spinach Soufflé

Serves 8-10

3 packages frozen chopped spinach
5 tablespoons butter, divided, softened
1/2 cup fresh breadcrumbs
1 tablespoon chopped onion
3 beef bouillon cubes dissolved in 2 cups boiling water
1 (8-ounce) package cream cheese, softened
Salt and pepper to taste
Dash nutmeg
3 eggs, well beaten

- Preheat oven to 400° F.
- Cook spinach according to package directions and drain very well.

Continued on next page

Spinach Soufflé *continued*

- Melt 2 tablespoons butter in a small skillet over medium heat.
- Stir in breadcrumbs and sauté until lightly browned. Set aside.
- Place spinach in a medium bowl and add remaining 3 tablespoons butter, onion, bouillon, cream cheese, salt, pepper, and nutmeg. Mix well.
- Add eggs and mix again.
- Pour into a soufflé dish and bake in preheated oven for 25 minutes.
- Sprinkle the browned breadcrumbs over the top and bake an additional 3 minutes

Anita Martin

Bear's Corn Pudding

Serves: 6-8

6 tablespoons melted butter
2 tablespoons self-rising flour
1 teaspoon salt
2 tablespoons sugar
4 eggs, beaten
2 cups fresh corn or 10 ounces frozen cream corn, thawed
1 cup milk

- Preheat oven to 325° F. and butter a baking dish.
- Blend butter, flour, salt, and sugar
- Add beaten eggs and mix well.
- Stir in corn and then milk. Mix well.
- Pour into the prepared baking dish.
- Bake in the preheated oven for 45 minutes.

This dish was a favorite of Alabama's famous football coach, Paul "Bear" Bryant. It is great served with meat and fresh vegetables. Good fried chicken makes it a real Southern meal.

Joyce Mason

Sautéed Carrots with Apricots

Serves 4-6

5 tablespoons unsalted butter
1 medium onion cut into thin strips
1 pound carrots peeled and shredded
4 ounces dried apricots, julienned
1/2 cup chicken broth
1 to 2 teaspoons Sherry wine vinegar
Salt and pepper

This is unusually good, doesn't taste sweet and looks pretty on a plate.

Susanne Hotte

- Melt butter, add onion and cook until lightly browned.
- Add carrots and apricots and stir-fry 2 minutes.
- Stir in chicken broth and cover. Cook 5 minutes.
- Uncover and cook until liquid evaporates.
- Season with vinegar and salt and pepper.

Asparagus in Dijon Mustard Sauce with Roasted Red Bell Pepper

Serves 4

1 pound asparagus, trimmed
2 tablespoons tarragon vinegar
2 tablespoons Dijon mustard, preferably coarse grained
A dash Tabasco sauce or to taste
1/4 teaspoon Worcestershire sauce
1/4 teaspoon dried thyme, crumbled
1/4 teaspoon dried tarragon, crumbled
Salt and pepper to taste
1/4 cup extra virgin olive oil
1 red bell pepper, roasted and cut into julienne strips

This recipe is based on one from the Ahwahnee Hotel in Yosemite National Park.

Albina Giardino

- Cook the asparagus in boiling salted water for 6-8 minutes or until it is tender and refresh it under cold water. Drain well on paper towels.
- In a bowl, whisk together the vinegar, mustard, Tabasco sauce, Worcestershire sauce, thyme, tarragon and salt and pepper to taste.
- Add the oil slowly in a stream, whisking the dressing until it is emulsified.
- Divide the asparagus between 4 plates, arrange the bell pepper on it and drizzle the dressing over the vegetables.

Green Beans with Bacon and Shallots

Serves 8

2 pounds green beans, trimmed, cut into 2-inch pieces
8 thin slices bacon
2 tablespoons butter
1/2 cup finely chopped shallots (about 3 large shallots)
1/4 cup dry white wine
1/2 teaspoon sugar

- Cook beans in large pot of boiling salted water until crisp-tender, about 4 minutes. Rinse under cold water. Drain well and pat dry with paper towels.
- Cook bacon in a large, heavy skillet over medium heat until crisp. Drain well. Reserve 3 tablespoons bacon fat in skillet.
- Melt butter with the bacon fat over medium heat.
- Add shallots, wine and sugar, and cook until tender and golden, about 5 minutes.
- Add beans and sauté until heated through, about 6 minutes.
- Crumble bacon and add to skillet. Toss to blend.
- Season to taste with salt and pepper. Serve warm

Anonymous

Peas with Scallions and Nutmeg

Serves 3

1 tablespoon butter
1/2 cup scallions or green onions, cut into 1/2-inch pieces
1 (10-ounce) package frozen peas
1 tablespoon water
1/4 teaspoon freshly grated nutmeg
Salt to taste

- Melt butter in a medium saucepan. Add scallions and stir. Remove pan from heat and set aside.
- Cook the peas in boiling water or microwave until barely tender, about 4 minutes. Drain well.
- Add peas and water to pan with scallions. Stir in nutmeg and salt to taste.
- Heat on medium-high until serving temperature is reached, peas are tender and water has evaporated. Add more water if needed.

These peas are delicious and the recipe doubles well. To make ahead, undercook the peas and drain. Place the butter, peas and one tablespoon water in a covered casserole. Sprinkle the uncooked scallions on top. Just before serving, reheat briefly in a microwave so that the peas are done, butter melted and scallions wilted. Stir in nutmeg and salt to taste just before serving.

Kim Batcheller

Black Beans with Yellow Rice ♥

Serves 8-10

2 pounds black beans
4 green peppers, diced
4 onions, diced
3 tablespoons olive oil
1 teaspoon salt or to taste
1 teaspoon black pepper
1 tablespoon cumin
1 tablespoon oregano
2 (8-ounce) cans tomato sauce
3 tablespoons cider vinegar
2 tablespoons white wine
2 tablespoons sugar or to taste
1 (4-ounce) jar red pimento, optional
1 package yellow rice

- Wash beans and check for stones. Cover with 3 inches of water and let soak overnight.
- Drain beans, rinse and drain again. Cover with water, bring to a boil, lower heat and simmer until beans are soft, adding water as needed. Stir several times.
- In a large skillet, sauté the green peppers and onions in the oil.
- Add seasonings, wine, vinegar, sugar and tomato sauce. Cook until the peppers are done. Add to beans, remove from the heat and let the flavors blend for an hour or so.
- When ready to serve, heat and add pimentos.
- Serve over yellow rice, cooked according to package directions.

To serve, sprinkle with chopped tomato, chopped onion, grated cheddar cheese and a dollop of sour cream or yogurt, as desired.
This recipe works wonderfully by cooking the beans in a crockpot. Cook 4 hours on high or 6-8 hours on low. This is a lowfat and vegetarian recipe.

Ruth Moose

Roasted Tomatoes ♥

The amount of each ingredient will vary depending on the number of tomatoes you are using.
Very ripe plum tomatoes
Pesto made with fresh basil, garlic, pine nuts and olive oil, homemade or purchased.
Salt and pepper
Freshly grated Parmesan cheese
Fresh breadcrumbs

These tomatoes are delicious as an accompaniment to lamb dishes or roast chicken. They may be served at room temperature as part of an antipasto platter. You may also top crostini or pizza with them. They are a terrific addition chopped into warm pasta with some olive oil and fresh herbs.

Continued on next page

Roasted Tomatoes *continued*

- Preheat oven to 375° F.
- Wash and dry the tomatoes. Trim any spotted areas and remove a 1/4-inch slice from the stem end.
- Cut each tomato in half lengthwise. Remove most of the seeds and some of the pulp leaving the tomatoes still juicy.
- Place the tomato halves cut side up in an oiled baking dish, drizzle some pesto over each one and salt and pepper them liberally.
- Sprinkle with just a little Parmesan, then a light dusting of breadcrumbs.
- Drizzle with a little more of the oil in the pesto container and add a bit more Parmesan.
- Roast in preheated oven for 25 minutes. Tomatoes should be medium brown and soft but not dry. If they are still very wet and not very brown, roast for another 5-10 minutes. Remove from the oven and serve hot.

At the market, choose Italian plum tomatoes of uniform size. Ripen at room temperature, turning every 2-3 days, until they have a good color and soften, about 5-7 days. Any brown spots or small moldy areas that may form will be discarded when you prepare the tomatoes.

Barbara Terry

Roasted Potatoes and Onions with Balsamic Vinegar and Thyme   ♥

Serves 4

12 boiling onions, golf ball size
16 new potatoes, golf ball size, peeled
2 tablespoons olive oil
3 tablespoons balsamic vinegar
3/4 teaspoon salt and freshly ground pepper to taste
6 sprigs fresh thyme, chopped

- Preheat oven to 350° F.
- Place onions and potatoes in a baking dish just large enough to hold them in one layer.
- Mix olive oil and vinegar and pour over potatoes and onions.
- Add salt and pepper and thyme. Turn until potatoes and onions are coated with oil-vinegar mixture.
- Cover tightly with foil and bake 2 hours, turning every 30 minutes and recovering lightly with foil.
- When done, onions and potatoes should be deep brown

This is a perfect dish to serve with roast pork or roast beef.

Michael Cotter

Well Dressed Asparagus ♥

Serves 6-8

2 bunches asparagus
3 cloves garlic
1/4 cup virgin olive oil
1/8 cup balsamic vinegar
Salt and pepper
1/2 cup freshly grated Parmesan cheese

- Preheat oven to 400° F.
- Snap off tough ends of the asparagus.
- Crush garlic in a garlic press and mix with the olive oil in a large glass rectangular baking dish.
- Add asparagus and roll to coat.
- Place in the oven and bake 6-10 minutes until tender.
- Remove dish from the oven and sprinkle on the vinegar, salt and pepper and Parmesan. Broil 1 minute.

You may roll the asparagus in the olive oil-garlic mixture and let it stand an hour or so until ready to bake.

Anne Kirkhoff

Grandma Davidson's Chili Sauce ♥

Makes 12-14 pints

36 ripe tomatoes, about 15 pounds, chopped
12 medium onions, chopped
8 green bell peppers, chopped
4 hot peppers to taste, chopped
3 cups sugar
3 cups vinegar
4 tablespoons salt
2 teaspoons each: allspice, nutmeg, cinnamon, paprika
1 teaspoon cloves
1 tablespoon celery seed
2 tablespoons mustard seed

This chili sauce was made by my Grandma from Macon, Georgia and is, therefore, a true Southern recipe. It is very good on fresh black-eye peas, collards, turnip greens, green beans and cabbage.

Continued on next page

Grandma Davidson's Chili Sauce *continued*

- Sterilize 12-14 pint jars and lids.
- Over medium heat combine tomatoes, onions and peppers in a large heavy pot. Bring to a boil, reduce heat and simmer uncovered for 30 minutes, stirring occasionally to make sure it does not stick.
- Add all other ingredients to the pot and mix well.
- Simmer slowly, uncovered, for 2 hours until thickened, stirring occasionally.
- Transfer to hot sterilized pint jars and seal with new caps. The caps should pop after the jars cool down or remain down in the center when pressed.

I make this for Christmas gifts to rave notices. Ideally, the tomatoes and peppers should be homegrown and ripened on the vine. The riper the tomatoes, the sweeter the sauce. It will keep in sealed jars for 2 years. It must be refrigerated after opening. This recipe makes a lot but it can be cut in half successfully if you prefer.

Joyce Baird

Pickled Cantaloupe ♥

1 large cantaloupe
1/2 cup vinegar
1 teaspoon whole allspice
1/2 cup sugar
1 teaspoon salt

- Cut cantaloupe lengthwise into quarters. Remove rind and seeds. Cut into crescent-shaped slices.
- Combine other ingredients and bring to a boil.
- Add melon and when syrup returns to a boil, remove from the heat and cool.
- Refrigerate overnight.

This different condiment is delicious as a garnish with ham, turkey or beef or on salad greens topped with fresh fruit.

Cynthia Jones

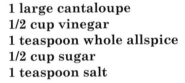

*This chutney is
excellent as a relish
with chicken, pork,
ham, or teamed
with cream cheese
on crackers, or
crostini for an hors
d'oeuvre. It is quite
easy to make, but
does take a while
from beginning to
end. May also be
frozen in small
containers.
The recipe is
adapted from one in
Family Circle
Magazine.*

Nancy Foster

*My mother, Effie
Lewis Blake, 1900-
1996, was the
author of this
recipe. Her recipes,
handwritten are
now in tatters. I
grew up on a farm
in eastern North
Carolina and my
mother, like all
Southern wives,
had a large
vegetable garden,
fruit trees and
pecan trees. My
mother naturally
used many of the
fruits of the earth in
her cooking,
canning and
preserving.*

Rosa Lee Tucker

Tomato Chutney

Makes 5 (8-ounce) jars

2 1/4 pounds ripe, red tomatoes, peeled, seeded, diced
1 cup raisins, dark preferred
3/4 cup cider vinegar
1/2 cup brown sugar
1/2 cup onion, finely dice
1 jalapeño chili, topped, halved, sliced, use seeds too
1 teaspoon mustard seed
1 teaspoon salt
1 teaspoon ground ginger
1/2 teaspoon cinnamon

- Sterilize 5 (8-ounce) jars and lids.
- Place all ingredients in a large, heavy pot. Bring to a boil, lower heat to a simmer.
- Cook uncovered until thickened, about 50 minutes, stirring occasionally.
- Ladle into hot, sterilized jars and seal with new caps. The caps should "pop" after the jars cool down or stay down in the center when pressed.
- Refrigerate chutney after opening sealed jars.

Pepper Hash ♥

Makes 4 quarts

12 sweet red peppers
12 sweet green peppers
6 bunches scallions
3 cups vinegar
3 teaspoons salt
2 cups sugar

- Seed the peppers.
- Grind the scallions and peppers.
- Scald with boiling water and let stand for 5 minutes. Drain, squeeze dry and repeat the process.
- Bring vinegar, salt and sugar to a boil. Add the peppers and onions and boil for 20 minutes.
- This may be served as a side dish, or added to potato salad.
- You may put this in sterile jars. Refrigerate after opening.

Semi-Dried Tomatoes ♥

2-3 pounds Roma tomatoes halved lengthwise.
Salt

- Arrange tomatoes on baking sheets, cut-side up. Sprinkle with salt.
- Place in warm oven, 180-200° F. overnight and possibly longer.
- Begin checking the tomatoes after they have baked for 8 hours. Tomatoes should be dried but still soft, not crisp. Be careful not to bake too long.
- Store in a sealed container in the refrigerator

This is a great way to recreate the real tomato taste that you crave in the winter. The flavor will be intense and wonderful to add to pasta and other dishes, or just eat as a snack. They will become chewier with time.

Carolyn Curtis

Cranberry-Walnut Conserve ♥

Makes 3 cups

3 cups fresh cranberries
1 cup water
1 stick cinnamon
1 3/4 cups sugar
3/4 cup golden, seedless raisins
1 large tart apple, peeled, cored and chopped
1/3 cup chopped, candied ginger
Grated rind and juice of 1 lemon and 1 orange
1/2 teaspoon salt
1/4 cup port wine
3/4 cup chopped walnuts

- In a large, heavy saucepan, combine cranberries, water and cinnamon stick. Bring to a boil.
- Reduce heat and simmer until skins pop, about 10 minutes.
- Add sugar, raisins, apple, ginger, lemon and orange rinds and juice and salt.
- Simmer, uncovered over medium heat 15-20 minutes, stirring occasionally.
- Remove from heat and cool to room temperature.
- Stir in port wine and walnuts.
- Store in tightly covered containers. It will keep refrigerated for several months.

This is adapted from a recipe more than 30 years old from a Detroit newspaper. My sister-in-law, Carol Bird, used it for several years and gave it to me. I have adapted the ingredients to fit the standard 3-cup packages of cranberries. I usually make a double recipe for Thanksgiving and keep some for Christmas "giving." It is still good for the Easter ham.

Shirley Schneerer

Sassy Cranberry Sauce ♥

Makes 2 1/2 cups

1 (16 ounce) can whole berry cranberry sauce
1/3 cup ruby port wine
1/4 cup honey
1 (8 ounce) can pears, drained and finely chopped
1 tablespoon balsamic vinegar
1/2 teaspoon apple pie spice or ground cinnamon
Zest of 1 orange

This may be made two days ahead and refrigerated in a covered container.

Ann Siebold

- Pour the cranberry sauce, wine and honey into a 1-quart saucepan and bring it to a boil over medium heat. Stir frequently.
- Add pears, vinegar, spice and zest. Raise heat to medium-high, cook at a rolling boil, stirring frequently, until sauce thickens slightly, about 5 minutes.
- Pour into serving bowl and cool for 5 minutes. Cover with plastic wrap and refrigerate. Sauce will continue to thicken as it cools.

Fig Chutney ♥

Makes 1 1/2 cups

1/3 cup raisins, dried cherries or dried cranberries
1/3 cup red wine vinegar or raspberry vinegar
1/4 cup honey
2 teaspoons slivered crystallized ginger
10 ounces fresh figs, trimmed and quartered, about 2 cups
1/2 teaspoon mustard seeds
3 whole cloves
1 teaspoon balsamic vinegar

This chutney is great with meat or curried dishes. It will keep for 2 weeks in the refrigerator. The recipe was adapted from one by Deborah Madison in Cooking Light magazine, August 2000.

Pat Bixby

- Combine raisins, cherries or cranberries, vinegar, honey and ginger in a non-aluminum saucepan and bring to a boil.
- Reduce heat and simmer 5 minutes or until syrupy.
- Add figs, mustard seeds, and cloves. Cover, reduce heat, and simmer 10 minutes or until figs are tender.
- Remove from heat. Discard cloves and add balsamic vinegar.
- Serve at room temperature or chilled.

Desserts

Desserts

Cakes
Almond Cappuccino Dacquoise, 196
Amaretti Torte, 195
Chocolate Amaretto Cheesecake, 198
Chocolate Chip Pumpkin Cake, 202
English Walnut Pudding Cake, 197
Hungarian Coffee Cake, 202
Poppy Seed Cake with Buttermilk, 201
Ruthie and Moe's Carrot Cake, 199
Warm Liquid Center Chocolate Cake, 200
White Christmas Fruit Cake, 203

Pies and Tarts
Brandy Alexander Pie, 204
Buttermilk Pie with Raspberry Sauce, 213
Cherry Cobbler, 212
Fresh-Spiced Pumpkin Pie, 214
Green Tomato Pie, 208
Holiday Pie, 211
Lemon Chiffon Bavarian, 206
Lemon Tart, 210
My Grandmother's Pumpkin Pie, 207
Nantucket Cranberry Pie, 209
Old Fashioned Pecan Pie, 212
Purple Plum Tart, 215
Red Raspberry Pie, 209
Rhubarb Delight, 205
Tipsy Blueberry Gin Pie, 204
Willa's Deep Dish Apple Pie, 224

Cookies
Apple-Pecan Squares, 216
Carolina Chew Cakes, 216
Chef John's Fabulous Chocolate Chip Cookies, 226
Chocolate Cappuccino Cookies, 219
Clipper Chippers, 217
Cranberry Biscotti, 218
Glazed Lemon Cookies, 222
Lacy Dessert Baskets, 219
Mama's Little Nut Cookies, 224
Mint Brownies, 220
Old Fashioned Gingerbread Boys, 223
Pistachio-Orange Cookies, 221
Triple Chocolate Biscotti, 225

Puddings
Cherry Clafouti, 229
Chocolate Christmas Trifle, 228
English Trifle, 228
Flan Crème Caramel, 227
Luscious Lemon Cream, 233
Mirage Famous Bread Pudding, 233
Pumpkin Pot de Crème, 230
Spirited Chocolate Mousse, 230
Tiramisu, 231
Victorian Cream with Chocolate Liqueur Sauce, 232

Fruit
Chamomile Dried Fruit Compote with Mascarpone, 235
Frozen Fruit Cups, 236
Prunes in Red Wine, 234 ♥
Roasted Figs with Candied Lemon and Sherry, 236
Slow Apples, 234 ♥

Ice Cream and Frozen Desserts
Delicious Pumpkin Ice Cream Pie, 237
Lavender Ice Cream, 239
Raspberry Ice Cream, 238
Walnut Frozen Fantasy, 238 ♥

Candy
GG's Virginity (Divinity), 240 ♥
Praline Pecan Crunch, 240

Daddy's Eggnog, 239

♥ Heart Healthy

Amaretti Torte

Serves 12

10 imported amaretti cookies
4 ounces semi-sweet chocolate
1 tablespoon water
1 cup unsalted butter at room temperature
1 cup sugar
5 eggs, separated, at room temperature
1/2 cup all purpose flour
Garnish:
Confectioner's sugar, mint leaves, raspberries or
strawberries

- Preheat oven to 350° F.
- Butter bottom and sides of a 9-inch round cake pan. Line bottom with wax paper. Butter the paper and dust the paper and sides of the pan with flour, shaking out excess.
- Break up amaretti, and pulverize in a food processor or blender. Set aside. You will need about 1/3 cup of fine crumbs.
- Melt chocolate with 1 tablespoon of water in the top of a double boiler over simmering water. Stir until smooth. Let cool while preparing the batter.
- In the bowl of an electric mixer beat 1 cup butter until creamy. Gradually beat in sugar until well blended. Beat in egg yolks, one at a time, and continue beating until mixture is light and fluffy, about 5 minutes. Gradually add flour alternately with amaretti crumbs, beating well after each addition. Fold in melted chocolate.
- In a clean bowl, beat egg whites until stiff peaks form and gently fold into the batter. Pour into the prepared pan.
- Bake in preheated oven 40-45 minutes or until a toothpick comes out clean. Cool in the pan on a wire rack about 10 minutes. Invert onto a serving plate, remove pan, peel off paper and cool completely.
- Sprinkle with powdered sugar just before serving. Garnish with mint leaves and berries.

Amaretti cookies are each paper wrapped and macaroon-like. They can be found in bags and tins at specialty and Italian food stores. This cake should be served in thin slices. For greater decadence you may add a small dollop of sweetened whipped cream and/or a little chocolate sauce on the plate. The torte keeps very well when wrapped in plastic after it has been thoroughly cooled.

Florence Johnson

Almond Cappuccino Dacquoise

Serves 12

Meringue layers:
1 cup shelled natural almonds, lightly toasted and cooled
1 1/4 cups sugar, divided
2 1/2 teaspoons cornstarch
5 large egg whites at room temperature
1/4 teaspoon cream of tartar
1/4 teaspoon salt
Filling:
4 1/2 cups heavy cream
1/3 cup instant coffee
6 tablespoons sugar
2 tablespoons Kahlua coffee-flavored liqueur
Garnish:
1 pint fresh raspberries

- Line 2 baking sheets with parchment paper and trace 3 13x4-inch rectangles on the paper, 2 on 1 sheet and 1 on the other. Set aside. Cut a piece of cardboard 15x6 inches. Wrap in foil and set aside.
- *For the meringue layers:*
- Preheat oven to 250° F.
- Grind almonds fine with 1/2 cup sugar and cornstarch; set aside.
- Beat egg whites, cream of tartar and salt with electric mixer until they hold soft peaks.
- Beat in remaining 3/4 cups of sugar in a slow stream, beating until meringue holds stiff, glossy peaks.
- Fold in almond mixture, and transfer to a pastry bag fitted with a 1/2-inch plain tip.
- Using the baking sheets with the traced rectangles, start along the inside edge of a rectangle, and pipe meringue to fill in the entire inside of each rectangle.
- Bake meringue layers in upper and lower thirds of oven, switching position of sheets halfway through baking. Bake 1 hour or until meringues are firm and dry to the touch.
- Cool meringues on baking sheets on wire racks.
- Slide parchment paper off sheets and peel the paper off the meringues. Set meringues aside. Meringues may be made 1 day ahead and kept tightly wrapped at room temperature.

Continued on next page

This makes a beautiful presentation and delivers in taste. Although it is a lot of work, it is worth it for that very special occasion. I often substitute Splenda for the sugar so that it is light in carbs... but of course, no comment on the fat!

Janet Lorant

Almond Cappuccino Dacquoise *continued*

For the Filling:
- Beat the filling ingredients in a large bowl with an electric mixer until the mixture holds stiff peaks.

Assemble the cake:
- Put 1 meringue, smooth side down, on the foil covered board.
- Using a long metal spatula spread a 1/2-inch thick layer of filling over the top of the meringue.
- Repeat meringue and filling layers ending with the last meringue smooth side up. Spread a thin layer of filling on top and sides of dacquoise. Place remaining filling in a pastry bag with a star tip. Pipe filling decoratively around top outside edge and base of the dacquoise.
- Arrange raspberries on top and around base of the dacquoise.
- Freeze dacquoise, uncovered, until hard, about 6 hours.
- The dacquoise may be used at this point, or wrapped in plastic wrap or foil and kept up to 2 days in the freezer.
- Let dacquoise stand in refrigerator 30 minutes before serving.
- To serve, slice dacquoise in 1 inch slices with a serrated knife. Make sure everyone gets some raspberries.

English Walnut Pudding Cake

Serves 6-8

2 tablespoons salted butter, softened
1 cup sugar
1/2 cup milk, room temperature
1 cup flour
1/4 teaspoon salt
2 teaspoons baking powder
3/4 cup chopped walnuts
1/2 cup raisins
1 cup brown sugar
1 teaspoon butter
1 1/2 cups boiling water

- Preheat oven to 350° F. and butter an 8 x 8-inch baking pan.
- Cream butter and sugar, add milk and combine.
- Sift flour, salt and baking powder together and add to mixture, stirring to combine.
- Add walnuts and raisins, stir, and pour into the prepared pan.
- Combine brown sugar, butter and water, and pour over cake mixture.
- Bake in preheated oven for 30 minutes.

My favorite cold weather dessert brings back happy childhood memories in Ohio. It is best served warm and can be reheated. Serve with dollops of whipped cream or vanilla ice cream on top of the cake. When serving, flip each piece over and spoon sauce from the bottom of the pan over cake.

Barbara Merten

Chocolate Amaretto Cheesecake

Makes 10 servings

Crumb Shell:
1 1/2 cups chocolate wafer crumbs
1 cup blanched almonds, lightly toasted and finely chopped
1/3 cup sugar
6 tablespoons butter, softened
Filling:
24 ounces cream cheese
1 cup sugar
4 eggs
1/3 cup heavy cream
1/4 cup Amaretto liqueur
1 teaspoon vanilla
Topping:
2 cups sour cream
1 tablespoon sugar
1 teaspoon vanilla
Garnish:
Chopped almonds

This cake is lovely as a dessert after a buffet supper. It is an especially light textured cheesecake. Garnish with fresh, unhulled strawberries.

Jean Green

- Preheat oven to 375° F.
- Butter a 9 1/2-inch spring-form pan.
- Mix together the chocolate wafer crumbs, almonds, sugar and butter.
- Press the mixture onto bottom and sides of the prepared pan.
- In a large bowl, cream together softened cream cheese and sugar.
- Add eggs one at a time, beating well after each addition.
- Add heavy cream, Amaretto and vanilla and beat until the mixture is light.
- Pour batter into shell and bake in the middle of the preheated oven for 45 minutes.
- Transfer the cake to a rack and let it stand for 5 minutes. The cake will not be completely set.
- Combine sour cream, sugar and vanilla, spread over the cake.
- Return cake to oven and bake for 5 more minutes.
- Transfer the cake to a wire rack. Cool the cake completely in the pan and chill, lightly covered, overnight.
- Remove the sides of the pan, transfer the cake to a cake stand, and press almonds around the top edge.

Ruthie and Moe's Carrot Cake

Makes 3 9-inch round cakes

Cake:
2 cups flour
3 teaspoons cinnamon
2 cups sugar
2 teaspoons baking powder
2 teaspoons baking soda
1 teaspoon salt
1 1/4 cups canola oil, or 1 cup applesauce and 1/4 cup oil
4 eggs
4 cups shredded carrots
1 cup finely chopped walnuts, optional
Frosting:
1/2 pound butter, room temperature
1 pound cream cheese, room temperature
1 teaspoon vanilla
1 pound powdered sugar

- Preheat oven to 350° F.
- Grease and flour 3 9-inch round cake pans.

Cake:
- Place dry ingredients in a mixing bowl, whisk together for 2-3 minutes.
- Add oil or applesauce and mix well, using electric beater.
- Add eggs and beat for 2 more minutes with beater.
- Stir in carrots and walnuts, mixing thoroughly.
- Pour into prepared pans and bake in preheated oven for 20-25 minutes. Cake will spring back to touch when done. DO NOT UNDER OR OVER BAKE. Check frequently and carefully from 18 minutes on.
- Cool on wire rack before removing cake layers from pans.

Frosting:
- Cream butter and cream cheese with electric beater until smooth.
- Add vanilla and sugar, beating well until it reaches spreading consistency.
- Spread generously on layers, assemble the cake and frost the top and sides.

Ruthie and Moe owned a famous diner in Cleveland in the 1980's and this cake was a huge favorite. I donate two cakes cut into 24 slices every year for the Fearrington Women's Club bake sale. Now I have let my secret out for this wonderful Carrot Cake. If nuts are a problem for some folks leave them out as I often do.

Kimball Page

Warm Liquid Center Chocolate Cake

Serves 8

250g (9 ounces) dark bittersweet chocolate
250g (9 ounces or 2 sticks plus 2 tablespoons) butter
5 large eggs
5 large egg yolks
120g (1/2 cup + 1 teaspoon) granulated sugar
125g (1 cup + 2 tablespoons) all-purpose flour
Zest of one orange, grated and finely minced

- Preheat oven to 350° F.
- Butter eight small ramekins 3 1/2 x 1 1/2 inches deep.
- Melt chocolate and butter in a double boiler, stirring until smooth.
- Combine eggs, egg yolks and sugar in a medium bowl and beat with an electric mixer until a pale lemon color.
- Add flour a little at a time, incorporating each addition well.
- Fold in the chocolate-butter mixture and the zest.
- Pour into the prepared ramekins.
- Place ramekins in a pan. Pour warm water in the pan until it reaches half way up the sides of the dishes.
- Bake for 20 minutes in the preheated oven. The center should still move when touched.
- Serve immediately.

This is good with Kirsch-marinated fresh sweet cherries and vanilla ice cream.

Graham Fox
Chef de Cuisine,
Fearrington House
Restaurant

Poppy Seed Cake with Buttermilk

Serves 16-20

1/4 cup poppy seeds
1 cup buttermilk
1 cup butter or margarine
2 cups sugar, divided
4 eggs
1 teaspoon vanilla
2 1/2 cups all-purpose flour
1/2 teaspoon salt
1 teaspoon baking soda
1 1/2 tablespoons cinnamon

- Preheat oven to 350° F.
- Mix poppy seeds and buttermilk in a small bowl.
- In a mixer bowl, cream butter or margarine and then gradually add 1 1/2 cups sugar and beat until fluffy.
- Add eggs, one at a time, beating well after each addition and then add vanilla.
- Sift flour, salt and soda together and add to the butter and sugar mixture alternately with the buttermilk and poppy seeds. Blend well.
- In a separate bowl, mix together remaining 1/2 cup sugar and the cinnamon.
- Grease a bundt pan with butter and coat the bottom and sides of the pan with some of the sugar-cinnamon mix, tapping out the mix that does not adhere. This will form a thin crust over the cake after baking.
- Pour the batter into the pan in 3 layers, sprinkling each layer with the sugar-cinnamon mixture before adding another layer. You will end with sugar-cinnamon on the top.
- Bake in the preheated oven for about 50 minutes, or until a toothpick inserted into the cake comes out clean.
- Cool the cake in the pan on a rack for an hour before unmolding. Do not wait longer or the cake will stick to the pan. Turn the cake upright after unmolding.

This unusual cake is good by itself or with ice cream. It is a cake that freezes well, either whole or cut into quarters.

Anne Bodner

Hungarian Coffee Cake

Serves 8-12

Topping:
1/2 cup granulated sugar
1 tablespoon cinnamon
1/2 cup chopped walnuts
Cake:
1 cup butter
2 cups sugar
3 cups sifted all-purpose flour
3 teaspoons baking powder
1 teaspoon baking soda
2 eggs
2 teaspoons vanilla extract
2 cups sour cream

This recipe was given to me almost 50 years ago by my mother-in-law Anna Seno. It is very light and delicious.

Edith Seno

- Preheat oven to 350° F.
- Grease an 11x14-inch baking pan.
- Mix topping ingredients together and set aside.
- With an electric mixer cream butter and sugar until light.
- Sift flour, baking powder and baking soda together in a separate bowl.
- Add eggs to the butter and sugar and beat until light and creamy. Add the vanilla and mix.
- Add the flour mixture and sour cream alternately, with flour as the first and last additions, folding into the egg mixture.
- Pour into the prepared pan and sprinkle with the topping.
- Bake in the preheated oven for 35-40 minutes.
- Cool on a wire rack.

Chocolate Chip Pumpkin Cake

Serves 15

2 cups flour
2 teaspoons cinnamon
2 cups sugar
4 eggs
2 teaspoons baking powder
1 teaspoon baking soda
1 cup oil
1 (16-ounce) can pumpkin
1 (12-ounce) package chocolate chips
1 cup chopped walnuts or pecans

This cake is very rich and moist and has always been well received. It can be made a few days ahead and will retain its moisture if well wrapped or kept in a covered cake holder. You could decorate the cake with powdered sugar, but it really speaks for itself.

Barbara Berke

Continued on next page

Chocolate Chip Pumpkin Cake *continued*
- Preheat oven to 350° F.
- Grease and flour a bundt pan. I use Baker's Joy. It combines oil and flour and makes the pan preparation and removing the cake much easier.
- In the bowl of an electric mixer combine flour, cinnamon, sugar, eggs, baking powder, baking soda, oil and pumpkin. Mix on low speed to combine well.
- With a large spoon, stir in chocolate chips and nuts.
- Pour into prepared pan and bake in preheated oven for 1 hour.
- Allow to cool in the pan on a wire rack before turning out onto a serving plate.

White Christmas Fruit Cake

Serves 12

2/3 cup sugar
1 cup butter, softened
1 egg
3 egg yolks, divided
1 cup crushed pineapple, drained, reserve 2 tablespoons juice
1 cup mixed candied fruit
1 cup white raisins
2 1/2 cups flour, divided
1 teaspoon baking powder
1/2 teaspoon salt

- Preheat oven to 300° F.
- Line a 9x5-inch loaf pan with waxed paper.
- Cream together sugar and butter.
- Add 1 egg and beat well.
- Add egg yolks one at a time and beat after each addition.
- Add pineapple juice and crushed pineapple.
- Coat the candied fruit and raisins with 1/2 cup of flour.
- Sift the remaining two cups of flour twice with baking powder and salt added to the second sifting.
- Add the creamed mixture to the flour mixture along with the fruit. Stir to mix well.
- Pour the cake mixture into the pan and level it so that it is an even depth.
- Bake in preheated oven for 1 1/2-2 hours.
- Remove from the oven and allow to cool in the loaf pan for fifteen minutes before removing from the pan.

This cake has been a traditional favorite in the Balfour family for generations. My mother, Mrs. Henry P. Balfour, baked this cake every holiday season for both family and friends. It was frequently given as gifts to many people. Serve with a glass of cream sherry for a festive treat.

Jean Green

Brandy Alexander Pie

Serves 6-8

1 envelope unflavored gelatin
1/2 cup cold water
2/3 cup sugar, divided
Pinch of salt
3 eggs, separated
1/4 cup cognac
1/4 cup crème de cacao
Pinch of cream of tartar
2 cups heavy cream, divided
1 (9-inch) graham cracker piecrust
Chocolate curls for garnish

- Sprinkle gelatin over the cold water in a saucepan.
- Add 1/3 cup of the sugar, the salt and egg yolks. Stir to blend.
- Heat over low heat while stirring until gelatin dissolves and mixture thickens. Do NOT boil.
- Remove from heat, stir in cognac and crème de cacao.
- Chill about 20 minutes.
- Beat egg whites and cream of tartar until stiff.
- Gradually beat in remaining sugar and fold into thickened egg yolk mixture.
- Beat whipping cream until stiff. Fold *1 cup of whipped cream* into mixture. Turn into crust. Refrigerate remaining whipped cream.
- Chill several hours or overnight.
- Before serving, spread remaining whipped cream over pie and top with chocolate curls. Chocolate will curl best when slightly warm.

Ethel D. Cunningham

Tipsy Blueberry Gin Pie

Serves 6-8

2 1/4 tablespoons arrowroot
1/4 cup gin
3/4 cup sugar, more if berries are not sweet
4 rounded cups fresh blueberries, divided
1 pre-baked piecrust

Continued on next page

This filling can be used in tart shells or on ginger cookies crumbled in the bottom of a compote instead of in a piecrust. Serve with vanilla ice cream or whipped cream.

Marietta Williams

Tipsy Blueberry Gin Pie *continued*

- In a medium saucepan dissolve arrowroot in gin.
- Add sugar and cook, stirring, over medium heat until the mixture boils and thickens.
- When the syrup coats a spoon, add 1 cup of berries and cook until the syrup is clear and thicker, stirring constantly.
- Add the remaining berries. Remove immediately from the heat. Stir until all berries are fully coated.
- Cool the filling for about 10 minutes until it is just warm. Pour into pie shell.

Rhubarb Delight

Serves 6

Pastry:
1 cup all purpose flour
2 tablespoons sugar
1/2 cup butter
Filling:
3 large egg yolks
1 1/4 cups sugar
3 cups rhubarb cut in 1/2-inch pieces
1/3 cup light or heavy cream
2 1/2 tablespoons cornstarch
Meringue:
3 large egg whites
4 tablespoons sugar

- Preheat oven to 350° F.
- Mix pastry ingredients together like a pie dough and pat into a 9x9-inch pan.
- Bake in the preheated oven for 20-25 minutes. Cool.
- Increase oven temperature to 375° F.
- Beat egg yolks until thick. Add remaining filling ingredients, mixing well.
- Cook in a saucepan until thick, stirring constantly. Cool, and pour into crust.
- Beat egg whites with 4 tablespoons sugar to peaks. Spoon over custard.
- Bake at 375° F. for 6-8 minutes to lightly brown the meringue.

What's all this fuss over rhubarb? It is delicious and nutritious and worth any fuss. Rumors note that Benjamin Franklin, scientist, bon vivant and America's ambassador to France sent the first rhubarb plants back to America for his relatives to cultivate. Rhubarb grows well in New York State and Connecticut and a healthy patch can triple every four years. It doesn't like North Carolina soil, or heat, or the absence of a long cold winter. With my EXCLUSIVELY RHUBARB COOKBOOK in hand, I am ready to go anytime in search of it.

Jewel Hoogstoel

Lemon Chiffon Bavarian

Serves 8

Crust:
2 cups crushed vanilla wafers
1/4 teaspoon ground cinnamon
1/2 cup melted butter
Filling:
4 eggs, separated
1/2 cup sugar
Juice of 2 large lemons
Grated rind of 2 or 3 lemons
1 envelope unflavored gelatin
1/4 cup cold water
1/4 cup hot water
1/2 cup sugar
1 cup heavy cream, whipped

Many friends have enjoyed this recipe at my home. They have always had wonderful comments about this dessert. Serve with freshly made coffee. Enjoy!

Jean Green

- This dessert should be made the day before serving.
- Combine wafer crumbs, cinnamon, and butter. Reserve 1/4 cup of the crumb mixture to sprinkle on top. Press the remaining crumb mixture onto sides and bottom of a 9-inch spring-form pan.
- Beat egg yolks with 1/2 cup sugar in small bowl of an electric mixer until thick and lemon colored.
- Add lemon juice and rind and transfer to the top of a double boiler. Cook, stirring constantly, until thickened. Set aside.
- Soften gelatin in cold water and dissolve in hot water. Stir well and add to custard.
- Continue to stir and cool until the custard is slightly congealed. You may hasten the process by placing the mixture in the refrigerator but watch it closely, as it congeals rapidly.
- Beat egg whites until soft peaks form. Add the remaining 1/2 cup sugar, a tablespoon at a time, beating until whites are stiff and glossy.
- Remove the custard from the refrigerator. Fold in the egg whites and then whipped cream.
- Pour into crust-lined pan, top with reserved crumbs and chill overnight.
- At serving time, remove the rim of the pan and place the Bavarian on a paper doily-lined cake plate.

My Grandmother's Pumpkin Pie

Serves 8

3 large eggs beaten with a wire whisk
1 cup light brown sugar
1 tablespoon cornstarch
1 1/2 cups half & half cream
1 (28-ounce) can pumpkin, not pumpkin pie mix
1/2 teaspoon salt
1 teaspoon ground cinnamon
1/2 teaspoon ground ginger
1/2 teaspoon allspice
1/4 teaspoon ground cloves
1 teaspoon pure vanilla extract
1/2 teaspoon maple extract

1 unbaked deep-dish pie shell
1 pint whipping cream, whipped and sugared to taste

- Preheat oven to 425° F.
- Mix eggs and sugar well in large bowl using a wooden spoon.
- Blend the cornstarch in a little of the half & half and add it, plus all the remaining ingredients, to egg-sugar mixture. Stir to combine well.
- Pour filling into the unbaked pie shell.
- Bake in preheated oven for 15 minutes.
- Reduce heat to 350° F. and bake for an additional 45 minutes, or until a knife inserted in the center comes out clean.
- Cool completely on a wire rack. Slice and serve with generous dollops of sweetened whipped cream.

This recipe was created by my grandmother, Katie Cecilia Moeller, born in Evansville, Indiana, in 1874. She married my grandfather and later moved to Brownsville, Texas in the Rio Grande Valley, where she died in 1955 at age 81. She made several of these pies every Thanksgiving and Christmas. Their six grown children and their families always congregated at their house for the main holiday meals. She "bribed" the numerous grandchildren by offering them an extra slice of her delicious pie if they helped clear the tables. I, for one, always took her up on the offer. I make these pies every Thanksgiving and Christmas. I wouldn't think of trying a different pumpkin pie recipe. This one evokes such warm memories and I cherish them!

Cleta F. Howell

Green Tomato Pie

Serves 6-8

Green tomatoes are hard to come by out of season, but the pie freezes well. To freeze the filling alone, line a pie pan with heavy-duty aluminum foil, pour in the filling and put it on the shelf in the freezer until frozen. The filling can then be removed from the pie pan, wrapped carefully in foil, sealed in a plastic bag and used later by putting the unwrapped frozen filling in a prepared crust. Cover with top crust. Protect with foil shield and bake at 450°F. for 20 minutes. Reduce temperature to 350°, remove foil shield and bake 45-55 minutes more until nicely browned and filling bubbling.

Jeanne Harrington

Pastry for a two-crust or lattice topped 10-inch pie, packaged, or your own recipe
4 cups green tomatoes, about 4 large very green ones, in thin vertical slices
1 medium lemon, very thinly sliced, seeds removed
1 1/4 cups sugar
1/4 teaspoon salt
1/2 teaspoon cinnamon
1/4 teaspoon nutmeg, optional
3 tablespoons flour
2 tablespoons butter or margarine
1 tablespoon milk for top crust

- Preheat oven to 450° F.
- Prepare piecrust and line pie pan, reserving second crust for solid or lattice top.
- In a large mixing bowl place the unpeeled green tomato slices and the lemon slices.
- Mix the sugar, salt, cinnamon, nutmeg and flour together and add, stirring, to distribute the mixture throughout the tomato and lemon slices.
- Turn tomato-lemon filling into the piecrust.
- Cut butter in small pieces and distribute over the top of the pie filling.
- Cover with top crust in which vent holes have been cut or use lattice top if preferred. Seal edges well.
- Brush top crust with milk.
- Bake in preheated oven for 15 minutes; reduce temperature to 350° F. and bake for 45 minutes more or until crust is nicely browned. Filling should be bubbling through the vent holes to ensure that it is thickened and will be set when time to cut and serve.
- Allow to cool to room temperature.
- Serve with vanilla ice cream or whipped cream.

Nantucket Cranberry Pie

Serves 12

2 cups chopped cranberries
1/2 cup chopped walnuts
2 large eggs
1 1/2 sticks butter, melted and cooled
1 cup sugar
1 cup flour
1/4 teaspoon salt
1/4 teaspoon almond extract

- Preheat oven to 350° F.
- Grease a 10-inch pie pan or spring-form pan.
- Scatter chopped cranberries and walnuts evenly into the pan.
- Mix eggs, butter, sugar, flour, salt and almond extract. Stir until batter is smooth.
- Pour the batter over the cranberry/nut mixture.
- Bake in preheated oven for 40 minutes until tester comes out clean.

This is a nice way to serve cranberries when in season and a festive addition to a holiday table. Chop the cranberries and nuts in a food processor and it's a snap to make!

Consi Scott

Red Raspberry Pie

Serves 10-12

Prepared pie shell, homemade or commercial deep dish
  plus top crust or crumb topping of your choice
4 cups red raspberries, picked over
1 cup granulated sugar
1/3 cup Crème de Cassis, black currant liqueur
4 tablespoons cornstarch
1 tablespoon fresh lemon juice
Pinch of salt

- Preheat oven to 425° F.
- Gently toss raspberries and sugar together in a mixing bowl.
- In a small bowl, whisk Cassis and cornstarch until smooth.
- Stir Cassis mixture, lemon juice, and salt gently into berries.
- Spoon the berry mixture gently into the prepared pie shell.
- Cover with the piecrust or crumb topping.
- Crimp edges of the pie dough and cover with a piecrust shield.
- Set on middle rack of oven and bake in preheated oven for 15 minutes. Reduce heat to 350° F. and bake for 30-40 minutes more until crust is golden brown and filling is bubbling.

This has been the #1 pie choice of our family for the past 25 years. A dip of vanilla ice cream with a piece of this pie and you are in heaven.

Julie Snyder

Lemon Tart

Makes one 9-inch tart, or 8-10 (2 1/2-3-inch) tartlets

Pastry:
8 tablespoons unsalted butter, melted and cooled, plus additional for buttering the tart pan(s)
1/4 teaspoon vanilla
1/8 teaspoon almond extract
Grated zest of 1 lemon, blanched and refreshed in cold water, drained
1/4 cup confectioners' sugar
A pinch fine sea salt
1 1/4 cups plus 1 tablespoon unbleached all purpose flour
Filling:
2 large eggs, room temperature
3 large egg yolks, room temperature
1 cup sugar
8 tablespoons unsalted butter, cut into 8 pieces, room temperature
Grated zest of 2 lemons, blanched, refreshed in cold water and drained
1/2 cup freshly squeezed lemon juice, strained
Pastry:
- Preheat the oven to 350° F.
- Lightly butter the bottom and sides of the tart pan(s).
- In a medium bowl, combine the butter, vanilla and almond extracts, grated zest, sugar and salt, and stir to blend well.
- Gradually incorporate enough flour to form a smooth, soft dough. Depending on the flour and the humidity, the full amount of flour may not be needed. The dough should resemble soft cookie dough.
- Place the dough in the center of the buttered pan. If using tartlet pans, divide the dough into appropriate portions. With the flat tips of your fingers, press the pastry evenly on the bottom and sides of the pan(s). The dough will be quite thin.
- To bake, you do not need to prick the shell or weight it. Place the shell(s) in the center of the oven and bake just until the dough is firm and lightly browned, 12-15 minutes. If using small tartlet pans check them after 10 minutes and remove when lightly browned. The small shells can easily overcook.
- Remove from the oven and set aside to cool for at least 10 minutes before filling. Do not remove from the pan(s).

Continued on the next page

This is always a spectacular dessert. The filling is bright with lemon flavor and light enough to finish a sumptuous meal. The lemon pastry shell is much preferred for this dish as you can prepare and fill the tart several hours ahead of serving time. The crust will be just as crisp as when it came out of the oven.

You may use a 9-inch tart tin, small tins for individual tarts or tiny ones for a mignardises tray. This pastry is ideal for lemon tarts but is quite nice with other fillings. The dough is not intended to be filled before baking.

This recipe is a variation of one in Patricia Wells' book PATRICIA WELLS AT HOME IN PROVENCE.

Barbara Terry

Lemon Tart *continued*

Filling:
- In the top of a double boiler set over simmering water combine the eggs, egg yolks and sugar. The bottom of the pan should not touch the water.
- Whisk the contents of the pan frequently until the curd is thick and pale lemon colored, about 8-10 minutes. If you have a very heavy bottomed saucepan such as Cruset you may not need to use a double boiler for this step.
- Add the butter, tablespoon by tablespoon. Allow each spoonful to melt before adding the next.
- Add the zest and lemon juice, whisking almost constantly until thick and custard-like. You will see the first bubbles beginning to appear on the surface of the mixture. This will take about 4 minutes. Do not allow the mixture to boil.
- Pour the curd into the pre-baked and cooled pastry shell. Smooth the top and set aside until set, about 30 minutes.

Holiday Pie

Serves 8

Pastry for 9-inch double crust pie.
3 cups whole fresh cranberries
4 apples, chopped
2 cups golden raisins
1 cup sugar
1 teaspoon salt
3/4 teaspoon nutmeg
1 teaspoon cinnamon
1 tablespoon butter to dot filling

- Preheat oven to 475° F.
- Combine all ingredients except butter and fill pie shell with mixture.
- Dot filling with butter and add top crust.
- Cut slits in crust.
- Bake in the preheated oven for 15 minutes.
- Reduce temperature to 375° F. and bake 35 minutes more.
- Cover the crust edge with foil to avoid over browning.

This pie has a nice combination of fruit flavors. It has become a family favorite, especially at Christmas.

Kathy Bowe

Old Fashioned Pecan Pie

Serves 6

This recipe belonged to my great aunt who was in her heyday of cooking in the 1930's. We would bring it out for all the South Alabama reunions. It's a nice change from the Karo syrup pecan pies. Serve when you want a lighter pecan pie.

Joyce Mason

1 (9-inch) pre-baked pie shell
2 egg yolks
4 tablespoons flour
1 teaspoon white vinegar
1/8 teaspoon salt
1 cup white sugar
1 cup milk
1/4 teaspoon vanilla

2 egg whites
1 cup brown sugar
1 cup chopped pecans

- Preheat oven 350° F.
- In a large bowl mix egg yolks, flour, vinegar, salt, sugar, milk and vanilla. Beat well.
- Cook in double boiler for 35 minutes, stirring.
- Pour into baked pie shell.
- Beat 2 egg whites until stiff but not dry.
- Add 1 cup brown sugar and mix well.
- Add 1 cup chopped pecans, stir and pour on top of the pie.
- Bake in the preheated oven for 15 minutes.

Cherry Cobbler

Serves 6-8

This is an easy and wholesome dessert that is versatile enough to make use of other fresh or frozen fruits. Fresh blueberry cobbler, when the berries are plentiful, is mouth-watering. Top with vanilla ice cream for real decadence.

Frank Galick

5 cups canned or frozen tart cherries
2 1/2 tablespoons lemon juice
1/3 cup sugar
1/3 cup brown sugar, packed
2 1/2 tablespoons cornstarch
1 teaspoon ground cinnamon
1/4 teaspoon nutmeg
Topping:
1 cup all-purpose flour
2 tablespoons sugar
1 teaspoon baking powder
1/2 teaspoon salt
2 tablespoons butter or margarine
1/3 to 1/2 cup milk

Continued on the next page

Cherry Cobbler *continued*

- Preheat oven to 450° F. Have ready an ungreased 8-inch square baking pan or dish.
- Drain cherries, reserving 1/4 cup juice. Combine cherries and lemon juice and set aside.
- In a saucepan combine sugars, cornstarch, cinnamon and nutmeg. Stir in 1/4 cup of the reserved cherry juice. Bring to a boil, stirring occasionally, and boil for 2 minutes. Add the cherries, stir, and pour into the baking pan or dish.

Topping:
- In a bowl combine flour, sugar, baking powder and salt. Mix well and cut in butter until crumbly. Stir in enough milk to moisten.
- Drop by spoonfuls over cherries.
- Bake in preheated oven for 10-13 minutes or until golden.

Buttermilk Pie with Raspberry Sauce

Serves 8

1/2 cup butter
1 1/4 cups sugar
3 eggs, beaten
1/8 cup flour
1 tablespoon water
1/2 cup buttermilk
1 teaspoon lemon juice
1 teaspoon vanilla
1 unbaked pie shell
Sauce:
1 package frozen raspberries, thawed
1/4 cup sugar
Fresh raspberries, optional

- Preheat over to 350° F.
- With an electric mixer, cream butter and sugar until fluffy.
- Add the beaten eggs and mix until creamy.
- Add flour, water, buttermilk, lemon juice and vanilla and beat until smooth.
- Pour into pie shell and bake in preheated oven for 50 minutes.
- Puree raspberries in a food processor. Strain into a bowl and add 1/4 cup sugar, stirring until the sugar is dissolved.
- When ready to serve, spread 2 tablespoons raspberry sauce on plates, add a slice of pie and top with fresh raspberries.

This is the easiest dessert I have ever served and everyone seems to love it. It was given to me several years ago by a good friend and wonderful cook who also allowed me to join his cooking class. The pie can be made ahead and refrigerated for several days. Blueberries or any fresh berries in season may be substituted.

Peggy Quinn

Fresh-Spiced Pumpkin Pie

Makes two pies

2 unbaked 9-inch deep-dish pie shells
4 eggs, beaten
1 1/2 cups sugar
1 teaspoon salt
2 teaspoons freshly ground cinnamon
  (Use cinnamon sticks and grind in a spice grinder or coffee mill. You may put through a fine sieve for the finest powder.)
1/2 teaspoon freshly ground cloves
  (Remove round heads from whole cloves and crush between fingers or with mortar and pestle, discarding the clove stems. You may put through a fine sieve for the finest powder.)
1 generous teaspoon fresh ginger, chopped <u>extremely</u> fine.
1 (29-ounce) can pumpkin
1 (12-ounce) can evaporated milk
1 (12-ounce) can non-fat evaporated milk
  (Have on hand several small custard cups in case there is extra filling.)

- Preheat oven to 425° F.
- In a large bowl beat eggs well.
- Add sugar, salt, cinnamon, cloves and ginger to eggs, mixing thoroughly.
- Add pumpkin and mix well.
- Add all evaporated milk and combine everything very well.
- Pour mixture into pie shells. Fill just to the point where fluted edge begins. This will allow for expansion during cooking. Extra mixture can be baked in custard cups while the pie is baking or later.
- Bake in preheated oven for 15 minutes.
- Reduce temperature to 350° F.
- Bake 40-50 minutes or until a knife inserted near the center comes out clean.
- Custard cups cook fairly quickly, in 30 minutes or less.
- Cool on wire rack for 2 hours. Serve immediately or refrigerate.

This pie is always a hit. When we lived in Micronesia, Palau and Saipan, many ingredients were impossible to find. I looked for substitutes in many of my recipes. Fresh ginger was readily available there. I started using the freshly ground cloves and cinnamon when we lived in Texas, A friend, Celia Stem, brought me fresh spices in bulk from Mexico. Having a five-pound bag of cloves on hand made me search for various uses! Celia keeps fresh cinnamon on one of her grandmother's metates, Mexican mortars, and grinds it periodically to produce a wonderful aroma in her kitchen.

Mexican grocery stores are good sources for easy-to-grind cinnamon sticks.

Rosie Batcheller

Purple Plum Tart

Makes 1 9-inch tart

Filling:
1 1/2 pounds purple plums
2/3 cup sugar
Pastry:
1 lightly filled cup plus 2 tablespoons unsifted unbleached
  flour
1/4 cup sugar
1/2 cup butter
1/4 teaspoon salt
Grated rind of 1/2 medium-sized lemon

- Preheat oven to 425° F.
- Wash and drain plums, cut in halves, discarding pits.
- Place plum halves in a single layer skin side down in a flat ovenproof dish. Sprinkle with the sugar.
- Bake in preheated oven for about 15 minutes to extract most of the juice.
- Remove from the oven and set aside.
- Reduce oven temperature to 350° F.
- Combine 1 cup of the flour, sugar, butter, salt and lemon rind in a medium bowl.
- Blend together with fingertips. When well blended, knead the dough by hand continuously for 15 minutes. This is the key to obtaining good results from this butter-rich dough.
- Sift in 1 tablespoon of flour during kneading and a second tablespoon near the end. This is a very soft dough.
- Turn the dough into a 9-inch ungreased tart pan or spring-form cake pan. Lightly press as you push the dough evenly over the surface of the pan and around the sides, making a rim of 1/2-3/4 inch high and about 1/4 inch thick.
- Place the cooked plums skin side down on the pastry, reserving the juice. Arrange them to look attractive and bake in preheated oven for 20-30 minutes. The crust should be light brown in color.
- Remove from the oven and allow to cool.
- Boil the reserved plum juice until it is reduced to a syrupy consistency. Do not let it burn. Spoon over the plums to form a beautiful glaze.

When I was growing up in Freetown, Virginia, plums of all kinds were looked upon as being very special. I chose plum tart over other fall fruits because I feel plums are the most fitting fruit for this butter-rich pastry.

Plums come in many different shapes, colors and textures. The bright red, round variety was the first to ripen and was used in preserving and winemaking. Damsons were always made into preserves. The pale green Greengages were stewed. And the dark purple ones were used for pies, tarts and fruit compotes. Everyone had plum trees and new plants were constantly seeded. The seedlings were passed from neighbor to neighbor.

Edna Lewis
Former Fearrington
House Chef

Apple-Pecan Squares

Makes 16 squares

Topping:
1 tablespoon granulated sugar
1/4 teaspoon ground cinnamon

1 cup sifted all-purpose flour
1 teaspoon baking powder
1/4 teaspoon salt
1/4 teaspoon ground cinnamon
1/4 cup unsalted butter, melted
1/2 cup light brown sugar, firmly packed
1/2 cup granulated sugar
1 egg, beaten
1 teaspoon vanilla
1/2 cup peeled and chopped apple
1/2 cup finely chopped pecans

- Preheat oven to 350° F.
- Grease an 8 x 8 x 2-inch baking pan.
- Mix topping ingredients together and set aside.
- Sift flour, baking powder, salt and cinnamon together.
- Melt the butter in a medium sized saucepan over low heat.
- Remove from the heat; beat in sugars, egg and vanilla with a wooden spoon until smooth.
- Stir in flour mixture, apple and nuts until well combined.
- Spread into the prepared pan. Sprinkle with topping.
- Bake in the preheated oven for 30 minutes or until top springs back when lightly pressed with fingertips.
- Cool completely in the pan and cut into squares.

I have been making this recipe since 1977 when it appeared in our neighborhood cookbook in North Attleboro, Massachusetts. It is easy to make, very little cleanup, and smells wonderful when it is baking. It freezes well. Fresh or frozen blueberries can be substituted for the apples. A scoop of ice cream, or a hot cup of tea and a friend make a fine accompaniment.

Diana Farley

Carolina Chew Cakes

Makes 2 1/2 dozen

1/2 cup margarine, softened
1 (16-ounce) package light brown sugar
3 eggs
2 cups self-rising flour
1 teaspoon vanilla
1 cup chopped pecans
Powdered sugar for garnish

This is my sister-in law's recipe. It was published in Southern Living.

Peg Perlman

Continued on the next page

Carolina Chew Cakes *continued*

- Preheat the oven to 300° F.
- Grease and lightly flour a 13 x 9 x 2-inch pan.
- Cream margarine and sugar until light and fluffy.
- Add the eggs, beating well.
- Blend in the flour and stir in the remaining ingredients except for the powdered sugar.
- Spoon batter into the prepared pan.
- Bake in the preheated oven for 45 minutes.
- Cool in the pan. The 'cake' will fall.
- Dust with powdered sugar and cut into squares.

Clipper Chippers

Serves a bunch!

1 cup softened butter
3/4 cup granulated sugar
3/4 cup brown sugar
1 tablespoon vanilla
2 tablespoons Tia Maria
2 eggs
2 1/2 cups flour
1 teaspoon baking soda
1/2 teaspoon salt
4 cups chocolate chips
1 cup walnuts, broken
1/2 cup pecans, broken
1/2 cup macadamia nuts, chopped

- Preheat oven to 325° F.
- Cream butter, sugar, vanilla and Tia Maria. Add eggs and beat well.
- Combine flour, baking soda and salt.
- Gradually add the dry ingredients to the wet mixture.
- Stir in chocolate chips and nuts. You may refrigerate the dough if you wish at this point.
- Drop by teaspoonfuls on an ungreased cookie sheet and bake in preheated oven for 15 minutes.

These cookies were served to us on a voyage aboard the Clipper Cruise Line, hence the name. We liked them so much that they gave us the recipe.

"My mother usually made these cookies bite sized but they are also great as a normal size".

Molly

Lucy Conley via her husband Patrick and her daughter Molly

Cranberry Biscotti

Makes 30 biscotti

2 1/4 cups flour
2 cups sugar
1 teaspoon baking powder
1/4 teaspoon salt
3 whole eggs, beaten, plus 1 for brushing the dough
2 egg yolks
1 teaspoon vanilla
3/4 cup dried cranberries
1/2 cup chopped pecans

This recipe is based on one used by Vince Tyler when he was chef at Carluccis in Rosemont, a suburb of Chicago. It is also good made with walnuts, chocolate chips or coconut instead of the cranberries and pecans. It is somewhat unusual in that it does not use any butter or other shortening.

Karen Vernon

- Preheat oven to 350° F.
- Butter and flour 2 baking sheets that are at least 15 inches long. You may use parchment paper.
- Combine flour, sugar, baking powder and salt. Mix well.
- Mix the 3 whole eggs, egg yolks and vanilla in separate bowl.
- Make a well in the center of the flour mixture and add the egg mixture, stirring. Gradually work the flour into the ingredients in the well and mix until smooth. A mixer with a dough hook may be used.
- Remove the dough from the bowl and place on a well-floured surface. Knead in the cranberries and pecans thoroughly and keep kneading, sprinkling with additional flour if necessary, 4-5 minutes in all.

Shaping:
- Divide the dough into quarters. Roll each piece of the dough on a floured surface into a 2 1/2-inch wide log.
- Place the logs at least 2 inches apart on the prepared baking sheets. Beat the remaining egg and brush it over the tops of the dough logs.

Baking:
- Bake in the preheated oven for 35 minutes.
- Remove from oven and reduce temperature to 325° F.
- Cut the logs diagonally into 3/4-1 inch thick slices and place them, cut side up, on the baking sheets.
- Return to the oven for another 15 minutes. Cool on racks.

Chocolate Cappuccino Cookies

Makes 4 to 6 dozen

1 cup butter
2 cups light brown sugar, firmly packed
2 large eggs
2 3/4 cups all-purpose flour
1/2 cup cocoa
2 tablespoons instant coffee granules
1/2 teaspoon baking powder
1/2 teaspoon baking soda
1/2 teaspoon salt
6 ounces semi-sweet chocolate chips

- Preheat oven to 350° F. Lightly grease a large baking sheet.
- Beat butter at medium speed with an electric mixer until creamy. Gradually add brown sugar, beating well.
- Add eggs and beat until well blended.
- Combine flour, cocoa, coffee granules, baking powder, baking soda, salt and stir to mix well. Gradually add to butter mixture, beating at low speed until just blended.
- Stir in chocolate chips and mix well.
- Drop by rounded tablespoons, 2 inches apart, on baking sheet.
- Bake in preheated oven for 8-10 minutes.
- Remove to wire racks to cool.

These are soft cookies. The original recipe called for cinnamon chips, but I could not find them so I used chocolate and they were delicious. When I decide to have a couple with my afternoon tea I pop them into the microwave for 5 to 10 seconds which is enough to soften the chocolate chips and they are wonderful!

Barbara Stoddard

Lacy Dessert Baskets

Makes 12 baskets

3/4 cup quick cooking rolled oats
1/2 cup granulated sugar
1/3 cup flour
1/4 teaspoon baking powder
6 tablespoons butter, melted, do not use margarine
2 tablespoons milk
2 tablespoons light corn syrup

- Preheat oven to 375° F. Grease a large baking sheet.
- Mix all ingredients in a mixing bowl with a fork.
- Drop by level tablespoonfuls on baking sheet, 4 to a sheet.
- Bake in preheated oven 8 minutes until a light caramel color.
- Let stand for a few seconds and remove with a spatula.
- Place over the bottom of a large custard cup; shape with fingers to form a basket and leave on until cool.

These may be filled with ice cream, custard or fruit. They are very delicate cookies and are susceptible to humidity which makes them break up easily. But even then these crispy treats do not have to go to waste. They can be crumbled up and used as topping for ice cream or fruit.

Wilhelmina De Graaf Hanrath

Mint Brownies

Serves 10-12

Brownies:
2 sticks butter or margarine
2 cups sugar
4 eggs
4 squares bittersweet chocolate, melted
2 teaspoons vanilla
1 cup flour

Frosting:
2 cups powdered sugar
2 tablespoons butter or margarine
1 teaspoon peppermint flavoring
2-3 tablespoons water or milk
Green food coloring, optional
Glaze:
3 squares of bittersweet chocolate
3 tablespoons butter or margarine

Brownies to die for!

Ruth Gerber

For Brownies:
- Preheat oven to 350° F.
- Prepare a 9 x 13-inch baking pan with cooking spray.
- Cream butter or margarine and sugar together. Add 1 egg at a time, mixing well after each addition. Stir in melted chocolate, vanilla and flour and mix well.
- Pour into the prepared pan.
- Bake in preheated oven for 30 minutes.
- Cool on wire rack.

For Frosting:
- Mix all frosting ingredients and spread on brownies when cool.
- Refrigerate.
- When frosting is set, cover with glaze.

For Glaze:
- Melt chocolate and butter or margarine, stirring well to combine. Spoon over mint frosting. Tilt pan to distribute evenly.
- Refrigerate at least 10 minutes. Cut into squares.

Pistachio-Orange Cookies

Makes about 24-30 cookies

2 tablespoons plus 2 teaspoons grated fresh orange zest, finely chopped
1 cup shelled pistachios
10 tablespoons unsalted butter, softened, and divided
1/2 cup sugar
1 tablespoon plus 1 teaspoon milk
2 tablespoons orange liqueur such as Grand Marnier or Cointreau
1/4 teaspoon vanilla
1 1/4 cups all-purpose flour
1/8 teaspoon salt

- Preheat oven to 300° F.
- Spread pistachios on a shallow baking pan or cookie sheet. Toast nuts, stirring once or twice, until they are golden and fragrant, about 10 minutes. Allow to cool.
- Raise oven temperature to 350° F.
- In a medium bowl or in the work bowl of a food processor fitted with the metal blade, cream 8 tablespoons of the butter with the sugar until light and fluffy.
- Add the milk, orange liqueur, vanilla, flour and salt and mix or process until well blended.
- Mix, or process in, the toasted pistachios along with the orange zest. Mix only long enough to combine ingredients. There should be noticeable pieces of pistachios present.
- Shape the dough into a cylinder 2 inches in diameter, wrap in plastic and freeze until firm, about 1 hour.
- Lightly coat a large shallow baking pan or cookie sheet with the remaining butter.
- Using a very sharp knife, slice the cylinder of dough into 1/4-inch thick rounds and place 1/2 inch apart on baking sheet. Refrigerate remaining dough until ready to bake.
- Bake the cookies until lightly browned but still soft, 15-18 minutes.
- Transfer the cookies to a wire rack to cool.

These crisp cookies elicit raves. The colorful green pistachios and orange zest make them attractive. This inspired marriage of nuts and orange recalls the sunny Mediterranean. The cookies can be stored in an airtight container for 1 week or can be frozen for up to 1 month. If you have leftover dough, wrap well, freeze and bake the rest of the cookies whenever you desire.
This recipe was adapted from THE BEST OF COOK'S MAGAZINE, volume two.

Barbara Terry

Glazed Lemon Cookies

Makes 30 cookies

Cookies:
3/4 cup granulated sugar
2 tablespoons grated lemon zest
2 tablespoons lemon juice
1 3/4 cups unbleached all-purpose flour
1/4 teaspoon baking powder
1/4 teaspoon salt
12 tablespoons cold, unsalted butter cut into 1/2-inch cubes
1 large egg yolk
1/2 teaspoon vanilla extract
Lemon glaze:
1 tablespoon cream cheese, softened
2 tablespoons lemon juice
1 1/2 cups confectioners' sugar

Cookies:
- In a food processor, process sugar and lemon zest until sugar looks damp, about 30 seconds.
- Add flour, baking powder and salt; pulse to combine, about 10 one-second pulses.
- Scatter butter pieces over mixture and pulse until it resembles fine cornmeal, about 15 one-second pulses.
- Beat together the lemon juice, egg yolk and vanilla.
- With the food processor running, add the juice mixture in a slow, steady stream. The process should take about 10 seconds. Continue processing until the dough begins to form a ball, 10-15 seconds longer.
- Turn the dough out onto a clean work surface. Working quickly, knead gently to insure that no dry bits remain and the dough is homogeneous.
- Shape the dough into a log about 10 inches long and 2 inches in diameter. Wrap the dough in plastic and chill until firm, about 45 minutes in the freezer or 2 hours in the refrigerator.
- Preheat oven to 375° F. Adjust oven racks to the upper and lower middle positions.
- Line 2 large baking sheets with parchment paper or spray with nonstick cooking spray.
- Unwrap the dough and slice dough into rounds 3/8 inch thick.

Continued on the next page

Glazed Lemon Cookies *continued*

- Place rounds on baking sheets, spacing them 1 inch apart.
- Bake until centers are beginning to color and edges are golden brown, about 14-16 minutes. Rotate the baking sheets front to back and top to bottom halfway through baking time.
- Cool on baking sheets for 5 minutes. Transfer to a wire rack and cool to room temperature before glazing.

Glaze:
- Whisk cream cheese and lemon juice in a medium, non-reactive bowl until no lumps remain.
- Add sugar and whisk until smooth.
- When cookies have cooled, spoon a scant teaspoon of glaze onto each cookie and spread evenly with the back of the spoon. Let cookies stand on wire rack until glaze is set and dry, about one hour.

Norma Berry

Old Fashioned Gingerbread Boys

1 cup butter, not margarine
1 cup light brown sugar
1/2 cup light molasses
3 cups flour
1 tablespoon ground ginger
2 teaspoons cinnamon
1 teaspoon baking soda
(Yes, there are no eggs)

- In the bowl of an electric mixer combine butter, sugar, and molasses. Beat on medium speed until creamy.
- Mix flour, ginger, cinnamon, and soda together and gradually add to creamed ingredients. Combine well.
- Divide the dough into 3 or 4 pieces. Flatten each piece and wrap tightly. Chill the dough for several hours, preferably overnight.
- Preheat oven to 350° F.
- Roll the dough out with as little flour as possible. Cut into desired shapes.
- Bake on ungreased cookie sheets for 10-12 minutes.
- Cool on a wire rack. Store in airtight containers.

These cookies are very crisp and melt in your mouth! They smell wonderful when baking. I bake the excess trimmings for immediate snacking and because the dough doesn't re-roll without leaving visible flour on the surface. You may frost the cookies with icing made of 1 1/3 cups sifted confectioner's sugar, and 1 egg white. The icing gets very stiff when dry. The cookies freeze well.

Nancy Foster

I mix the dough by hand, like biscuits. This way I can tell if each addition is mixed properly. Also, the flour is merely folded in to prevent toughness. This way of mixing takes about 10 minutes. The dough rolls may be frozen, thawed slightly, then sliced and baked when company is coming. "Mama" was Florence Norwood Keener, my mother. She was a wonderful cook. She died in 1991 at age 94. She lived in Charlotte.

Sarah Watkins

Mama's Little Nut Cookies

2 cups all purpose flour, sifted before measuring
1/2 teaspoon baking powder
1/4 teaspoon salt
1 cup salted butter, softened
1/2 cup light brown sugar, firmly packed
1/2 cup granulated sugar
1 large egg, lightly beaten, room temperature
1/2 teaspoon pure vanilla
1/2 cup chopped pecans

- Sift baking powder, salt and sifted flour together.
- Cream butter and sugars. Add egg and vanilla and beat.
- Add flour mixture in fourths, mixing well after each addition.
- Add chopped pecans and mix to distribute. Chill the dough.
- Divide the dough into 4 equal portions. Place each portion on a piece of waxed paper and form a roll 1 1/2 inches in diameter and about 8 inches long. Refrigerate for several hours.
- Preheat the oven to 350° F.
- Lightly butter a large baking sheet.
- Remove one roll at a time from the refrigerator and slice it very thinly, about 1/4 inch.
- Place 3/4-1 inch apart on the prepared baking sheet.
- Bake in preheated oven until the edges are light brown, approximately 8-10 minutes.
- Remove cookies from the baking sheet and cool on a wire rack.

Willa's Deep Dish Apple Pie

From Willa Fearrington's recipe card file, courtesy of her husband, Jesse Fearrington.

Deep Dish Apple Pie
6 or 7 apples sliced to make about 1 quart
1 cup water
1 tsp. cin.
3/4 cup sugar
1/2 cup flour
6 tblsp. butter
Place apples, water + cin in dish. Blend rest until crumbly. Place over apples bake in 400° oven 1 hr.

Triple Chocolate Biscotti

Makes about 30

1 3/4 cups all purpose flour
1/3 cup unsweetened cocoa powder
2 teaspoons baking powder
1/2 teaspoon salt
1 cup sugar
6 tablespoons unsalted butter, room temperature
3 large eggs
1 1/2 teaspoons vanilla extract
8 ounces semisweet chocolate chips
4 ounces bittersweet chocolate chips. Ghirardelli double
   chocolate chips are excellent bittersweet chips or you can
   chop bittersweet chocolate.

- Line two large baking sheets with parchment paper.
- Sift flour, cocoa, baking powder, and salt into a medium bowl.
- With an electric mixer, beat sugar and butter in a large bowl
  to blend.
- Beat in the eggs 1 at a time. Add the vanilla. Slowly beat in
  flour mixture.
- Stir in the semisweet and bittersweet chocolate and mix well.
- Drop dough by heaping spoonfuls onto prepared sheet in
  2 (10-11-inch long) strips, spaced 3 inches apart.
- Using spatula or your wet hands, shape the strips into
  11 x 2 1/2-inch logs. Refrigerate 30 minutes.
- Preheat oven to 350°F.
- Bake logs until tops are cracked and dry and tester inserted
  into center comes out clean, about 25 minutes. Remove from
  the oven and cool 10 minutes on the baking sheet.
- Reduce oven temperature to 300° F.
- Using foil as aid, lift the logs onto a work surface.
- Line two baking sheets with a single thickness of foil.
- Using a sharp chef's knife, gently cut warm logs diagonally
  into 3/4-inch thick slices. Arrange the slices, cut side down, on
  prepared baking sheets.
- Bake biscotti until just dry to touch, about 8 minutes.
- Turn the biscotti over and bake until the top is dry to the
  touch, about 8 minutes.
- Remove from the oven and cool on the baking sheets on wire
  racks.

These biscotti have an astoundingly rich flavor. Your guests will not believe you made them! This is a modification of a recipe that appeared in Bon Appétit Magazine. Using a serrated knife to score the logs when they are warm from the oven and then using a chef's knife for the complete cut eliminates most of the crumbling. These biscotti are not as hard as traditional biscotti, and are very good with a cup of strong coffee.

Barbara Terry

Chef John's Fabulous Chocolate Chip Cookies

Makes 2 batches of mix. Each batch makes about 4 dozen cookies

Making the "Cookie Stash"
4 1/2 cups unbleached flour
2 teaspoons baking soda
1 teaspoon salt
2 cups firmly packed dark brown sugar
1 1/2 cups granulated sugar
1 (16-ounce) can of Crisco or 2 cups vegetable shortening
2 (12-ounce) packages semi-sweet real chocolate chips
1 (12-ounce) package Heath Bar Toffee bits

- Combine flour, baking soda, salt and both sugars in a large bowl.
- Mix in shortening with fingers.
- Stir in chocolate chips and toffee bits.
- Divide into two batches, about 7 cups each and place each batch into an airtight, plastic bag.
- Store the dough in the refrigerator. It will keep indefinitely in the refrigerator or freezer.
-

Baking the "Cookie Batch"
7 cups of the above cookie mix.
1 teaspoon vanilla
2 eggs, slightly beaten

- Preheat the oven to 375° F. Grease a large cookie sheet.
- Place the cookie mix in a large bowl. Stir the mix to distribute chips evenly.
- Add the vanilla and eggs, mixing well. This creates a heavy batter.
- Drop the batter by heaping tablespoons on the prepared cookie sheet.
- Bake in the preheated oven for 10-12 minutes.
- Cool slightly on baking sheets before transferring to a wire rack for final cooling.

For avid cookie lovers: To save effort, it is easy to double this recipe to yield approximately 28 cups of mix, enough for 16 + dozen cookies. The mix stores indefinitely and you'll find the extra batches don't last long.

John Stoller

Flan
Crème Caramel

Serves 4

Caramel:
3 tablespoons granulated sugar
2 tablespoons water
Fresh lemon juice, a few drops
Flan:
1/2 quart milk
Pinch of salt
6 tablespoons granulated sugar
1 (8-ounce) package vanilla sugar, Oetker brand or 1/2
  vanilla bean pod, split
3 or 4 eggs, well beaten

Caramel:
- Melt the sugar in a mold together with 2 tablespoons of water and a few drops of lemon juice. You may make the caramel in a small saucepan and pour it into the mold.
- When the mixture begins to turn golden, tip the mold gently to coat the interior sides of the mold. Remove from the heat.

Flan:
- Preheat the oven to 400° F.
- Boil the milk with the salt, sugar and either vanilla sugar or vanilla bean. Remove from the stove.
- Slowly add a bit of the boiled milk mixture to the beaten eggs in a mixing bowl, whisking well. Add the mixture to the remaining milk, stirring briskly as you pour.
- Strain the mixture through a fine screen into the mold.
- Place the mold in a pan containing about 1 inch of water.
- Bake in the preheated oven for 35-40 minutes. The flan is done when there is a golden crust on the top, the center feels firm to the touch and a knifepoint comes out clean when inserted in the center.
- Remove from the oven; place the flan on a wire rack to cool one or two hours at room temperature. Chill the flan in the refrigerator.
- Just before serving, loosen the edges of the flan in the mold by turning a knife around the edge of the mold. Then turn the flan over carefully into a deep platter.

Serve with cookies. It can be made the day before serving. You may make the flan in individual small custard cups.

Nicole Shadday

Chocolate Christmas Trifle

Serves 30

4 Heath Bars, frozen
1 devil's food cake mix
3 packages Oetker Double Chocolate Mousse Mix
3 cups half & half
3/4 cup coffee liqueur
1 (4-ounce) carton whipping cream

- Preheat oven to desired temperature (see cake mix).
- Grease and flour cake pans. You can use a 9 x 13-inch rectangular pan or two 9-inch round pans. Have a large clear glass bowl ready for the trifle.
- Prepare the chocolate cake according to the package directions and bake as directed.
- Make the Mousse using half & half (recipe on box calls for milk). Place the Mousse in the refrigerator to set.
- When the cake is done, remove from the oven and immediately pierce the entire cake with a fork. Pour liqueur over the cake while the cake is still warm and then allow it to cool. When cool, break the cake into medium sized pieces.
- Beat the whipping cream to a very stiff stage.

To assemble the cake:
- Remove Heath Bars from freezer and crack into small pieces.
- Divide cake and Heath Bar pieces into three equal portions.
- Layer trifle components in glass bowl in the following order: cake, Mousse, heath bar pieces; cake, Mousse, Heath bar pieces; cake, whipped cream. Garnish with Heath Bar pieces.
- Chill until ready to serve.

This is a beautiful and delicious dessert for a large crowd. It is easier than it looks. Heath Bars are sometimes hard to find. I buy them whenever I see them and put in my freezer. Oetker Double Chocolate Mousse is usually available at specialty food stores.

Vaughn Owen

English Trifle

Serves 8-10

2 packages ladyfingers
1 can raspberries, or 1 package frozen, drained, and
  reserve juice
1/3 cup Sherry
1 1/2 packets Bird's Custard powder
2 1/2 cups milk
Whipping cream
Chopped nuts as desired

Continued on the next page

English Trifle *continued*

- Line the bottom and sides of a glass bowl with the ladyfingers, making sure that they fit closely together.
- Place the drained berries in the bottom of the bowl and add the sherry, sprinkling part of it on the ladyfingers. You may also add some of the reserved berry juice as desired. Set aside.
- Prepare the Bird's Custard according to the directions on the package, combining the milk and the custard powder. Cook on medium heat, stirring all the time until the custard is thick. Cool until warm and then pour over the contents in the bowl.
- Refrigerate until ready to serve.
- Whip cream and spoon over custard. Garnish with chopped nuts.

This is really delicious and easy. It is a traditional dessert in the UK where I was born. Bird's Custard powder is available at local grocery and specialty shops.

Joyce Kirkbride

Cherry Clafouti

Serves 6

Batter:
1 1/4 cups milk
1/3 cup sugar
3 eggs
1 teaspoon vanilla
1/8 teaspoon salt
1/2 cup all purpose flour

1 can sweet black cherries, drained well
Sugar for sprinkling

- Preheat oven to 350° F.
- Prepare a baking dish with cooking spray or butter.
- Place all the ingredients for the batter in a blender in the order listed above. Cover and blend at top speed for one minute. Refrigerate if not using immediately.
- When ready to cook, stir gently and pour a very thin layer of batter into the dish.
- Place in oven for about 5 minutes until a film of batter has set in the bottom of the dish.
- Spread the cherries over batter and sprinkle with the sugar.
- Pour remaining batter over cherries.
- Bake in the middle of the preheated oven for 1 hour.
- The clafouti should be puffed and browned, and a knife inserted into the center should come out clean.
- Serve immediately or while still warm. It will sink as it cools.
- Serve with a dollop of whipped cream or crème fraîche.

You may marinate the drained cherries in 1/4 cup kirsch or cognac. Let stand for at least one hour. Reduce the amount of milk to 1 cup and omit the sugar.

Gillian Cell

Pumpkin Pots de Crème

Serves 4

1 1/2 cups cream
1 cinnamon stick
5 large egg yolks
1/3 cup sugar
1/3 cup canned pumpkin
1/8 teaspoon freshly grated nutmeg
1/8 teaspoon freshly ground cloves

- Preheat oven to 300° F.
- Bring cream and cinnamon stick to simmer in heavy saucepan over medium heat. Remove from heat, cover and let steep for 30 minutes to one hour.
- In large mixing bowl combine egg yolks, sugar, pumpkin and spice and whisk to combine.
- Bring cream back to a simmer. Remove cinnamon stick.
- Gradually whisk hot cream into egg mixture. Strain.
- To bake, divide the mixture evenly among 4 (3/4- cup) custard cups or ramekins and place in a small baking pan.
- Cover pan with foil and place on oven rack. Lift one corner of foil and pour water into baking pan to halfway up sides of cups. Keep covered with foil.
- Bake for 40 minutes to one hour until custards are just set.
- Remove from water and refrigerate, covered, until well chilled.
- To serve, unmold on a dessert plate that has some caramel sauce squeezed across it. Add a dollop of whipped cream at side of plate and a little on top of custard.

If making this ahead you may refrigerate the egg mixture for up to two days after straining. Mark Tachman at Restaurant 411 in Chapel Hill, N.C, prepares this dessert. Garnish with a sprig of mint and serve with Ginger Spice thins.

Jewel Hoogstoel

Spirited Chocolate Mousse

Serves 6-8

1 cup milk, divided
1 envelope unflavored gelatin
1/3 cup dark rum
1 egg
1/4 cup sugar
1/8 teaspoon salt
1 (6-ounce) package semi-sweet chocolate morsels
1 cup heavy cream
2 ice cubes

The preparation is quick and the mousse can be made ahead and refrigerated or kept in the freezer. When placed in parfait or champagne glasses and served on a glass plate with a wafer, or cookie, it is fancy and light.

Marilyn Worth

Continued on the next page

Spirited Chocolate Mousse *continued*

- Combine 1/4 cup milk and the gelatin in a blender. Cover and blend at low speed to soften gelatin.
- Place remaining milk in a small saucepan and bring to a boil.
- Add boiling milk to mixture in blender. Blend until gelatin dissolves. Scrape down sides of container with a spatula.
- When gelatin is dissolved and the mixture is still warm, add rum, egg, sugar and salt. Blend a few seconds.
- Add chocolate morsels and blend on high speed until smooth.
- Add cream and ice cubes. Blend until ice is liquefied.
- Pour mixture into parfait or wine glasses and chill until firm.
- Serve with whipped cream or garnishes such as strawberries, raspberries or shaved chocolate.

Tiramisu

Serves 10-12

6 egg yolks, room temperature
1 1/4 cups beverage fine granulated sugar
1 1/4 cups mascarpone
1 3/4 cups whipping cream
3/4 cup water
2 teaspoons instant coffee granules
1 1/2 tablespoons brandy
2 (3-ounce) packages ladyfingers
Garnishes: grated semi-sweet chocolate; use a potato peeler
Piped whipped cream, optional

- Prepare a 9-inch spring-form pan with cooking spray.
- Combine egg yolks and sugar in top of double boiler.
- With an electric mixer beat until thick and lemon colored.
- Reduce heat to low. Cook for 8-10 minutes, stirring constantly.
- Remove from heat. Add mascarpone and beat until smooth.
- Whip cream to soft peaks and fold into cheese mixture.
- Combine water, coffee and brandy and brush on both sides of ladyfingers to wet well. Line the sides and bottom of the prepared pan with the ladyfingers. You may also use a 3-quart soufflé dish.
- Pour in half the filling, layer with ladyfingers and cover with the remaining filling.
- Garnish, cover and chill for at least 8 hours.

This should be served in very small amounts, as it is very rich.

Marcia Gest

Victorian Cream with Chocolate Liqueur Sauce

Serves 6

Victorian Cream
1 envelope gelatin
2 tablespoons cold water
1 cup heavy cream, 36% fat
1/2 cup sugar
1 cup sour cream
1 teaspoon pure vanilla extract
Sauce
1 1/4 tablespoons arrowroot
1 cup very strong cool coffee, reserve 2 tablespoons
1/2 cup sugar
3 tablespoons Vandermint Liqueur

Victorian Cream
- Sprinkle gelatin over water to soften.
- Combine cream and sugar in a pan over low heat stirring until sugar dissolves.
- Remove from heat and stir in softened gelatin.
- Mix in sour cream and vanilla.
- Pour into 1 1/2-pint mold. Chill until firm, 5-6 hours.
- Unmold onto a plate with a rim to hold sauce.
- Pour sauce around mold.

Sauce
- Soften arrowroot in reserved 2 tablespoons of coffee and mix to a paste.
- Heat remaining coffee with 1/2 cup sugar until sugar dissolves.
- Stir in arrowroot mixture.
- Stir mixture over low heat until sauce thickens.
- Remove from heat and stir in liqueur.

Victorian Cream remains good the next day. It can also be served with fresh fruit sauces. The Vandermint chocolate sauce lasts for 2 weeks or more and is also delicious over ice cream or pears.

Marietta Williams

Luscious Lemon Cream

Serves 8

1 pint heavy cream
1/2 cup granulated sugar
Grated zest of 4 lemons
Juice of 4 lemons
2 tablespoons sweetened condensed milk

- Combine all ingredients in a chilled mixing bowl. Beat until very thick.
- Serve in a crystal bowl or individual champagne glasses garnished with strawberries, blueberries, blackberries and/or raspberries in any single or multi-fruit combinations.
- Serve alone or with cookies of your choice.

For variations:
- Fill the bottom of a crystal bowl with berries and heap on lemon cream or layer berries and cream. Blueberries and strawberries or raspberries are great for Fourth of July.
- Fill a meringue piecrust or individual meringues with lemon cream and sprinkle berries on top.

Janet McCarthy

Mirage Famous Bread Pudding

Serves 12

16 ounces half & half
8 ounces whipping cream
8 eggs, beaten
1 1/4 cups sugar
1 tablespoon vanilla
8 slices French or good sandwich bread, crusts removed
2 teaspoons cinnamon
2 teaspoons sugar

- Preheat oven to 400° F. and butter a 9 x 12-inch baking dish.
- Combine half & half, whipping cream, eggs, 1 1/4 cups sugar and vanilla and mix well.
- Arrange the bread on the bottom of the prepared dish.
- Pour the egg mixture over bread.
- Mix sugar and cinnamon and sprinkle over the pudding.
- Cover with foil and bake in a water bath in the preheated oven for 75-90 minutes.

This is the best bread pudding you will ever taste. The first time I had it at the Mirage in Las Vegas I went into the kitchen and asked for the recipe. Now when we go to Las Vegas, I order and eat this first before my meal. Serve warm, with or without a sauce. Enjoy!

Dorothy Alexander

Prunes in Red Wine ♥

Makes approximately 6 cups

1 to 1 1/2 cups prepared infusion of strong tea. Any plain black tea can be used but not flavored.
1 orange
1 lemon
4 cups red wine such as Beaujolais
2 pounds sugar
1 vanilla bean
1 teaspoon cinnamon
3 pounds whole pitted prunes
6 2/3 ounces brandy or cognac

- Prepare black tea and allow to steep. Strain.
- Peel the lemon and orange, removing only the peel and no white pulp. Cut into 1/2-inch wide strips. Set aside.
- Juice both fruits, discarding the pulp, and reserve the juice.
- Bring the red wine to a boil in a large saucepan and set it aflame. Shake the pan gently and when the flame dies down add the sugar, orange and lemon peels and their juice.
- Cut the vanilla bean in half lengthwise and then in 1-inch lengths. Add it to the wine mixture.
- Add the cinnamon, tea and the prunes. Boil for 5 minutes.
- Allow prunes to cool. Add brandy and stir to mix.
- Place prunes and liquid in jars and cover tightly. Refrigerate.
- Allow the prunes to 'age' for at least 2 or 3 weeks. Waiting 2-3 months is even better and if you eat them after 6 months they will have become a melt-in-the-mouth delight.

These prunes are wonderful served over vanilla ice cream, ricotta cheese, or with yogurt for breakfast. They can be drained and used with pork roasts or chicken, or made into delicious tarts.
Thirty years ago we had these prunes at the restaurant of George Blanc in Vonnas, Burgundy. Along with several of the other delicious desserts, we tried one prune. It was so extraordinary that we asked for more. This recipe is an adaptation of one in George Blanc's book, MES RECETTES.

Jim Terry

Slow Apples ♥

Serves 6

1 teaspoon of sweet butter
6 medium size apples, about 2 1/2 pounds, Golden Delicious, Stayman or Granny Smith
1 tablespoon lemon juice in 1/3 cup water
1/3 cup honey
1/2 teaspoon of grated nutmeg

Serve warm or at room temperature. Great with vanilla ice cream.

John Karvazy

Continued on the next page

Slow Apples *continued*

- Preheat oven to 300° F.
- Butter the sides and bottom of a 9 x 13-inch baking dish.
- Peel and core the apples. Slice them 1/4 inch thick. Layer the sliced apples in the baking dish, overlapping.
- Pour the lemon water over the apples.
- Drizzle the honey over the apples and sprinkle nutmeg on top.
- Cover with foil and bake in the preheated oven for 1 hour.
- Remove the foil and bake until apples are golden, about 1 1/2 hours more.

Chamomile Dried Fruit Compote with Mascarpone

Serves 4-6

3 1/2 cups water
3 1/2 tablespoons granulated sugar
4 chamomile tea bags
4 dried peach halves
4 dried pear slices
12 dried apricots
12 dried pitted prunes
12 dried apple slices
1/3 cup dried cherries
4 ounces mascarpone cheese, room temperature
1 teaspoon orange liqueur such as Grand Marnier or Cointreau
1 1/2 teaspoons confectioner's sugar

- Bring water and sugar to a boil in a medium saucepan.
- Add tea bags, remove from heat and let steep for 15 minutes.
- Remove tea bags and bring the liquid back to a boil.
- Add peaches and pears, reduce heat to medium and simmer for about 4 minutes.
- Add apricots, prunes and apples and simmer for 2-3 minutes.
- Add cherries and simmer for 1 minute more.
- Remove from the heat and set aside.
- In a bowl, mix together the mascarpone, orange liqueur and confectioner's sugar.
- To serve, divide fruit among bowls, pour some of the poaching liquid over and top with the mascarpone.

The fruit mixture will keep in the refrigerator for 3 or 4 weeks.

Jewel Hoogstoel

My father, Philip, often cooked for the family. This was his recipe. These fruit cups are great to have on hand in the freezer. They are delicious for desert, a quick snack, or to accompany a light meal. They are especially good in the summer and are well loved by kids of all ages. They keep very well when wrapped with plastic and stored in zip-lock plastic bags.

Sam Mason

Frozen Fruit Cups

Serves 18

16 ounces sour cream
2 tablespoons lemon juice
3/4 cup sugar
1/8 teaspoon salt
3 bananas, peeled and cubed
1 (8 1/4-ounce) can crushed pineapple, undrained
1/4 cup chopped maraschino cherries
2/3 cup chopped pecans

- Line 18 muffin cups with paper liners
- Combine all ingredients and pour into the prepared muffin cups.
- Freeze until firm and then store in plastic bag in the freezer.
- Remove from the freezer to soften a few minutes before serving.

This is a very light dessert. The crème fraiche gives it a piquant richness that other creams do not have. The dish may be assembled ahead and refrigerated. Bring to room temperature before baking.

Jim Terry

Roasted Figs with Candied Lemon and Sherry

Serves 4

1 tablespoon butter
12 ripe black figs
2 tablespoons candied lemons or peel, chopped, homemade is best
3 tablespoons medium dry Sherry such as amontillado
2 teaspoons granulated brown sugar.
4-8 tablespoons crème fraîche, or to your taste

- Preheat oven to 400° F.
- Butter a shallow baking dish just big enough to hold the figs
- Trim off the tips of the fig stems and discard
- Cut an X about 2/3 of the way through the base end of each fig opposite the stem end.
- Place 1/2 teaspoon candied lemon or peel in each fig and reform the fig firmly.
- Place stuffed figs base down in the buttered baking dish.
- Sprinkle the Sherry then the brown sugar over the figs.
- Bake the figs for 10 minutes in the preheated oven.
- Remove the figs from the oven; allow to rest for 10 minutes.
- Serve each guest three figs with some of the juices in the baking dish and a dollop of crème fraîche.

Delicious Pumpkin Ice Cream Pie

Serves 8

Pie Crust:
1 package Anna's Ginger Thins cookies
1/4 cup sugar
1/4 cup melted butter
Filling:
1 quart vanilla ice cream
1 cup 100% pure canned pumpkin
1/2 cup brown sugar
Dash of salt
1/2 teaspoon ground cinnamon
1/2 teaspoon ground ginger
1/4 teaspoon ground nutmeg

Whipped cream and cinnamon for garnish

Crust:
- Preheat oven to 350° F.
- Crush Ginger Thins finely in plastic bag with rolling pin and mix in a bowl with the sugar and melted butter.
- Press the mixture into the bottom and sides of an 8 or 9 inch pie pan. Bake in the preheated oven for eight minutes. Allow to cool.

Filling:
- Let ice cream soften until easy to handle.
- Mix the other filling ingredients in a large bowl.
- Add the softened ice cream and blend thoroughly.
- Pour the filling into the crust. Cover with plastic wrap and freeze.
- Remove from the freezer 1/2 hour before serving.

Before serving, garnish the edge of the pie with whipped cream sprinkled with cinnamon. May be made well in advance of a party.

Nina Falconer

Raspberry Ice Cream

Serves 4

2 pints fresh raspberries
1 cup sugar
1 cup whipping cream
2 tablespoons Cointreau

- Process the raspberries in a blender until pureed.
- Strain into a bowl, discarding the seeds.
- Add sugar, cream and liqueur to the raspberry puree and mix.
- Pour into an ice cream freezer container.
- Freeze using the manufacturer's directions

Rhoda Berkowitz

Walnut Frozen Fantasy   ♥

Serves 8

1 egg white
2 teaspoons water
1 cup Kretschmer Wheat Germ
1/2 cup chopped walnuts
1/4 cup lightly packed brown sugar
1 teaspoon ground cinnamon
6 cups fat free vanilla ice cream or frozen yogurt, softened
1/3 cup fat free chocolate, caramel or strawberry topping
Optional toppings such as walnuts or fruit

- Heat oven to 350° F.
- Spray a 9-inch pie plate with cooking spray.
- Beat egg white and water with a fork until frothy.
- Combine wheat germ, walnuts, brown sugar and cinnamon.
- Add egg white mixture.
- Stir until dry ingredients are evenly moistened.
- Press the mixture onto bottom and sides of the pie plate.
- Bake 7-8 minutes until golden brown. Cool completely.
- Spoon softened ice cream into cooled crust.
- Drizzle ice cream topping over the ice cream. Carefully run a knife or spoon through ice cream, creating swirls.
- Cover and freeze until firm, about 5 hours.
- Remove from the freezer 10-15 minutes before serving.
- Slice and top with chopped walnuts or fruit.

Donna Dicker

Lavender Ice Cream

Serves 4-6

1 1/2 cups whole milk
1 1/2 cups heavy cream
1 inch section vanilla bean, sliced lengthwise
6 egg yolks
1/3 cup granulated sugar
2 tablespoons fresh lavender flowers

- Heat milk and cream to a scald.
- Remove pan from heat, add vanilla bean and cool.
- In a double boiler whisk egg yolks and sugar.
- Slowly pour in the milk-cream mixture, whisking constantly.
- Cook mixture, whisking until it thickens enough to coat a wooden spoon.
- Add lavender flowers, stir, remove from heat and cool for 1 hour.
- Chill in refrigerator for one hour.
- Strain and pour liquid into an ice cream maker. Freeze as directed by manufacturer.

This ice cream is delicate and rich at the same time. English lavender, Lavandula angustifolia, tastes sweet, perfumy, and intense. A little goes a long way.

Marietta Williams

Daddy's Eggnog

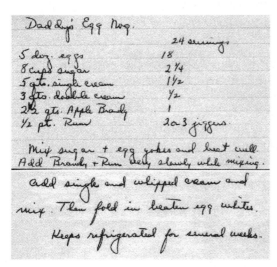

Daddy's Egg Nog.

	24 servings
5 doz. eggs	18
8 cups sugar	2 1/4
5 qts. single cream	1 1/2
3 qts. double cream	1/2
2 1/2 qts. Apple Brandy	1
1/2 pt. Rum	2 or 3 jiggers.

Mix sugar + egg yokes and beat well. Add Brandy + Rum very slowly while mixing.

add single and whipped cream and mix. Then fold in beaten egg whites.

Keeps refrigerated for several weeks.

Made for a large crowd or for 24 guests, this eggnog was traditionally enjoyed during the Christmas holidays. It was then that the extended family gathered at the Fearrington home on Eureka Farm. The home is now the Fearrington House Restaurant.

You must make this recipe on a day with low humidity. This is a prized family recipe. When I was a little girl, Mama made this candy and hid it so we couldn't eat it all. I found it and ate it anyway. When my daughter, Hannah, was a little girl, she and GG (what she calls my 81 year old mother) used to make this candy together. Hannah always asked GG to make "Virginity" when she came to visit us from Atlanta. And so it became GG's Virginity. I'm not sure if it actually restores one's virginity.

Joyce Baird

I put some of these in a plastic bag with a ribbon and give to friends for Christmas.

Barbara Stoddard

GG's Virginity (Divinity) ♥

2 cups sugar
1/2 cup water
1/2 cup light corn syrup
2 egg whites
1/8 teaspoon salt
1 teaspoon vanilla
1/2-3/4 cup chopped pecans
Powdered sugar as needed

- Cook sugar, water and corn syrup in a heavy saucepan until hard-boil stage, 265° F., 25-30 minutes. Use a candy thermometer. The sugar will form a thread when poured off the spoon. Do not stir while cooking.
- Beat the egg whites and salt until stiff.
- Pour the sugar mixture slowly into the egg whites while beating continuously.
- Add vanilla and continue to beat the mixture until stiff.
- Add pecans and stir.
- Add powdered sugar if the candy consistency remains too soft.
- When thickened to candy consistency, drop by spoonfuls onto waxed paper.

Praline Pecan Crunch

Makes 10 cups

1 (16-ounce) package Quaker Oat Squares cereal, 8 cups
2 cups whole pecans
1/2 cup light Karo Syrup
1/2 cup firmly packed dark brown sugar
1/4 cup butter or margarine
1 teaspoon vanilla
1/2 teaspoon baking soda

- Heat oven to 250° F.
- Combine the cereal and pecans in a 9 x 13-inch aluminum pan.
- Combine the syrup, brown sugar and butter or margarine in a saucepan and bring to a boil.
- Stir in vanilla and baking soda. The mixture will foam up so make sure the saucepan is large enough to accommodate doubling in quantity. I use a 2-quart pan.
- Pour the sugar mixture over cereal and pecans. Stir to coat.
- Bake 1 hour, stirring every 20 minutes.
- Spread on a baking sheet to cool; break into pieces.

Wine

and Food

WINE	CHEESE	SEAFOOD	POULTRY	MEATS
CHARDONNAY WHITE BURGUNDY	Gruyere, Brie Jarlsburg, Livarot	Crab, Lobster, Halibut, Cod, Sole	Chicken, Game Hen, Turkey	Pork, Veal, Baked Ham, Sweetbreads
SAUVIGNON BLANC SANCERRE	Aged Chevre, Triple Creams	Sole, Snapper, Oysters, Sushi	Chicken, Game Hens, Turkey	
RIESLING	Gorgonzola, Swiss, Gouda, Morbier	Crab, Shrimp, Sole, Scallops, Trout	Goose, Duck, Turkey	Baked Ham, Pork
GEWÜRZTRAMINER	Roquefort, Swiss, Munster	Crab, Shrimp, Smoked Salmon	Spicy Dishes, Turkey, Foie Gras	Pork, Sausage, Ham
PINOT GRIS PINOT GRIGIO	St. Nectaire	Oysters, Sushi Lobster, Crab, Calamari	Spicy Chicken, Chicken Breast, Game Hens	Pork, Foie Gras
PINOT NOIR RED BURGUNDY	Brie, Gruyere, Camembert, Port Salut	Salmon, Tuna (Ahi), Swordfish	Duck, Squab Roast Chicken, Coq au Vin	Lamb, Pork, Veal, Rabbit, Ham
MERLOT ST. EMILION POMEROL	Smoked Gouda, Cheddar	Salmon, Tuna	Duck, Guinea Hen	Lamb, Pork, Veal, Beef, Venison
SYRAH/SHIRAZ RED RHONE	Gruyere, Aged Chevre, Tallegio, Cheddar		Goose, Duck, Turkey	Barbecued Meats, Chili, Beef, Venison, Beef Stews
ZINFANDEL	Smoked Gouda, Cheddar	Blackened Fish	Game Hens, Turkey	Sausages, Beef, BBQ, Grilled meats
CABERNET SAUVIGNON BORDEAUX	Hard Cheeses Gouda, Gruyere, Cheddar	Swordfish, Tuna	Duck	Beef, Sausage, Lamb
TUSCAN RED SANGIOVESE BARBERA	Tallegio, Parmesan	Tuna, Bluefish	Chicken with Tomato Sauces	Pasta with meat sauces, Italian Sausage
RIOJA, TEMPRANILLO SPANISH REDS	Manchego, Petit Basque		Guinea Hen, Quail, Duck	Lamb, Richly Flavored Roasts
PORT	Stilton and Chocolate			

Wine and Food Pairing

Wine is sunlight, held together by water. Galileo

Good food, good friends to share it, and a bottle of wine to enhance the flavors and enjoyment of the meal.... these are ingredients for a memorable dining experience. Food and wine have always been natural companions. With growing interest in wines across the United States and growing numbers of prize-winning wineries around the world, the choices are limitless. Regional cuisines travel the globe influencing the many flavor combinations of recipes and increasing the choices of wines to pair with them. Although the wine world can be a bit mystifying, there is help for the hosts who wish to multiply the pleasure of their cooking efforts with a perfectly paired wine.

Choosing A Wine

What is the definition of a good wine? According to William Sokolin, wine merchant, it should start and end with a smile. A smile, a nod, a slight nip of the tongue to the lip, and an audible, "AH.....," this is what one wants to experience with the first and last sip of a good wine well paired with an excellent meal. With the old standby rule...choose a red wine to go with red meat, and a white with fish and white meat.... life was simpler. But cooking methods, seasonings, and sauces may suggest exceptions to this rule. For example, a meat dish with a cream sauce such as veal scaloppini with mushrooms or many pork dishes match well with a white wine. Salmon or any fish poached in red wine or roasted with a tomato topping goes well with Pinot noir. Red wines complement roasted chicken, coq au vin or chicken cacciatore. With so many exceptions, guidelines rather than strict rules are a reasonable approach to wine and food pairing.

The most important guideline is that the wine should complement the food and the food should accentuate and blend with the qualities of the wine. Consider the food and its cooking method; the flavors in the food suggest which wine to serve with the meal. Taste the dish and decide what flavor, body and strength the wine should have. Foods with strong flavors can support full flavored wines, while delicate foods call for more delicately flavored wines. Tomato flavors, meaty, creamy, robust, delicacy, richness, and buttery...these are some of the flavors and textures to marry with wine.

Both white and red wines range from lighter to more full-bodied. Light, dry white wines include Chablis and Sancerre. They go well with broiled fish, oysters, cold meats and egg dishes.   White Burgundy, Chardonnay and Sauvignon blanc are usually more full bodied and complement poultry, veal, and fish in cream sauce. Light red wines such as Pinot noir and Beaujolais are excellent served with roasted chicken or ham, while duck and roast lamb are best served with such full-bodied reds such as those from the Rhone Valley, a Cabernet sauvignon, or a Shiraz from Australia.

Ethnic and regional foods are best accompanied by wines of the same region. For example, when pairing wine with pasta the sauce is the deciding factor. For a rich, meaty tomato sauce dish such as spaghetti and meatballs or fettuccine with Bolognese sauce, a flavorful zesty red wine from Tuscany, such as Chianti or Sangiovese, would be a good choice. In contrast a very crisp white wine like a dry Pinot grigio from northern Italy would be enjoyable with pasta in a light seafood sauce. With Asian foods keep in mind the heat and the sweetness of the dish. If the main dish is either fairly sweet or hot, choose an off-dry wine preferably with lower alcohol, such as a German Riesling or Gewürztraminer.

Dessert wines should be sweeter than the dessert they accompany. For example, a sweet Muscat beautifully complements a fruit tart. Champagne goes with most desserts, but many sweet wines served with a very sweet dessert will seem sharp and tart. Such desserts are probably best served just with coffee.

Cheese and Wines

Wine and cheese are both natural products served together for hundreds of years. Generally one drinks red wine with hard, hearty, ripe cheeses, and white wine with soft milder cheese. For example, white wines are especially wonderful with many of the soft ripened cheeses such as Camembert, or Pont l'Évêque, or with many goat cheeses. Cheddars and other hard cheese generally pair well with red wines. A good Port is wonderful with blue cheeses such as Stilton, Roquefort, or Gorgonzola. There are also other interesting combinations such as those in the accompanying table. When serving a cheese course with multiple cheese types, it is advisable to offer both a white and red wine.

Serving Wines

Proper serving temperature enhances the wine experience. White wines are often served too cold and red wines too warm. To obtain the maximum enjoyment serve white wines cold but not icy, somewhere between 43 and 53° F. Note that normal refrigerator temperature is around 40°. Pour sparkling wines and Champagnes on the cooler side, closer to 43°. Red wines should be served at "cellar" temperature, between 55 and 65°, not at room temperature. Beaujolais and other light red wines are enjoyable when served lightly chilled to about 50-55°. To achieve these serving temperatures bring white wines out of the refrigerator about twenty minutes before serving. Chill red wines in the refrigerator about twenty minutes before drinking them.

Cooking with Wine

Cooking with wine adds layers of flavor and richness to dishes. The flavor of wine blends with other flavors to create complexities not otherwise achievable. If a recipe calls for dry white wine, a Sauvignon blanc or Pinot grigio is usually a good choice. If a recipe requiring lengthy cooking calls for dry red wine, a red Burgundy, Syrah or Zinfandel would complement the dish. For recipes such as lamb shanks with a red wine sauce, or Coq au Vin, traditionally calling for a dry red wine, simply serve the same type of wine with the dish. Conversely, cook with the same type of wine that will be served. Cooking wines should be drinkable, but need not be as expensive as the wine served with the meal. Do not save an undrinkable wine for cooking. If a wine is not good enough to drink, do not cook with it.

It has been said that food is love, and one of the most marvelous qualities of wine is that it marries well with food. Although there are general guidelines about the right accompaniment for each dish, experimentation can lead to wonderful discoveries. True lovers of wine and food know that a certain amount of adventure is in order. They also realize that many of the guidelines used in selecting the right wine serve as a base from which one playfully wanders. Good wine pairing, whether at home or in a restaurant, makes the difference between a routine occasion and a memorable event. To your health and the adventures ahead, SALUT!

Cookbook Development

For nearly a year more than 200 Fearrington residents worked to create this very special book. We extend heartfelt thanks to the committees, consultants, photographers, graphic designers and computer experts who have made this project to benefit Fearrington Cares such a great success.

Coordinating Chairs
Lorant, Janet
Mason, Joyce
Terry, Barbara

Finance
Green, Charles-Chair
DiGiano, Ann
Tauriainen, Marvin
Weinress, Ron
Williams, Ruth

Fundraising
Snelling, Rod and Anne
  Louise-Chairs
Alexander, Dorothy
Martin, Anita
Mellencamp, Ginny
Snyder, Julie
Williams, Marietta
Vernon, Karen

Marketing
Mason, Sam-Chair
Angevine, Chuck
Heaton, Mary and Forrest
Hunt, George
Johnson, Sally
Mellencamp, Jim
Patterson, Tina

Publications
Morse, Phil; Alter, David;
  Schultzberg, Alvin-Chairs
Ayers, Carey
Cotter, Joanne
Greenslade, Carol-Ann and
  Forrest
Hess, David
Hobbs, Fredda
Luberoff, Renee
Levine, Lilyan
Lorant, Reg
Myers, Gloria
Oliver, Elizabeth
Owen, Carol

Reese, Barry
Reilly, Don
Terry, Jim
Tharaldsen, Mary
Troutman, Laverne

Recipe
Quinn, Peggy-Chair
Burke, Judith
Foster, Nancy
Goodman, Barbara
Hotte, Suzanne
Johnson, Florence
Jones, Cynthia
Landriau, Elaine
Taft, Linda

Wine and Food Pairing
Terry, Jim-Chair
DiGiano, Fran
Mones, Ray
Zehl, Sue and Don

Testing
Green, Jean-Chair
Angevine, Joan
Berke, Barbara
Berry, Norma
Birnham, Dorothy
Bodner, Anne
Bonahue, Lyn
Brauer, Sue
Carson, Barbra
Cell, Gillian
Comey, Sallie
DiGiano, Fran
Ebert, Jean
Edwards, Mary Clare
Gaudet, Maggie
Genovese, Carol
Gest, Marcia
Giardino, Albina
Hanrath, Wilhelmina
Harrington, Jeanne
Hoogstoel, Jewel
Johnson, Sally

Jones, Cynthia
Karvazy, Betts and John
Kelley, Sandy
Kerrigan, Mary
Levine, Lilyan
Long, Beverly
Lorant, Janet and Reg
Marshall, Karen
Mason, Joyce and Sam
McCarthy, Janet
Merten, Barbara
Morse, Phil
Nicholson, Ruth
Owen, Vaughn
Raysich, Mary Anne
Reilly, Janet
Richardson, Joan
Salsbury, Joe
Scott, Consi
Slotnick, Rita
Smith, Julie
Snelling, Anne Louise
Snotherly, Barbara
Stewart, Pat and Don
Terry, Barbara and Jim
Toumbalakis, Barb
Troutman, Laverne and
  Paul
Vesley, Pan
Weinress, Diane
Williams, Marietta

Consultants
Delany, Richard
Fearrington, Jesse
Fitch, R.B.
Fox, Phoebe
Young, Mary Anne

Graphics and Photography
Mann, Wallace
Owen, Carol
Shillito, John
Terry, Jim
Vatter, Fred

Special Event Fundraising

The hugely successful *Affair to Remember* was an evening of champagne and friends, food and fun. The auction, along with other sales and contributions, provided sufficient funds to print this book. Without the efforts of many people this memorable occasion would not have happened. We wish to express our sincere gratitude to the committee chairs and members whose hard work made the event one to remember.

Coordinating Chairs
Lorant, Janet
Martin, Anita
Mason, Joyce
Snyder, Julie
Terry, Barbara

Food Committee
Snyder, Julie, Chair
Berke, Barbara
Green, Jean
DiSabatino, Debbie
Perlman, Peg
Stuneck, Mary
Vernon, Karen

Registration
Mellencamp, Ginny-Chair
Johnson, Florence
Milliken, Liz

Wine and Libations/Special
Sales
Terry, Jim-Chair
DiGiano, Fran
Harrington, Dick
Martin, Anita and Bob
Mason, Sam
Mellencamp, Jim

Mones, Ray
Richardson, Ken
Snyder, Larry
Zehl, Sue and Don

Finance
Green, Charles-Chair
DiGiano, Ann
Tauriainen, Marvin
Weinress, Ron
William, Ruth

Marketing
Mason, Sam-Chair
Hunt, George
Mellencamp, Jim
Patterson, Tina
Johnson, Sally
Angevine, Chuck

Auction
Terry, Barbara-Chair
Alexander, Dorothy
Graye, Vera
Heaton, Mary
Morse, Phil
Perlman, Peg
Rogerson, Nancy
Smith, Julie

Snelling, Rod
Snyder, Julie
Taft, Linda
Vernon, Karen

Decorations
Mason, Joyce-Chair
Gribbin, Jane
Siebold, Ann
Snotherly, Barbara
Owen, Vaughn

Music
Terry, Barbara-Chair
Lorant, Reg

Aprons
Snyder, Julie-Chair
Belden, Joan
Bowe, Kathryn
DeHart, Frances
Goetz, Pat
Jones, Cynthia
Marshal, Karen
McGrain, Karen
Milliken, Liz
Rockwell, Harriet
Taft, Linda

Contributors

At the heart of this book is a caring community. Fearrington residents, friends, businesses, sponsors and supporters contributed the recipes for this book, auction items for *An Affair to Remember*, services, and monetary support. Their exceptional generosity is greatly appreciated.

A Stone's Throw
A Touch of Class – Jan Ritchie
Abrahamson, Marigold
Adams, Annie
Aesthetic Solutions
Ahern, Betsy
Alexander, Dorothy
Allan, Don
Allen & Sons BBQ
Allen, Ralph
Alperin, Nina
Alter, David
Anderson, Marylou
Angevine, Joan
Atwater, Kay
Austin, Christie
Ayres, Carey & David
Baird, Ingrid
Baird, Joyce
Barker, Ben (chef)
Baron, Irma
Batcheller, Roselyn & Kim
Belden, Joan
Bensen, Vidabeth
Berke, Barbara & Jerry
Berkowitz, Roger & Rhoda
Berry, Connie
Berry, Norma
Bird, Sally
Birnham, Dorothy
Bixby, Pat
Bodner, Anne & Stephen
Bogle, Betsy
Botto, Anne
Bowe, Kathy
Boychuck, Shirley
Bratton, Mary
Brauer, Sue
Brennan, Janet
Brown, Irene
Brown's Tire & Auto
Bruce, Jane
Burke, Judith & Phil
Buyze, Pat
Cameron's, University Mall
Carew, Amelia
Carolina Club, Gary Hibbert
Carson, Barbra & Douglas
Cathy Fogelman
Cell, Gillian
Chapel Hill Tire Company
Chapel Hill Wine Company
Chapman, Margaret
Chas, Ann & Gus

Childress, Virginia
Ciao Bella Restaurant
Cole Park Cleaners
Comey, Sallie
Conley, Lucy
Connolly, Suzanne
Cook, Betty Anne
Cotter, Michael
Cunningham, Ethel
Curry, Kathy
Curtis, Carolyn
Daly, Janet
Darwin Design
Davidson, Ellie
DeHart, Frances
Delany, Richard
deSherbinin, Betty
Dicker, Donna
DiGiano, Ann & Fran
Dillard's at University Mall
Dina Porter Dress Shop
Dixon, Barbara
Doublier, Janet
Dry Clean Warehouse
Dunlap, Doris
Earnest, Sally
Eastgate Hair Salon
Ebert, Jean
Edwards Antiques
Edwards, Mary Claire
Ewing, Rosemary
Falconer, Nina
Farley, Diana
Fearrington House Inn
Fearrington, Jesse
Fenson, Shiffra
Feuer, Carol
Fink, Rene
Fitch, R.B.
Foster, Nancy
Fox, Graham (chef)
French Connections
French, Margaret
Galick, Jeanne & Frank
Galloway Ridge - Stan Finch
Garvin, Cheryl & Skip
Gaudet, Maggie & Jerry
General Store Café
Genovese, Carol
George, Margaret
Gerber, Ruth
Gerow, Sandy
Gest, Marcia & Henry
Giess, Rosemary

Gill, Jack
Gillham, Carol & Nick
GNC
Goetz, Bob
Goodman, Barbara & Eric
Graye, Vera & Alex
Green, Jean & Charles
Greenslade, Forrest
Gribbin, Jane
Griffin, Shirley
Grooves Fitness for Women
Gross, Ina
Grubbs, Tom and Jeannie
Hagen, Jeanne
Hairspraye – Jo Lucas
Hairspraye – Patrick Hawker
Hairspraye – Skincare by Marta
Hall, Dorothy & Don
Hall, Dortha
Halpern, Emily
Hanrath, Wilhelmina & Jan
Hansen, Joan
Harrington, Jeanne & Dick
Harris, Jerry
Heaton, Mary & Forrest
Heisserman, Mary
Herskowitz, Elliot
Hobbs, Fredda
Holliday, Joan
Holmgren, Robert
Holton, Sandy & Bob
Hoogstoel, Jewel & Robert
Hotte, Susanne
Howell, Cleta
Hunt, Barbara
Hunt, Janice
Hunt, Kay & George
Ingram, Shane (chef)
Investor's Trust, Inc.
Irwin, Barbara & Whitney
Ising, Judy
Ivey, Anne
Joan Belden, Joan
Johnson, Beverly
Johnson, Florence
Johnson, Sally
Jones, Clyde
Jones, Cynthia
Karvazy, Betts & John
Keady, Nancy
Kealey, Eleanor
Keepsakes Custom Framing
Kelley, Sandra
Kerrigan, Mary & Anthony

Kirby, Jean
Kirby, Peggy Jo
Kirkbride, Joyce
Kirkhoff, Anne
Kitchenworks
Koehler, Stacy
Kurtz, Beatrice
Landriau, Elaine
LaPine, Joyce
Larry Stroud Upholstery
Leuteritz, Jerrie
Levine, Annette
Levine, Lilyan & Sid
Levy, Susan
Lewis, Edna (chef)
Lindsay, Betty
Long, Betty Lu
Long, Beverly
Lorant, Janet & Reg
Lowe's Foods
Lucas, Jo
Lucey, Don
Lyn Morrow Pottery
MacCloy, Joyce
Mahon, Dorothy
Mann, Wallace
Marcus, Rosalie
Marrow, Nancy
Marrs, Goldie
Marshall, Karen
Martin, Anita & Bob
Mason, Joyce & Sam
Mattson, Cory (chef)
Maurer, Alice
McCarthy, Janet
McClendon, Nancy
McDaniel, Gilda
McGrain, Karen
McKinney, Lucy
Medical Supply Super Store
Mellencamp, Ginny & Jim
Mennear, Maggie
Merten, Barbara & David
Michael's Bar and Grille, Heather
  Coore
Millennium Sports Club
Minata
Mones, Raymond
Moose, Ruth
Morse, Phil
Myers, Gloria & Larry
Nagy, Robert
Nenninger, Patricia
Neufer, Nancy
Newman, Lenni
Nicholson, Ruth & Steve
North, Suzanne
O'Loughlin, Carole
Olson, Judy
Owen, Carol & Gwil
Owen, Vaughn

Page, Kimball
Palkoski, Jane
Palmer, Betty
Patterson, Bettina
Pazzo Restaurant
Performance Bicycle
Perlman, Peg and Alvin
Perry, Shirley
Peterson, Ralph
Piercecchi, Willie
Pittsboro Appliance Center
Pope's Hardware
Potts, Welshie
Preminger, Gloria
Pressley, Bill
Quinn, Peggy & Jarus
Quinn, Zina
Ramsdale, Barbara
Reece, Barry
Reilly, Janet & Donald
Repp, Donna
Restivo, Bernice
Richardson, Joan & Ken
Ritchie, Jan
Roberts, Floydine
Rodemann, Jinny
Rogerson, Nancy
Rosemary House B&B
Row, Betty
Ryder, Susan
S & T Soda Shop
Salon 135
Salsbury, Julia
Samitz, Dorothy
Sanderling Resort
Sawyer Termite & Pest Control
Schneerer, Shirley
Schuller, Ruta
Schultz, Peg
Schultzberg, Fran & Alvin
Scott, Consi
Seno, Edith
Shadday, Nicole
Shapiro, Florence
Sher, Betty
Sherman, Cuddy
Sherrod, Carol
Shillito, Bunny & John
Shumate, Mervin
Siebold, Ann
Silverstein, Jane & Stanley
Slotnick, Rita
Smith, Anne & Charlie
Smith, Barbara & Dale
Smith, Julie & Phil
Snelling, Anne Louise & Rod
Snelling, Sandy & Don
Snotherly, Barbara
Snyder, Julie & Larry
Speser, Teddy
Spina, Rita

Stempfle, Jacqueline
Stephens, Warren (chef)
Steward, Suzanne
Stewart, Pat & Don
Stoddard, Barbara
Stoller, John
Stroud Upholstery
Stroud, Larry
Stuneck, Mary
Stutz, Gerry
Taft, Linda
Tarr, Kay
Tashner, Judith LCSW
Tauriainen, Zana & Marvin
Temple Theater
Terry, Barbara & Jim
Thomas, Carolyn & Peter
Thomas, Grace
Tiemann, Ruth
Toumbalakis, Barbara
Tredinnick, Dody
Tremblay, Barbara
Troutman, Laverne & Paul
Tucker, Rosa Lee
University Florist & Gift Shop
VanHorn, Anjanette
Van Iten, Helga
Vansuch, Jo Anne
Vatter, Fred
Vernon, Karen & John
Vesley, Pan & Allan
Video Booth
Vietri, Inc.
Village Beauty Shop – Allison
  Womack
Village Beauty Shop – Theresa
  Robertino
Watkins, Sarah
Watts, Patricia
Webster, John
Weiner, Rita
Weinress, Dianne & Ronald
Weiss, Adair
Weiss, Burton
Whaling, Liz
Whole Foods Market
Wilkins, Gloria & Robert
Williams, Marietta & Robert
Williams, Ruth
Williamson, Anne
Wimer, Rita
Windy Oaks Inn
Worth, Marilyn & Jack
Young, Mary Ann
Zehl, Sue & Don
Zempel, Lynn
Zinsmeyer, Kay
Zollinger, Joan

Recipe Index

The Barn in Winter 2004